BLUFF, BLUSTER, LIES AND SPIES

BLUFF, BLUSTER, LIES AND SPIES

The Lincoln Foreign Policy, 1861–1865

DAVID PERRY

CASEMATE
Philadelphia & Oxford

Published in the United States of America and Great Britain in 2016 by
CASEMATE PUBLISHERS
1950 Lawrence Road, Havertown, PA 19083, USA
and
10 Hythe Bridge Street, Oxford OX1 2EW, UK

Copyright 2016 © David Perry

Hardcover Edition: ISBN 978-1-61200-362-7
Digital Edition: ISBN 978-1-61200-363-4

A CIP record for this book is available from the British Library

Printed in and bound in the United States of America

For a complete list of Casemate titles, please contact:

CASEMATE PUBLISHERS (US)
Telephone (610) 853-9131
Fax (610) 853-9146
Email: casemate@casematepublishers.com
www.casematepublishers.com

CASEMATE PUBLISHERS (UK)
Telephone (01865) 241249
Fax (01865) 794449
Email: casemate-uk@casematepublishers.co.uk
www.casematepublishers.co.uk

CONTENTS

Dedicated to Dr. Francelia Butler
Professor of English, University of Connecticut
and
Jane Marjorie Perry

PREFACE

More often than not, the story of the American Civil War is about generals and battles. Foreign policy and diplomacy are often given much less attention. With this in mind, I started my research to find out if there was a foreign policy during the Lincoln administration, and if so, how effective it was.

I first became interested in the topic of diplomacy and foreign relations during the American Civil War when reading William Henry Seward's *Some Thoughts for the President's Consideration.* Contemporary historians like Doris Kearns Goodwin tell us that Seward gets "high marks" for his work as secretary of state. When she didn't adequately explain why he earned those good grades, I decided to look further. Seward's contemporary, Charles Francis Adams, believed that the secretary saved the Union through his skillful handling of the 1861 *Trent* Affair. On the other hand, British prime minister Lord Palmerston thought Seward was a "vaporing, blustering, ignorant man." So, who was William Henry Seward, and why have most historians given the secretary of state a "free pass"? Didn't he threaten to "wrap the world in flames" over European talk of recognition of the Confederate States of America? I wondered if those threats had any material impact on the conduct and outcome of the war, or was this just posturing that was recognized as such and ignored by the powerful men of the Foreign Office and the Tuileries? Did anyone else get a "free pass"? My research began with Seward and the Lincoln State Department, but quickly led South to people like Seward's counterpart in the Confederate State Department, Judah Philip Benjamin and his boss, Jefferson Davis. Like Seward, Benjamin was mistrusted and vilified in the press. He was both the "dark prince" and the "brains of the Confederacy". However, Seward published his official correspondence, and saved his private letters. The Rush-Rhees library contains almost 50,000 Seward communication items.

Unfortunately, Benjamin burned all of his personal papers after the war. With less evidence to help evaluate his work, how can we better understand the part people like Judah Benjamin played in Confederate foreign relations?

One of the complications in analyzing Confederate foreign relations at this time is the fact that President Jefferson Davis initially did not have a foreign policy. On the one hand, he believed that cotton was his best choice for commissioner to Europe. On the other, he still needed guns to fight the Yankees and clear his harbors of the Union ironclads that stood in his way. Without recognition as a sovereign nation, the representatives of the Confederacy lacked the "accreditation" to be formally received by the men of the Foreign Office in either London or Paris. No matter. As secretary of war under Franklin Pierce, Davis knew he needed guns first. Southern farmers and plantation masters didn't know how to make them, but Northern gunsmiths did. So, Davis' first ministers to Europe were a small group of purchasing agents whose job it was to get there before Union representatives and buy as many guns as they could. Don't bother with old smoothbores that Europe was trying to unload. Just get the better rifled guns like Lincoln had from Springfield. As the war dragged on, I could begin to analyze the impact of a more organized and formal Confederate State Department structure on the European Foreign Office. Most of this, however, came too late.

Beyond Union and Confederate ministers, consuls and purchasing agents, what part did international law play at that time? Lord John Russell of the London Foreign Office was guided by the two leading exponents of international law: Emmerich de Vattel and Henry Wheaton. He and the Crown law officers also paid attention to the Admiralty judgments of William Scott, the First Baron Stowell. Nevertheless, Vattel, Wheaton and Stowell told him how things ideally should be. Men like Seward, Napoleon, Palmerston and many others were acting out of immediate need as dictated by sometimes novel circumstances not addressed by any of the legal "experts".

The language and craft of diplomacy and diplomats, then and now, is often deliberately vague and ambiguous to be able to gain advantage and/or deniability at a later date. Knowing the complexity of the American Civil War, I was left with the fact that this diplomatic "vagueness" resulted in too many questions unanswered by the existing research on Civil War foreign relations. Minister to France, William Lewis Dayton, wrote to Seward about his frustration in dealing with French diplomacy. He wrote, "No man but a Frenchman would ever have thought of Talleyrand's famous *bon mot*, that the object of language was to conceal thought."

A few of the many unanswered questions which arose during the course of research for this book include but are not limited to:

1. If we are still to believe that Britain was the most powerful nation on Earth at this time, what would have happened if she had recognized the Confederacy? Could she have backed up her actions with the force necessary to break the blockade and subdue a fully-mobilized Union army? Or was Britain a paper tiger who maintained her illusion of power by staying out of the American conflict?

2. Were people like Richard Lyons the real heroes of the diplomatic war that ultimately saved the Union? Was he in control of U.S. foreign relations?

3. Was Europe really so distracted by events at home that they paid less attention to the war in America thus doing more for the Union war effort than all of the diplomatic work at the state department?

4. If Benjamin Disraeli was correct in his assertion that Seward and Russell had a secret agreement that Britain would not break the blockade and that the Laird Rams would never leave an English port, was Seward the *de facto* president and hero after all? He wasn't crazy, but crazy like a fox all along?

As I began to dig deeper, I also realized that there were many unsung heroes who played significant parts in this complex drama. A good example of this is the story of the undercover agents who spied upon and frustrated Confederate activities in Europe. Thomas Haines Dudley, U.S. consul in Liverpool, is well-known and credited with being "Lincoln's spymaster". The reality is that Dudley was employed, supervised and paid by another, lesser-known man, Henry Shelton Sanford, U.S. minister resident to Belgium. Sanford's correspondence makes it clear that he was actually in charge of the surveillance, intelligence and arms purchasing operations for Lincoln in Europe.

The vital role played by diplomacy and foreign relations during the American Civil War has been well documented by earlier historians like Lynn Case and Warren Spencer as well as more recent historians like Amanda Foreman and Howard Jones. *Bluff, Bluster, Lies and Spies* does not attempt to cover the broad, complex entirety of foreign relations during the American Civil War. Most researchers have focused on a short, ten-month period from March 4, 1861 to the settling of the *Trent* crisis in December, 1861. Issues with Mexico and Napoleon III are not ignored, but given much less attention. Rising tensions and a shooting war were also erupting in Japan that are not often addressed. At the same time that the *Alabama* and *Kearsarge* were battling off Cherbourg in the summer of 1864, Robert Pruyn, U.S. minister to Japan, warned Seward that war with that country might break out at any moment.

Truth is always stranger than fiction. Keeping this in mind, the account of diplomacy and foreign relations during the American Civil War finds the men and women of North and South fascinating for different reasons. Lincoln's Union was a better-funded, better-articulated machine which fought hand-to-hand with the Confederacy which improvised and did everything "by the seat of their pants". Jefferson Davis and his team achieved much more than would otherwise have been expected. With this in mind, this research takes a revisionist look at diplomacy during the American Civil War. It also hopes to shed more needed light on a complex subject that always seems to have another side and so many more unanswered questions.

David D. Perry
West Haven, Connecticut, 2015

INTRODUCTION

Nothing can be more virulent than the hatred that exists between the Americans of the United States and the English.

Alexis de Tocqueville, *Democracy in America*, 1838

In order to better understand the American Civil War, it is also important to know something of the background of an empire that controlled one quarter of the world's land mass, and another that was to soon challenge that empire "upon which the sun never sets". The nineteenth century was a period of Manifest Destiny for many of the then developed countries of the world. For England and France, "Arrogance and resolution were respected as virtues and the rest of the world was there to be dominated."[1] Those countries maintaining the balance of power in Europe were sensitive about their national honor. If Britain's prime minister was prepared to use gunboat diplomacy to protect British pride, U.S. secretary of state William Henry Seward was equally prepared to use bluster and threat to ensure the integrity of the United States.

Abraham Lincoln claimed that he had no foreign policy experience and would defer to Seward. The secretary had little diplomatic experience, but at least he had been to Europe and made contact with many of those with whom he would now be negotiating. James L. Orr, chairman of the Confederate House Committee on Foreign Affairs, claimed that the Confederacy never had a foreign policy at all.[2] The government of Jefferson Davis was up against some "hoary and shrewd men" in the

London Foreign Office, the slippery Napoleon III at the Tuileries in Paris and in Washington at the U.S. State Department. The primary objective of the Lincoln foreign policy was to ensure that Europe did not intervene in a domestic rebellion. Britain and the Union did not want to fight each other. Palmerston thought such a war was a risky waste of time, money and effort. Lincoln often said that he wanted "one war at a time." Conversely, Jefferson Davis desperately needed that European intervention to help him ensure the sovereignty and survival of the Confederate States of America. That would be accomplished through formal, diplomatic recognition of Confederate independence. He had no foreign policy designed to achieve that objective because he didn't believe that he needed one. He could blackmail England and France with cotton.

William Henry Seward and Lord Palmerston were experienced politicians who had considerable impact on national policy and foreign relations during their tenure in public life. Lord Palmerston died in his bed at 10:45am on Wednesday October 18, 1865. He was just two days short of his eighty-first birthday. William Henry Seward died a much harder death that took place in stages.

At 10:15pm on April 14, 1865, a large, muscular man wearing a pink and brown overcoat and carrying a knife and pistol stabbed Secretary of State William Henry Seward on the right side of his face and neck with such force that the victim's tongue could be seen through the wound in his cheek. The assailant was Lewis Powell.[3] He was part of the conspiracy designed by John Wilkes Booth to kill President Abraham Lincoln, his secretary of state and Vice President, Andrew Johnson all in the same night, and at the same time. Seward survived, but died in 1872 at the younger age of seventy-one. He carried the deep physical scars of that night in 1865 for the rest of his life. The last photograph of Seward shows him staring with bitter defiance at the camera with that gash in his right cheek and chin. Before the lens cap came off the camera, Seward pulled his right shirt collar tight over the deep wound on his neck. Powell nearly severed Seward's right common carotid artery. The aging secretary didn't want the world to remember him this way.

The purchase of Alaska, attempted assassination, service as secretary of state, and defeat by Lincoln in 1860, are the general, historical highlights of Seward that stand out for the average American today. If one digs deeper, however, William Henry Seward had a record of success and failure that went far beyond those highlights. Although *Bluff, Bluster, Lies and Spies* is not about the tumultuous and colorful political life of William Seward *per se*, it ultimately filters those critical moments of U.S. and Confederate diplomacy during the American Civil War through the political lens of Lincoln's secretary of state. From the standpoint of diplomacy, everything seemed to come back to Seward.

The ideal world of Vattel, Wheaton and Stowell is contrasted with the real world of the key players in this intense political drama.[4] The respective honors of England, France, Spain, Mexico, Prussia, Russia, Japan, the United States and the "so-called Confederate States of America" are threatened and defended by bluff, bluster, lies and spies throughout this critical period. The student of history is always told that Europe was distracted by its own issues, and preferred to look at the American Civil War as a side-show that might have unpleasant consequences in the distant future. However, the fate of upcoming generations the world over was at stake because the success or failure of the democratic experiment was on trial in America.

Secretary Seward was a seasoned domestic politician with little foreign policy experience. Fortunately, he worked for a man who had the self-confidence and wisdom to ignore or excuse Seward's faults and take advantage of his strengths.

Judah Benjamin was not as lucky. He worked for a man whose apparent self-confidence was more an indication of fear and self-doubt. Nevertheless, Davis trusted Benjamin to the same degree that Lincoln eventually came to trust Seward. Many modern historians have praised Seward and deified Lincoln. For many, Benjamin remains a mystery and Davis the prime mover in a "lost cause" whose mistakes were highly publicized by men like the editor of the *Richmond Examiner*, Edward A. Pollard. Some claim that Seward was one of the most successful secretaries of state, second only to John Quincy Adams. Adams' son, Charles Francis Adams, credited Seward with creating the most effective state department up to that time. From 1861 to 1865, however, Seward was often vilified, mistrusted, blamed and critically underestimated by many experienced diplomats and politicians on both sides of the Atlantic. Many in the Davis government suffered the same fate. Through bluff, bluster, competent legation personnel, and an extensive ring of spies, propagandists and skillful agents all over Europe, Seward was able to make many valuable contributions to the successful prosecution of the American Civil War. Davis also employed spies, purchasing agents and publicists, but they were compromised by the fact that they had little money to do their work. Unlike Seward's men, some of Davis' agents ultimately came to doubt the mission of the Confederacy itself.

One of the problems in getting to know the real characters in this drama is the fact that public and private perceptions of them are vested in controversy. Where does the truth really lie? For example, Charles Francis Adams had one view of Seward, and Gideon Welles another. Other than Lincoln's closest secretaries, Nicolay and Hay, very few people were neutral about Lincoln's Secretary of State. Benjamin and Davis fared no better. Seward basically learned on the job. Through inexperience, he made some mistakes early on in his career that led to him gaining a reputation as something of a rogue – a reputation that followed him and the work of the U.S. State Department throughout the war. That reputation had some serious consequences for U.S. diplomacy and foreign relations at that time. Seward was doing business with some of the most skillful and experienced politicians, then performing on the diplomatic stage. They included Lord Palmerston, British prime minister during the Civil War; Lord John Russell at the Foreign Office; Richard Lyons at the British Legation in Washington; Queen Victoria, Napoleon III of France, and Charles Francis Adams at the U.S. legation in London. The men of the Confederate government dealt with many of the same adversaries. Through his commissioners James Mason and John Slidell, Judah Benjamin worked on Lords Palmerston, Russell, Thouvannel and Drouyn de Lhuys just as hard as did Seward.

If, for example, Seward biographer Walter Stahr is correct in stating that the *Trent* affair of November–December 1861 "was the Cuban Missile Crisis of the nineteenth century"[5], then British prime minister Palmerston was second only to Henry Seward in running a dangerous bluff of his own. The threat of war with Great Britain may have helped to free the Confederate representatives Mason and Slidell in 1861. The issue of Confederate recognition and the consequent risk of war with

Britain over that contested recognition was always lurking in the background. The possibility of war with Britain, France, Spain or Japan was that sobering factor that forced Seward to act with more deliberation and care than might otherwise have been the case. Jefferson Davis had neither the time nor the opportunity for bluff and bluster. He needed help, and he needed it fast. Unfortunately for Davis, he was restrained by a new Constitution and state's rights philosophy, which initially restricted his authority and ability to even ask for help. Just communicating with his commissioners in Europe became a problem, as the Confederate Constitution determined that the post offices were to be self-supporting. Even if they could generate the money necessary to sustain a viable postal service, the blockade made it difficult and then almost impossible to get mail through – to Europe or anywhere else. In a timely and thus effective manner, how were Davis, Benjamin, Treasury Secretary Christopher Memminger and Navy Secretary Stephen Mallory supposed to communicate with their agents and commissioners working on their behalf in Europe?[6]

Ironically, if Palmerston's bluff had been called and war erupted over Confederate recognition, the British Royal Navy would have been exposed for weaknesses that would have threatened the security of the British homeland and the empire as well. For offensive operations against the unique coastal conditions of the United States in the mid-nineteenth century, the Royal Navy was a paper tiger.[7] In addition, neither the French *Gloire* nor the rebuilt Spanish fleet could have broken the blockade and seriously threatened critical harbors in the Union or the Confederacy.[8] Fortunately, men like Palmerston, Russell, Richard Lyons in Washington, Prince Gorchakov in Moscow and Thomas Corwin in Mexico City exercised the diplomatic judgment necessary to avert a possible world war and to give Abraham Lincoln the room necessary to restore the union and emancipate the slaves.

Bluff, Bluster, Lies and Spies examines the *de facto* conduct of foreign relations during the Civil War as performed by the key players in that event. Even though U.S. foreign relations involved people and events in far-away places from Tokyo to London, American diplomacy issues always came back, directly or indirectly, to the Lincoln and Davis state departments.

International law in Western Europe was evolving along with those nations who were working and fighting with each other to better define themselves and flex their muscles. In 1758, Emmerich de Vattel's *The Law of Nations* attempted to create some guidelines for the conduct of affairs between nations in war-time.[9] Subsequent to this, ground-breaking work was done by William Scott, aka Lord Stowell, relative to such issues as neutral rights and Continuous Voyage.[10] Sitting as judge of the High Court of Admiralty, his prize court decisions provided more specific guidance regarding maritime issues that were soon to be put to the test.[11] That test was the Crimean War and the resulting 1856 Treaty of Paris which did the most to develop more realistic maritime rules by which enemies and neutral nations should conduct themselves in time of war. Unfortunately, both the Treaty, Vattel and the Stowell judgments were used and abused by the powers of Western Europe, the U.S. and the "so-called Confederate States of America" as they attempted to remain neutral yet still profit from the American Civil War. Vattel's "laws" were not always appropriate to apply because they dealt primarily with sovereign nations and their relations with each other. William Seward insisted that this was a rebellion and not a war between sovereign countries. Vattel's admonition that "Neutral Nations are those who, in time of war, do not take any part in the contest, but remain common friends to both parties without favoring the arms of the one to the prejudice of the other" was quickly side-stepped by both Britain and France as private citizens supplied the Confederacy with the money, guns and ships to fight the Union for four, bloody years.[12]

Like the British Foreign Office, the U.S. State Department was a busy place. While the Lincoln State Department was built specifically for the purpose of housing state documents and conducting state business, the Davis State Department was hastily arranged on the top floor of the Richmond Customs House. During this time, Seward had competition for the work of managing foreign relations. Both the House of Representatives and the Senate had standing committees on foreign affairs. Charles Sumner of Massachusetts chaired the Senate committee and Henry Winter Davis of Maryland chaired the House committee. Some historians consider Sumner to have been the *de facto* secretary of state who shared the president's greatest trust. Sumner was powerful, outspoken and could block Senate legislation to prevent it from reaching the House. One of his biographers stated, "As head of the prestigious Committee on Foreign Relations, Sumner could expect, and did usually receive, implicit obedience … to all his requests dealing with diplomatic affairs."[13] Nevertheless, Henry Seward worked hard to retain primary control of foreign affairs within the state department. In addition to Sumner and Davis, who were some of the other "key players" in a drama which almost brought Abraham Lincoln to a two-front war with the Confederacy and the Anglo-French alliance?

The British legation in Washington was headed by a career diplomat, Lord Richard Bickerton Pemmel Lyons. The Union legation in London was run by Charles Francis Adams, Sr. Both men were careful and methodical in their response to the many crises that demanded attention at this time. Adams, Seward, Napoleon III and even Lyons used bluff and bluster against each other throughout the war period to secure their objectives. All four men were ultimately central and critical to the foreign policy politics which had a controlling impact on the outcome of the Civil War. Jefferson Davis' first "ministers" to Europe were William Loundes Yancey of Georgia, Ambrose Dudley Mann of Virginia, and Pierre Rost of Louisiana. Again, despite their presence in London, Paris and Brussels, King Cotton was the real minister plenipotentiary.

That was foreign relations plan A. Unfortunately, Jefferson Davis had no effective, organized plan B.

From 1861–1865, nobody really wanted war. Abraham Lincoln wanted one war at a time. Lord Palmerston was wary of war as an instrument of diplomacy after Crimea. Jefferson Davis did the best he could to stir up trouble and start a war between Britain and the Union. What prevented a conflict that might have involved so many countries from Britain to Japan? Was it skillful state department diplomacy? Despite his threats, was Seward "crazy like a fox?" Did issues in Europe provide the necessary distraction to allow Lincoln to succeed? Was Jefferson Davis so incompetent that the war was Lincoln's to lose? Were those "hoary and shrewd men" of the British Foreign Office the real heroes? These are just a few of the issues examined in *Bluff, Bluster, Lies and Spies*.

On the morning of April 15, 1865, William Henry Seward awoke in pain. That morning was the first time that the secretary was able to get out of bed and look out the window at the warm spring sunshine. Seward was not comforted by the beautiful day – he was upset. He wasn't angered by the pain and swollen right cheek that was now twice its normal size. Henry Seward was concerned that of all those who came to see him and wish him well, the president never came. At nine o'clock that morning, Edwin Stanton and Frances Seward came to his room and broke the news that Lincoln was dead. As Seward slowly got out of bed and pulled the curtain to his third floor bedroom aside, he saw black bunting hanging from the windows of all the houses that bordered Lafayette Square. Lincoln was at that moment lying in an open casket in the East Room of the White House. Although the association between Lincoln and Seward and Davis and Benjamin is a critical one, an analysis of those relationships is beyond the scope of this research.

In the end, Seward was not alone in a "bad-boy" attitude that sometimes got in the way of good judgment and sound diplomacy. Palmerston, Russell, Napoleon III and a large cast of players were all involved in writing a new and more realistic book of rules in foreign relations.

CHAPTER 1

THE ENIGMA AND THE MYSTERY

*If you know the enemy and know yourself, you need not fear the result of
a hundred battles. If you know yourself but not the enemy, for every victory
gained you will also suffer a defeat. If you know neither the enemy nor
yourself, you will succumb in every battle.*

Sun Tsu, *The Art of War*, second century BCE

War and the threat of a "world wrapped in flames"[1] can bring out the best
and the worst in those expected to win the war and secure an honorable
and lasting peace. During the American Civil War, guns and diplomacy
needed to work skillfully together to achieve that objective. West Point
graduates of high and low standing manned the guns while two college
men, William Henry Seward and Judah Philip Benjamin, tried to work
foreign relations in their favor. As secretary of state, Seward worked for
Abraham Lincoln, and Benjamin for Jefferson Davis. Although Seward
claimed that he was an enigma to himself, Benjamin was a brilliant
Jewish lawyer who burned all of his personal papers after the war. We
know him professionally though his official dispatches as secretary of war,
and then secretary of state. We know him personally through the words
of those who were close to him. Varina Davis was kind in her assessment,
but *The Richmond Examiner* was not so generous. Personally, he remains
a mystery. Seward sought publicity, and Benjamin ran from it. However,

Jefferson Davis may be the least understood and most maligned of them all. As with both Seward and Benjamin, the newspapers were merciless in their criticism. Sometimes this was justified, and sometimes not. Davis suffered the same fate and thus remains an enigma and a "leader without a legend."[2]

William Henry Seward, the "wise macaw", was a complex and entertaining man who enjoyed Havana cigars, swore like a company sergeant and worked with an impulsive speed that sometimes frustrated people like British minister Richard Lyons and thus impacted U.S. foreign relations during the American Civil War. Many who knew Seward commented that he also wrote quickly. Those letters in his own hand marked "personal and confidential" sometimes display impatience, and always show a barely legible script that suggests Seward was often in a hurry. If he couldn't be president, he would secure his place in history as the *de facto* president who saved the union and showed the seasoned diplomats of Europe "how it's done".

Henry Seward was a small man who always stood out. In the Frances Carpenter painting showing the Lincoln cabinet at the first reading of the Emancipation Proclamation, the scene is one of black broadcloth and serious faces.[3] One figure, however, stands out. William Henry Seward sits right in the middle of the canvas wearing yellow pants that visually force everyone else into the background.

The Union representative in London, Charles Francis Adams, confirmed Seward's impulsivity. "Mr. Seward was never a learned man. In the ardor with which he rushed into affairs, the wonder is that he acquired what he did. To his faculty of rapid digestion of what he could read, he was indebted for the attainments he actually mastered."[4] Adams and his sons were consistently inconsistent in their estimation of the talents of William Henry Seward. That inconsistent estimate of Seward is a common theme in the letters of those who knew him. That contradiction is a hazard through which the historian must navigate to understand the real man, and the true motivation behind him.

After battlefield losses and bread riots at home, Jefferson Davis also received little praise for his work. Many considered him cold, inflexible and difficult to work with. The same stress that etched those creases into the second life mask made of Lincoln also made Davis look older than he was. His right eye was covered with a cataract and he slept badly. "[Judah Benjamin and Varina Davis] shared a dangerous knowledge that must never be revealed to anyone: that the president could go for days unable to function, brought down into deep depression by war news and bedridden with neuralgia, causing him throbbing headaches and stomach pains."[5] Davis and Lincoln took the heavy toll on young life personally. Nevertheless, the estimates of the administrative skills of Davis and Benjamin were consistently negative. Both men worked long hours together. Where Lincoln knew how to delegate, Davis took on a level of administrative responsibility that almost killed him. So, where Seward and Lincoln had both supporters and critics, Davis and Benjamin were more consistently condemned. With all four men, however, criticism made them focus more on their respective goals. Lincoln wanted to win on the field of battle and diplomacy. Davis wanted help from Europe so his Confederacy would be left alone to live as it wished.

But what else do we know of these men? The basic facts of the life of William Henry Seward are simple. He was born in Florida, New York on May 16, 1801. He was one of five children who grew up with black servants employed by his parents. Henry studied law at Union College and was admitted to the bar in 1821. A successful lawyer by 1826 earning almost $5,000 per year, Seward tired of the detail and the pace of jurisprudence. He was always in a hurry, and he preferred the excitement of politics and dealing directly with people. He was a small man with reddish hair, an unexpected husky voice and eyes that looked right through you and tried to read your mind. When he married Frances Miller, the daughter of his law partner, he moved and spent the rest of his life in Auburn, New York. He and Frances had five children. Seward served in the New York State senate and was elected governor in 1838. As senator and governor, he favored such progressive policies as prison reform and strong public education as then advocated by Horace Mann in Massachusetts.

Henry, an anti-slavery Whig, was elected U.S. senator from New York in 1849. In 1850, he acknowledged that slavery was protected by the Constitution, but claimed that there was a "higher law" that superseded the Constitution. Seward defended runaway slaves in court, and may have allowed his home in Auburn to be used as a hideout for slaves accessing the underground railroad. He joined the newly-formed

Republican party in 1855, and looked forward to his expected nomination for president in 1860. Anticipating his election, he had already written his senate resignation speech. His loss to Lincoln shocked the political establishment, and humbled Seward to an extent that his optimistic personality had never experienced before. He was crushed, angry and confused. However, Seward accepted the most prestigious of cabinet posts, secretary of state. When not in Washington, Seward lived in a spacious house in Auburn, New York. His library was large with many volumes on diverse subjects. Henry Seward, as he was known by friends, was a smart man. Strangely, numbered pictures of kings, queens, politicians and powerful people lined the staircase wall leading to the second floor. Seward's collection contained 132 numbered pictures. Most of the people in the collection directly or indirectly represent every country with which the United States had a diplomatic relationship. It is revealing that Seward called those in the collection his "tormentors".

Among the images were the photographs of Lord Richard Lyons, British representative in Washington and Lord John Russell, foreign secretary. Initially, neither man trusted Seward; both expressed unkind words about him during the early days of the Civil War.

It is also interesting to note that Seward numbered the picture of Abraham Lincoln as "66", and the portrait of himself as "66 ½". Does this suggest the relationship was a close personal one designed to mean that the secretary was almost the president? Was he the *de facto* president that Gideon Welles claimed that Seward considered himself to be? There may be some truth to both suggestions. In some respects, he was a surrogate president, friend, advisor, rival and enigma to Abraham Lincoln. Seward served Lincoln and Andrew Johnson as secretary of state until he retired in 1869 upon the election of Ulysses Grant. His counterpart in the Davis government was Judah Philip Benjamin, sometimes referred to by historians as the "Confederate Kissinger".

Judah Philip Benjamin may arguably be considered one of the most mysterious personalities of the entire Civil War period. Unlike Seward, we only know Benjamin vicariously through the eyes of those who knew and worked with him. William Seward left a long paper trail for historians to follow, but Benjamin left a short one. "I have never kept a diary or kept a copy of a letter written by me. No letters addressed to me by others will be found among my papers when I die ... for I have read so many American biographies which only reflected the passions and prejudices of their writers, that I do not want to leave behind me letters and documents to be used in such a work about myself."[6]

After the war, Confederate archives were hidden in barns and attics. Attempts were made to sell them through their "owner", Col. John Pickett, to the federal government. However, when the representative of the U.S. government, William Henry Seward, was approached about purchasing what was left of the Confederate records, the secretary asked to see the archives first. Although Pickett never showed up with those documents, they were eventually sold to the U.S. for $50,000. Referred to as the "Pickett Papers", these records contain some official dispatches and correspondence of Benjamin both as secretary of war and secretary of state. Official dispatches are those which the sender was prepared to eventually publish and make public. As secretary of war, Benjamin's official dispatches shed considerable light on his legal focus and surprising lack of tact when dealing with the military.

Judah Philip Benjamin had many similarities with William Henry Seward. Both men were lawyers and senators, ambitious and smart. Both were also in a hurry.

Benjamin was born in the British Virgin Islands and moved as a young child to Charleston, South Carolina. He was Jewish, and lived at a time when Jews were suspect and stereotyped; the newspapers of the day oozed anti-Semitism. Benjamin went to Yale University at 14, but left under a cloud of suspicion two years later.[7] He then moved to New Orleans, and became an attorney so successful that he earned $50,000 per year.[8] Soon, he befriended John Slidell, argued successfully before the U.S. Supreme Court, and at 23 wrote what soon became a standard reference text on Louisiana common law. Before the first shot was fired in the Civil War, he turned down an offer to become a U.S. Supreme Court justice. Wishing to settle down, he married into a well-known Louisiana Creole family, built a large plantation and purchased 140 slaves.

Another enigmatic figure of the Civil War was Jefferson Davis. Contemporaries either respected him or hated him. Other than his family, few people loved him. A hero at Buena Vista in the war with Mexico,

Davis was wounded, "his leg bloody and swollen, pieces of brass spur driven into the wound and imbedded there so that his boot filled with blood."[9] Somehow, Judah Benjamin and Jefferson Davis worked together to the same extent that Lincoln and Seward did during the war. Davis respected and trusted Benjamin's great intellect and judgment. Seward was primarily an opportunist, but a skillful politician as well. Benjamin was a legal scholar who especially enjoyed legal research. He was most at home in the law library. By contrast, Davis is described by Varina Howell to her mother, "The fact is, he is the kind of person I should expect to rescue me from a mad dog at any risk, but to insist upon a stoical indifference to the fright afterward."[10]

While Davis was a risk-taker in battle, Seward was a risk-taker in politics and loved to play the political game. He had no problem with playing for very high stakes. Later in life, Henry Seward was described on both sides of the Atlantic as a devious politician driven by personal ego. After marrying Frances Miller, Seward spent so much time in political pursuit that his marriage suffered. His wife felt that his children no longer knew him. One of his biographers, Glyndon Van Deusen, described Seward in terms that also describe aspects of the French emperor, Napoleon III:

> "Politicians of the Seward stripe act from a mixture of motives. They have a real desire to serve the people, to make the country a better place than they found it. They are aggressive by nature, and at the same time seek to bolster self-esteem by political activity. Gamblers by instinct, they are fascinated by the element of chance in a political contest. They covet power, and if convinced that a given political course rides the wave of the future they will be loyal to it, even though its triumph may be of dubious social value. But they are reluctant to commit themselves to a cause the success of which is doubtful, and once convinced that it has outlived its usefulness they abandon it without reluctance."[11]

Benjamin also neglected his marriage, but to an extent that his wife took other lovers, and ultimately moved to Paris with their only child. They were never divorced, but lived apart for the rest of their lives. Seward had six children, and after ten years of marriage, Benjamin had one daughter.[12] Both men were dedicated to themselves and their work. Seward admitted that he was, "an enigma" to himself. Benjamin just maintained that constant, mysterious smile that many remarked upon. "Benjamin's voice seemed a silver thread woven amidst the warp and woof of sounds which filled the drawing room ... from the first sentence he uttered, whatever he said, attracted and chained the attention of his audience." Varina Davis spoke of Benjamin in a manner that could never be applied to either Lincoln or his secretary of state.

Seward's enigmatic personality manifested itself in many ways. He believed in union and graduated emancipation, but not at the price of war. He had a desire to serve the people, as long as that service suited his personal objectives. Seward was aggressive in the context of being a risk-taker who took chances to further advance his own agenda. He coveted power to the extent that he tried to act as an alternate president for a man who was so preoccupied by the Civil War that foreign policy devolved to one of the most polarizing personalities of the era. By contrast, Judah Benjamin actually acted as an alternate president when Davis was away or suffered such depression that he could not get out of bed, let alone hold cabinet meetings and plan strategy. Seward knew that some liked him and others hated him. He closed his letters to his friend Thurlow Weed, "Your friend who has faith in everybody, and enjoys the confidence of nobody."[13] Seward knew many people on both sides of the Atlantic. Ironically, when traveling to Europe in 1859, he met and was entertained by his future antagonists, Henry Temple (Lord Palmerston), John Russell, and Louis Napoleon. Although he knew many, he lacked intimate friends. He, Benjamin and Davis remained enigmatic and mysterious figures.

The American Civil War represents an era of historical significance. The people who worked with Abraham Lincoln and Jefferson Davis knew that they were involved in something important. They believed that the part they played would be recorded for posterity. People like William Henry Seward, John Hay, Charles Sumner, Gideon Welles, John Bigelow, Richard Cobden, John Bright and Salmon Chase kept diaries, wrote letters, sent dispatches and filed reports that have been preserved for research. The common thread that runs through much of the communication at this early stage of the Civil War confirms that the U.S. secretary of state was perceived to be more concerned with politics than ideology. All thought of him as an intelligent man, but he was also thought of as someone who could not be trusted. Gideon Welles and

Seward were competitors, and the Navy secretary did not trust the secretary of state. Both came to know Lincoln well, in part because they were the only two to serve in the cabinet throughout Lincoln's presidency. Personally and socially, Welles claimed to enjoy Seward's company, and attended many of the social events that were often held at the Seward home in Washington. Both the Welles and Seward homes bordered Lafayette Park. With just one entry gate to the park, the Navy secretary had to walk around the square to the red, brick house that Seward rented for $1,800 per year. According to Welles, "My opposition to him [Seward] has always been political ... There was a freshness and a heartiness in his manner, and his conversation so abounded in humor ... I always found his society attractive."[14] Professionally, however, Welles, Senator Charles Sumner and others thought little of Seward. Sumner was a powerful senator from Massachusetts who also chaired the Senate Foreign Relations Committee. He maintained a regular correspondence with British members of parliament John Bright and Richard Cobden. Writing to Bright on November 18, 1862, he says that, "Seward has talent and prodigious industry, but little forecast and a want of seriousness." This is a common complaint by some about Seward, and perception became reality for many people. That perception had consequences. In addition to Gideon Welles, Salmon Chase, secretary of the treasury, often clashed with Seward. One of Chase's biographers stated, "To the inflexible and austere secretary of the treasury, Seward's geniality seemed ingratiation, his laughter at the president's jokes, sycophancy, and his shrewd advice self-promotion."[15] According to Chase, "He is too much of a politician for me." However, neither Chase nor Sumner saw Seward as an enigma, just a tricky politician. Lord Richard Lyons, British legation minister to Washington, was offended by what he interpreted as typical American brash behavior. Henri Mercier, French minister to Washington, saw the secretary's behavior as a form of braggadocio which helped drive the pace and direction of the Seward state department. In early 1861, did anyone else see Seward in a more objective light? Can anyone bring us closer to the truth?

Other than Mary Lincoln, there were only two people who had more daily contact with Abraham Lincoln than any other: John George Nicolay and John Milton Hay. Both men were secretaries who worked and slept on the second floor of the White House, right across the hall from Lincoln's cabinet room. Hay's diary, Nicolay's letters to his fiancée Therena Bates in Pittsfield, Illinois, and their ten-volume biography, *Abraham Lincoln: A History* preserve an interesting and generally more balanced picture of the Lincoln cabinet. Nicolay and Hay were guilty of overstating their case for Lincoln, but more objective than Welles and Sumner regarding William Henry Seward. Nevertheless, even with greater objectivity, the observations of Nicolay and Hay confirm the problematic personality of the secretary of state.

Although a polarizing figure, Seward has been credited by Charles Francis Adams with being the prime mover in growing and strengthening the U.S. Department of State. This, however, is an example of one of those overstatements, which are common among contemporaries and modern historians. From the standpoint of personnel (numbers and locations of legations and consulates) the State Department grew considerably from 1790 to 1863.[16] For example, in 1790, there were two diplomatic positions filled, one for England and one for France. By 1863, the number of diplomatic positions had increased to thirty-three. The growth of the consular service was much greater. Consuls were primarily intended to support and protect American business, security and commerce in their respective countries. The consular service employed ten people in 1790, 282 in 1863. The numbers tell a different story, however, when comparing the size of the state departments of Daniel Webster, 1851 (Millard Fillmore); Lewis Cass, 1859 (James Buchanan); and William Seward, 1863 (Abraham Lincoln). During the Civil War, relations with England were more critical than were relations with any other single country. Each of these presidents maintained a legation and minister in London. However, the size of the consular service grew only modestly from Fillmore to Lincoln. Daniel Webster listed eight consuls in London in 1851; Lewis Cass registered nine consuls in 1859, and Seward registered just one more to list ten consuls in London in 1863. The growth of support personnel was much greater, however. Daniel Webster employed only one clerk, but Cass had 23 on the payroll, and Seward 25. In addition to that modest increase, Seward hired five clerks from the Buchanan department and carried them over to his own state department. The record indicates that the greatest physical growth of the U.S. State Department actually came from Lewis Cass and James Buchanan, not

William Seward and Abraham Lincoln. More interesting than the personnel numbers are the rates of compensation for the heads of the legations.[17] History has subsequently shown where the diplomatic "hot spots" were during the Civil War. Unquestionably, the management of foreign relations was the most critical with England and France. Buchanan and Lincoln paid their legation ministers (George Dallas and Adams respectively) the same, $17,500 per year. Following in diplomatic significance were Russia, Prussia, Austria, Mexico and Spain. Ministers in all of these countries were also paid the same under Buchanan and Lincoln, $12,000 per year. As such, neither the physical growth nor the more complex determination of diplomatic sensitivity, as evidenced by annual compensation, can be attributed to the Seward State Department. Was Adams perhaps referring to the more subjective "effectiveness" of the Department? Clearly, a definition of the term "effective" will be relative. However, research has shown that Seward's political orientation also helped him place the right people in the right places at the right time. Men like Charles Francis Adams, John Bigelow, Thomas Corwin and Henry Shelton Sanford worked hard to ensure that the primary Lincoln war aim, a united union, could successfully defeat the Confederacy on the battlefield as well as the hearts and minds of those in power in Europe. Adams labored to help ensure that England did not formally recognize the Confederacy and thus ensure that Lincoln had a chance to win on the battlefield. Henry Sanford occupied a lesser Ministry in Brussels, Belgium. However, correspondence marked "personal and confidential" between Seward and Sanford clearly indicate that they were involved in a large, expensive espionage and arms purchasing operation that kept both men busy from December, 1861 to the end of the war. In Seward's words:

> "You can readily imagine how vast a machinery has been created in the War Department, in the Navy Department, and in the Treasury Department, respectively. The head of each is a man of busy occupations, high responsibilities, and perplexing cares. You would hardly suppose that a similar change has come over the modest little State Department of other and peaceful days; but the exactions upon it are infinite, and out of all that offers itself to be done, I can only select and do that which cannot be wisely or safely undone."[18]

In 1861, the U.S. State Department, as well as the legation offices in Washington, became active places. According to Frederick Seward, assistant secretary of state, "Unusual activity and unwonted industry pervaded the Washington legations of all the maritime powers. The attachés of the British legation found themselves as busy as hard-working attorneys' clerks".

Jefferson Davis didn't have the benefit of an established state department with accredited representatives and established lines of communication. At the start of the war, Union post offices still located in the seceding states were closed. The existing foreign legations were located in Washington, not Montgomery or Richmond. What about all of the consuls who were then working in every major Southern city from Charleston to Galveston? Consular work was critical to England and France. Consuls worked to protect foreign business interests as well as the many foreign-born men who had lived in the United States for many years and were now being drafted into the Union army. When this happened, they ran to the consular office for help. But, without competent men in London and Paris to represent the Confederacy, what was to be done with the many consuls who were appointed by presidents from Pierce to Lincoln and still at their desks in the new Confederacy? Where were their loyalties? Were they going to be spies for Lincoln and Seward? If necessary, who would replace them? Initially, Jefferson Davis decided to let them all stay at their posts and carry on as they did before Fort Sumter. Richard Lyons wisely told the British consuls that they should communicate directly with the Foreign Office and not through him. He was in Washington, and Davis might suspect that he would tamper with dispatches to Europe. It was a wise decision that helped Davis make his choice to allow the consuls to remain – but with a blockade, how would they be able to communicate with their respective home offices?

Initially, the blockade was not very effective, and communication was relatively easy. As the blockade tightened by 1862, communication between the consuls and their home offices in London and Paris became difficult. Sending critical dispatches to London eventually took three to four months. Mail was sent aboard blockade runners to try and make it to Europe.

Beyond the dispatch issue, one of the problems which increased as the war progressed were the ships which attempted to run the blockade and sell cotton for guns in the ports of Charleston, Wilmington, and others. Those critical blockade runners were shallow-draft and built with powerful steam engines that were faster than the slower Union warships blockading the harbors.[19] British neutrality provoked Seward into recommending that blockade to Lincoln. English captains complained that their neutral status should allow them to lawfully pass through the blockade and sell non-contraband goods to Southern merchants. Lincoln and Seward drew no distinction between contraband and so-called non-contraband. They felt that any assistance to the Confederacy would help sustain them and prolong the war. Frederick Seward told his father that the State Department was seizing guns that were being labeled as farm equipment, and gunpowder marked as "white lead".[20]

During the Civil War, the state department negotiated twenty-six treaties with foreign countries. In addition, the state department was monitoring an active political scene in Europe. Nicolay and Hay confirmed this in stating, "One of the gravest doubts which beset the Lincoln administration on its advent to power was how foreign relations would deal with the fact of secession and rebellion in the United States."[21] Seward's two-room office was on the second floor of a two-story building on the corner of Pennsylvania Avenue and Fifteenth streets. His son Fredrick was right across the hall. All thirty rooms overflowed with the books, archives and papers covering the details of the complex business of foreign policy. Some of these were the personal papers of William Seward which contained lists detailing the number of official dispatches which went from the secretary's office to the legations and consuls around the world, neatly tallied by hand. Charles Francis Adams' office in London led the list with 1,829 dispatches from Washington to London from 1861–1865. One thousand such dispatches were issued in 1863 alone. Paris was next with 1,240 dispatches, St. Petersburg received 323, and The Hague recorded 321. Seward's department communicated most often with London, Paris, The Hague, St. Petersburg, Copenhagen, Lisbon, Rio de Janiero, Brussels, Mexico, Peking, Berlin, Madrid and Vienna.[22]

On March 22, 1861, detailed instructions went from the State Department to all foreign legations. The first such dispatch was to Lincoln's personal friend Norman Judd in Prussia. Lincoln was sensitive to the opinions of the large German population in America. His senior secretary, John George Nicolay, was a German immigrant. Lincoln also bought a German language newspaper during the first campaign to act as a means for reaching this audience and securing their support. The Judd dispatch consisted exclusively of a lecture on the wrongs committed by the seceding Southern states. Seward ends by warning Judd not to say or do anything that might cause offense to the Prussian government. This first dispatch was nothing provocative. It was more than capable of surviving public scrutiny.

The more sensitive communication to Charles Francis Adams in London wasn't dated until April 10, 1861. In that dispatch, Seward initially states that the only serious issues between the Union and England were a boundary dispute in Puget Sound and the termination of a contract with the Hudson's Bay Company. Halfway through Seward's lecture to Adams, however, he threatens England and flatters Adams. Seward's risk-taking eclipsed anything that the more cautious Richard Lyons would have written. A Lyons dispatch of this type would have been marked *Confidential*. The secretary tells Adams, "The president does not doubt that you fully appreciate the responsibility of your mission. An honored ancestor of yours was the first to represent your whole country, after its independence was established, at the same court to which you now are accredited. The President feels assured that it will happen through no want of loyalty or of diligence on your part if you are to be the last to discharge that trust." Believing that possible recognition of the seceding states might be the first diplomatic problem, Seward warned Adams, "If, as the President does not at all apprehend, you shall unhappily find her Majesty's government tolerating the application of the so-called seceding states, or wavering about it, you will not leave them to suppose for a moment that they can grant that application and remain the friends of the United States. You may even assure them promptly in that case that if they determine to recognize, they may at the same time prepare to enter into alliance with the enemies of this republic."

Seward's first instructions to Adams and the other legation representatives were essentially lectures which justified the position of the Union and the error of the seceding states. This is exactly what the first Confederate secretary of state, Robert Toombs, did when composing his first instructions to commissioners Yancey, Mann and Rost. Seward had accredited ministers and consuls already in place around the world, whereas Davis and Toombs had no accredited representatives, and nobody to receive a first dispatch. The first commissioners went armed with instructions similar to those issued by Seward. Davis' instructions consisted of a lengthy dissertation on the rights of secession and the veiled threat of what would happen if the cotton supply dried up. The style and didactic tone of Seward's dispatches and Toombs' instructions suggest that neither man wanted to be misrepresented. Unfortunately, Seward also had a bad habit of publishing personal and confidential correspondence with his legation personnel and releasing this to the newspapers without permission. In this, he was sometimes a threat to his own staff. Charles Francis Adams and the minister to France, William Lewis Dayton, were angry recipients of this practice.

Seward's need for public recognition was always near the surface. Dayton complained about this as early as May 32, 1861. "May I be permitted to beg of you that the contents of my Dispatches do not get into the newspapers at home."[23] Dayton was a plodding but hard-working and diligent minister in Paris who expected more from the secretary. Seward didn't respect Dayton and sometimes ignored him. He continued to publish sensitive, private communications in the newspapers. Ironically, this was often the only credible intelligence that the Davis administration had available on activities in the North. Judah Benjamin read as many Northern newspapers as could be smuggled South.

Who was in charge of foreign policy in the Lincoln administration at this time? Charles Sumner, chairman of the Senate Committee on Foreign Relations? Henry Winter Davis, chairman of the House Committee on Foreign Affairs? Between the November election and the March 4th inauguration, the Buchanan State Department was in charge. Buchanan had tried to resupply Major Anderson at Fort Sumter in Charleston. When the *Star of the West* was fired upon, the ship returned North and ended any further attempts by the president to avert secession. The months which followed the March inauguration of Lincoln were full of greater tension and uncertainty. On April 12, 1861 at 3:30am, a small row boast pulled away from the shore in Charleston and headed for Fort Sumter. Four men worked hard at the oars in the dark. One of them carried a polite note from the man in a grey uniform standing at water's edge straining to make sure the little boat made it to its destination.

The soldier in the uniform was a handsome man with neatly combed hair, narrow chin whiskers, and a quiet stare through piercing eyes that didn't blink. The man was Confederate General P.G.T. Beauregard. His note stated:

"Sir: By authority of Brigadier General G.T. Beauregard, commanding the Provincial Forces of the Confederate States, we have the honor to notify you that he will open the fire of his batteries on Fort Sumter in one hour from this time. We have the honor to be, very respectfully, your obedient servant, James Chestnut, Jr. Aide de Camp, Stephen D. Lee, C.S. Army, Aide de Camp."[24]

The fort commander had already notified Confederate forces that he didn't need to start firing because he only had four days of food anyway. When that ran out, so would he and his men. No matter. Fearing that Lincoln would also try to resupply the fort, the man with the piercing stare opened fire anyhow.

The perception at home and abroad was that Seward was regarded as the real power in Washington. In April, 1861, the secretary of state made plans that were risky and potentially dangerous if it backfired. His desire for peace at home and a desire for personal fame quickly exposed the secretary's bluff.

The year 1861 started out with tension and uncertainty. Lincoln's election was the signal to the South that there would be trouble. During his debates with Senator Stephen Douglas, Lincoln made it clear that he did not intend to interfere with slavery as it existed already in the South. His concern was for the potential spread of slavery into the new territories that were then becoming populated. Kansas and Nebraska territories were huge tracts of land that would later be divided up into smaller states. If they were slave, their congressional representation in Washington would tip the balance of power in favor of the slave states. Lincoln drew the line there. Nevertheless, fear of control by abolitionists caused South Carolina to secede from the Union even before Lincoln was inaugurated. She was followed by six other states, Mississippi, Florida, Alabama, Georgia, Louisiana and Texas. What would happen with Virginia, Arkansas, Tennessee and North Carolina? Virginia was important because she was on the border with Washington. From her railroad depot in Manassas, it was only two days' march to the Capitol.

Tennessee was just as important because control of that state by the Union would give her easy access to Arkansas, Mississippi, Alabama, Georgia and North Carolina. Tennessee also provided access to important border states like Missouri and Kentucky. President Buchanan was anxious to hand his problems off to Abraham Lincoln, but he refused to surrender the federal forts to the states in secession. Nerves frayed further in March when Lincoln was inaugurated as the sixteenth president.

In April, knowing that another relief ship was being sent to Sumter by the new president, South Carolina ordered Pierre Beauregard to open fire and reduce the fort. Major Anderson surrendered, and four more states joined the new Confederacy. France and England were dependent on the South for cotton and wheat. What if they were now cut off from their supply? Could the secretary of state help?

Seward saw political opportunity in this first crisis of the Lincoln presidency. Seeking to fill a perceived void in foreign policy, stake his claim on history, and control Lincoln's foreign relations, Seward immediately put Lincoln on the spot with his *"Some thoughts for the President's consideration"* memo of April 1, 1861.[25] There was nothing vague in Seward's frontal attack. The secretary began his memo with, "1st. We are at the end of a month's administration and yet without a policy either domestic or foreign." Seward was impatient. The head of the Union legation in London, Charles Francis Adams, had just left for England on the same day. His trip was delayed by the wedding of his son, Charles Francis, Jr. Adams arrived in London on the 13th. But foreign policy administration couldn't wait. "If satisfactory explanations are not received from Spain and France, would convene Congress and declare war against them." Seward's solution to the anticipated problem of not receiving quick and satisfactory answers from Spain and France (regarding French interest in Mexico and Spanish designs on Santo Domingo) was war. Beneath the threat of war, however, the secretary wanted to maintain peace between North and South at almost any cost. Seward believed that many in the South did not want secession and would unite with the North in a war with a common enemy. He believed that an attack by Europe on America would make "all the hills of South Carolina pour forth their population to the rescue."

After admitting his own limitations, Lincoln took one of his most significant steps in foreign affairs – he tried to control Seward and put him in his place. Significantly, he also sought foreign relations advice from another, more reliable source: Charles Sumner.

However, before turning to Sumner, Lincoln responded to Seward. The secretary of state's memo is dated April 1st. Lincoln's response was also dated April 1st. He realized the dangers of Seward without a bridle and immediately set out to remind the secretary who was the boss, closing his response to Seward by indicating that the foreign policy responsibility rested with the president:

> "Upon your closing propositions, that whatever policy we adopt, there must be an energetic prosecution of it. For this purpose, it must be somebody's business to pursue and direct it incessantly. Either the President must do it himself, and be able all the while active in it, or devolve it on some member of his cabinet. Once adopted, debates on it must end, and all agree and abide. I remark that if this must be done, I must do it. When a general line of policy is adopted, I apprehend there is no danger of its being changed without good reason, or continuing to be a subject of unnecessary debate; still, upon points arising in its progress, I wish, and suppose I am entitled to have the advice of all the cabinet. Your Obt. Servt. A. Lincoln".

Seward's memo was marked "confidential". We don't know if Sumner ever saw it.

In writing to his friend, the Duchess of Argyll, on June 4, 1861, Sumner warned, "The president is honest and well-disposed. There has been a sinister influence." Yet Lincoln had knowingly taken his chief rival for the presidency into his cabinet. He believed that Seward was a capable but tricky politician; it was better to keep this man close where Lincoln could better control him. Although Lincoln told Seward that he, Lincoln, would assume responsibility for administration policy, he never said that he disagreed with the secretary's aggressive approach.

The president still knew that he needed help.

One source of help in the foreign relations department was Charles Sumner. The senator's ego was well fed with the knowledge of the president's call for aid. Writing to Richard Henry Dana on June 30, 1861, he stated, "The statement on our foreign relations is that All's Well – in a single sentence. The secretary of state has changed immensely during the last month, and is now mild and gentle."[26] Was there really a change in Seward? If so, what caused that change? Did the president's response have the intended impact? Did Seward know that he had a rival secretary of state? Did this slow him down? We know that Seward learned on the job, and became more careful with his written communication. However, Sumner's statement that the secretary was now "mild and gentle" is not consistent with the historical facts. The Civil War drama was just beginning to unfold.

Even after Lincoln's scolding, Seward didn't think the president was up to the job. Abraham Lincoln was a man who sometimes carried important papers in his stovepipe hat. Unlike Seward, he didn't smoke or drink, but always enjoyed Seward's jokes and stories. Nevertheless, Lincoln had little knowledge of foreign policy and was frank enough to say so. In the President's own words, he told Rudolph Schleiden, the minister from Bremen, that "I don't know anything about diplomacy. I will be very apt to make blunders." Charles Francis Adams stated in 1873, "In the history of our government, no experience has been made so rash as elevating to the head of affairs a man with so little previous preparation for his task as Mr. Lincoln ... It is eminently so in respect to foreign relations, of which he knew absolutely nothing."[27] John Lothrop Motley, the U.S. minister to Vienna, was a friend of Henry Seward. Writing to Seward in June, 1861 he also saw the limitations of the new president, and wrote to Seward that he thought Lincoln ignorant about foreign affairs but honest enough to admit it. Adams was a sour critic of anyone whose views differed from his. He thought little of either Seward's or Lincoln's foreign relations background. When asked to give the eulogy at Seward's funeral in 1873, Adams further detailed Lincoln's amateurish attempts at helping to set up the foreign policy machinery. "Moreover, the president, in distributing his places, did so with small reference to the qualifications in this particular line. It was either partisan service, or geographical position, or the length of the lists of names to commendatory papers, or the size of the salary, or the unblushing pertinacity of personal solicitation, that wrung from him many of his appointments."[28]

Nevertheless, in his first message to Congress on December 3, 1861, Lincoln elevates foreign relations to the opening paragraphs. This was done at the recommendation of Charles Sumner. He was concerned with foreign intervention. The president warned Congress that "A nation which endures factious domestic division is exposed to disrespect abroad; and one party, if not both, is sure, sooner or later, to invoke foreign intervention." He stated that Union success didn't depend on foreign assistance.[29] Lincoln went on, however, to state that we needed to be careful to guard our shores from any foreign interference. He wanted "one war at a time." This was a constant Lincoln theme and would later prove critical to foreign relations and Union success in the Civil War.

The Union wanted help from Europe, but initially had some trouble. Lincoln was turned down for a loan as well as a request for ships and other war supplies. The loan request came after the defeat at Bull Run on July 21, 1861. The circumstances were very different for the Confederacy, however. They needed money, ships, guns and any other war material that Europe was willing to sell.

Seward knew that the Confederacy was at a serious material disadvantage. In 1859, he purchased the latest best-seller and added it to his library in Auburn. The book was by a South Carolinian named Hinton Rowan Helper, entitled *The Impending Crisis of the South: How to Meet It*. The volume was published and marketed by anti-slavery factions in the North.[30] It is significant that the book was written by a man from the South, but detailed in graphic terms the disadvantages crippling the Confederacy because of the reliance on slave labor. Helper described the North in comparison to the South in terms of per capita income, farm output, industrial output, population growth, extent of rail capacity and more. Although the Union was more financially stable than the Confederacy, the South borrowed from wherever they could. Rothschild and Barrings said "no", but Erlanger later said "yes". This was fortunate for Davis because critical to Confederate success was money. Helper showed bank capital in the Northern states in 1856 to be $230,100,340. In the Confederate states, the cash holdings in all banks amounted to less than half of that found in the North, $102,078,940. This was 1859. During the war, Confederate finances continued to suffer. The Dutch financial newspapers quoted new CSA bond prices 500 times in less than one year. In addition to credit abroad, the Confederacy also needed an organized diplomatic corps to help achieve that second objective, official recognition. Jefferson Davis, however, was as ill-suited as Abraham Lincoln to the demands of international relations.

Most people in government, foreign and domestic, were aware of Lincoln's ignorance of international affairs. Underneath, however, Abraham Lincoln knew his objectives and put his stamp on U.S. foreign policy during the Civil War as best he could given his preoccupation with the conflict.

Lincoln was the commander-in-chief. He charted the basic course, and left the diplomatic details to Seward. Sometimes this backfired. In several significant instances, the president outlined his basic policy, foreign and domestic, to his secretary of state. First, he wanted to deal with the South without interference from Europe. Lincoln would do nothing to cause a war with England, France, Spain or Russia. Three of these countries, for example, had loaned money to Mexico and were anxious to collect. Mexico was politically unstable, and Europe was concerned that those debts would never be paid back. Setting foot on Mexican soil to force repayment was a potential challenge to the Monroe Doctrine. France, Spain and the Netherlands had colonies and possessions immediately off the coast of Key West, Florida. Confederate privateers saw English ports in the Caribbean as safe refuge from Union warships attempting to put a stop to the piracy then practiced by privateers sneaking past the blockade to bring in war supplies in exchange for cotton that was shipped out at night.

The domestic front was more complex than European foreign relations at this early stage and quickly brought out Seward threat. Lincoln claimed that the South lacked the Constitutional authority to secede. However, on August 14, 1861, the first Confederate commissioners in Europe wrote an explanation as to why the Southern states had seceded at the request of Lord John Russell, head of the Foreign Office. To the Right Honorable Earl Russell, Her Majesty's principal secretary of state for foreign affairs, the confederate commissioners avoided any mention of slavery. They defended secession as a means of protecting life, liberty and property. They neglected to mention that the property was human "property". Their letter stated, "Governments are instituted among men deriving their just powers from the consent of the governed; that whenever any form of government becomes destructive of these ends (security to life, liberty and the pursuit of happiness), it is the right of the people to alter or to abolish it and to institute a new government."

Secession had been threatened by states North and South ever since the nation was founded. Although South Carolina fired the first shot at Fort Sumter on April 12, 1861, those first shots were provoked by Lincoln himself. Before Sumter, Lincoln and many others in Washington were not convinced that the South would go to war. Many believed that the South contained many loyal to the Union. Most Southerners did not own slaves. Jefferson Davis was not popularly elected, but selected by a small group of seven wealthy plantation owners. For this reason, many in the Lincoln administration believed that the South would not secede and go to war to maintain that separation.

Lincoln initially only wanted to retain control over federal government property. That property included the forts that were guarding the harbors of America's largest seaport cities. Fort Sumter, in the harbor at Charleston, South Carolina, was federal property. The problem was that Lincoln needed to reinforce Major Anderson, commander at the fort. The major was running out of food. Lincoln could have waited until lack of supplies forced the inevitable surrender. Instead, he made plans to send a relief ship to resupply the fort. Cabinet discussions related to the relief of either Fort Pickens in Florida or Sumter in South Carolina were extensive. Initially, the vote was five to two against relief of Sumter.

At this time, many Senators and House members from the South were still in Washington and at their desks at the unfinished capitol. Seward knew most of them from his years as a senator from New York. Believing that he was the power behind the president, Seward held private meetings with selected members from the South regarding his promise to ensure that Fort Sumter would not be resupplied. Believing that Seward was the real authority in the Lincoln government, the Southern congressmen were convinced that federal property in the South would be left alone and war would be avoided. Seward made promises that he had no right to make and ultimately could not keep. Robert Toombs, Confederate secretary of state under the early provisional government, believed that Seward's promise not to resupply Sumter was an empty promise, and warned the Davis government not to fire on the fort.

Secretary Toombs was one man in the Montgomery Cabinet who was not deceived by Seward's sophistries. He knew the temper of Mr. Lincoln better than Mr. Seward did. He appreciated the feeling in the North, and gave his counsel in the Davis Cabinet against the immediate assault upon Sumter.

There was a secret session of the Cabinet in Montgomery. Toombs was pacing the floor during the discussion over Sumter, his hands behind him, and his face wearing that heavy, dreamy look when in repose. Facing about, he turned upon the president and opposed the attack. "Mr. President," he said, "at this time, it is suicide, murder, and will lose us every friend at the North. You will wantonly strike a hornet's nest which extends from mountains to ocean, and legions, now quiet, will swarm out and sting us to death. It is unnecessary; it puts us in the wrong; it is fatal." He clung to the idea expressed in his dispatches to the commissioners, that "So long as the United States neither declares war nor establishes peace, the Confederate States have the advantage of both conditions." But just as President Lincoln overruled Secretary Seward, so President Davis overruled Secretary Toombs.[31]

In Washington, the evidence about the resupply effort was unclear. Did Seward and Lincoln have plans to resupply both Pickens and Sumter, but not tell anyone else? Fort Pickens was in the harbor at Pensacola, Florida. Sumter was more sensitive because it was right in the middle of the harbor at Charleston South Carolina which was at the center of the drive for secession. Pickens, however, was also important for control of the Gulf and could provide assistance to New Orleans and the Mississippi. That river provided easy access to the South. Seward considered Pickens to be vital and worth the risk of war. He did not favor the resupply of Sumter. He believed this this would provoke war and force Virginia into the Confederacy. At this stage, the Navy secretary agreed. Gideon Welles was one of the five who initially voted not to resupply Fort Sumter. Seward underestimated Lincoln's determination to test Southern resolve, however. The cabinet finally voted five to two to relieve Sumter. When the president made plans to send the supply ship, did Seward panic? In his capacity as *de facto* president, had he overstepped the limits of his office? Was there no secret plan with Lincoln to resupply both forts? The secretary of state had promised influential Southern Congressmen that the fort would be evacuated, not relieved. At this stage, historians refer to the Welles diary wherein the Navy secretary states that Seward deliberately substituted his plan to support Fort Pickens instead of Fort Sumter. In many instances Nicolay and Hay offer a more balanced view of Secretary Seward. However, in 1890, they relied on Welles' diary and published accounts to help them tell the story of the *Powhatan*. Nevertheless, Edward Bates was present for all of the discussions on Sumter. What does his diary say about the role of Seward in this situation? Bates is brief, and only stated on March 16, 1861, "But I did not see any great national interest involved in the bare fact of holding the fort ... Upon the whole, I do not think it wise to attempt to provision Fort Sumter. Mr. Seward gave his advice for the immediate evacuation of Fort Sumter." Unfortunately, Welles maintained a personal antipathy towards Seward, and his diary remains one of the primary sources of information on this critical incident.

Welles claimed that Lincoln trusted his secretary of state enough to sign papers submitted for signature without reading the actual content. We know that many did this with Lincoln. At this early stage of his presidency, Lincoln encouraged both his secretaries and his cabinet officers to read their dispatches and other proposed written communications to him. It has always been assumed that Lincoln was busy with new and unfamiliar duties as president, and reading to him saved time. Recent research has shown that Lincoln was more of an auditory than a visual learner.[32] Although Lincoln was a good reader, and decoded and literally read the words on a page with ease, he comprehended better when he heard the words rather than reading them. Part-time secretary to Mary Lincoln, William O. Stoddard, often read the daily newspaper to Lincoln. When Lincoln first made the request to read newspapers to him, Stoddard stated that Lincoln told him, "Sit down. I can always tell more about a thing after I've heard it read aloud, and know how it sounds. Just the reading of it to myself doesn't answer as well either." This is significant because, if we believe Welles, Seward brought papers for Lincoln to sign which countermanded the president's order to re-supply Sumter and activated the secretary's plan to help Fort Pickens. Comprehending better in the auditory capacity, Seward may have read the papers that Lincoln was to sign. He selectively read what he needed to read to set his secret plan for Pickens in motion. As late as 1864, Seward himself noted and complained of Lincoln's habit of not reading important dispatches. In a letter to Francis Lieber May 17, 1864, Charles

Sumner stated, "Goldwin Smith's pamphlet is excellent. I doubt if it would interest the president, who reads very little. Seward said to me two days ago 'there was a great cry last year on the question whether the president reads despatches [sic] before they are sent; but I am sure he never reads a d---ed one which we receive."[33] From the Bates diary, we know that Seward initially voted not to reinforce Sumter. According to Welles, Lincoln expressed surprise when he learned of the issue. Lincoln may not have known of the secretary's switch at this point.

Potential relief for Fort Sumter was openly discussed in Washington at this time. Federal property that was now within the bounds of the seceding states was obviously vulnerable and an issue to the federal government. That was no secret. The actual decision to relieve Sumter, however, was not intended to be open for public discussion. Nevertheless, vigorous activity at the Navy yard was clear evidence to anyone with interest that a naval relief effort might be underway. Perhaps unnecessarily, Secretary Seward's panic over the decision to support Sumter may have been leaked by the secretary to Charleston. According to Gideon Welles, "To the surprise of the administration, information of the confidential order to reinforce Sumter was promptly sent to Charleston. It was subsequently ascertained that this telegram was sent by Mr. Harvey, a newspaper correspondent, who was intimate at the State Department."[34] Although Seward dissented in the Sumter resupply plan, the rest of the cabinet agreed with Lincoln.

The steamship *Powhatan* was provisioned and sent on its way to Charleston. Before going to sea, however, Seward had gone over the head of the Navy secretary and installed a new captain on the ship with orders to go to Pensacola, not Charleston. When Welles discovered the plan, he went to Lincoln who immediately demanded that word be sent to the *Powhatan* to redirect it to the original destination. A tug boat, straining at 14 knots, tried to catch the *Powhatan* and deliver the message. According to Welles, "The president, who, without giving the subject much consideration, had assented to the scheme of the secretary of state to reinforce Pickens, was not aware that the flagship of the squadron had been detached, and its commander superseded until the evening of the 6th of April, on which day the *Powhatan* sailed under a different officer for a distant destination, carrying off supplies, munitions and boats which the

Navy Department had ordered for Sumter. I was not made acquainted with this secret proceeding until the *Powhatan* sailed ..." Again, we only have Welles' diary as the primary source of information on this matter.

Some historians claim that Lincoln knew about a plan to supply both forts. The Seward papers contain the telegrams from the Magnetic Telegraph Company from Captain David Dixon Porter to both Seward and Lincoln. At a time when the Lincoln administration was young, untested and under intense scrutiny, it is unfortunate to read telegrams where the captain of one of the relief expeditions is exasperated and confused about who was in charge and what to do. It is not possible to determine which telegram was sent first. Both messages were dated April 6, 1861. However, the telegram to Lincoln was sent at 11:17am. The note to Seward did not contain a time. Porter didn't know what to do because he was supposed to relieve Fort Pickens, as per an alleged order of Lincoln, but Gideon Welles had also ordered him to Sumter. Welles wanted the more powerful of the relief ships, the *Powhatan*, to go to Charleston. Cabling Seward, Porter says, "Mr. Welles has altered the destination of the *Powhatan*, the ship selected to carry out the order given to me by the President. Is the President's order of April first to be obeyed or Mr. Welles' order of today? Of the latter, Col. Brown will be entirely crippled." By 11am on the morning of the 6th, Porter sent this message to the president. "The Secretary of the Navy has issued an order in conflict with yours of the first of April and this complicates matters seriously. The original destination of the *Powhatan* has been changed. Shall I or shall I not carry out your original order delivered in the presence of Captain Meigs?" It is difficult to tell whether this was a mix-up caused by Seward alone or Seward and Lincoln together. However, the cabinet vote not to resupply Sumter would suggest that Seward was acting alone. The secretary of state kept Welles out of the loop. This was dangerous politics. Seward's polarizing personality and bad-boy reputation convinced Welles that Seward was the sole culprit. Domestic issues like Sumter quickly yielded to foreign policy concerns as Europe considered recognition of the Confederacy.

Although William Henry Seward was an enigma to himself, he wasn't the enemy. Lincoln knew who he was dealing with, and took advantage of the secretary's skills. Nevertheless, after putting Seward in his place on

April 1, 1861 over *Some Thoughts*, Lincoln became so absorbed in other aspects of the Civil War that the administration of foreign policy fell to William Henry Seward and the "key players" by default. As the hero of Buena Vista and former secretary of war, Jefferson Davis was also totally absorbed in the war. However, Davis was his own secretary of war. After many cabinet changes, he wisely came to trust his secretary of state. In Washington, Seward knew himself to the extent that at least he knew he was an enigma. Benjamin and Lincoln probably knew themselves to the same extent.

Jefferson Davis was convinced that cotton was king, and that England and France would do his bidding out of a desperate economic need for the raw material. He didn't know his enemy, and he was wrong. The Confederacy paid the price.

The military campaign immediately consumed the attention of both presidents. On April 10, 1861, Fort Sumter was attacked. On the 17th, Virginia seceded. On June 10, the Battle of Bethel Church commanded consideration. On the 17th, the Battle of Boonville secured control of the Missouri. On July 5th, Carthage; on the 11th Rich Mountain; on the 18th Blackburn's Ford and on July 21, 1861, First Manassas (Bull Run). Seward expressed concerns about repercussions from European recognition of the Confederate States. He believed that this could lead to war with the Union. Seward didn't know his enemy either. Lincoln didn't say no to a war with England; he didn't want to fight two wars at the same time. He preferred to chart the course, and leave the details to Seward and the legation representatives throughout the world. When the shooting war started, it was increasingly difficult for Lincoln to re-visit foreign policy. He didn't have the time. "He (Lincoln) was a sort of Japanese emperor withdrawn into his Kyoto White House, a shadowy figure in a distant retreat. Time and time again Shogun Seward would remark that he had spoken to the president or that he had shown a certain dispatch to him and that the president had ... etc."[35]

At this early stage in the Lincoln administration, what were the issues facing the State Department that were of the greatest concern to the government? Those issues were the threat of European recognition of the seceding states and the economic disruption that lack of cotton and wheat exports were causing in England and France. Thus, a man for whom the more experienced diplomats of Europe thought they knew was now in charge of a foreign policy machine that would have serious, practical consequences for the Union, and the conduct of the war. A man who considered himself to be an enigma was in a position of considerable power and authority. The new secretary of state set out to expand the size, authority and power of the State Department. In this he was partially successful. Nevertheless, before the end of his first term in office, the secretary of state had alienated and confused ministers, consuls, cabinet members and presidents alike. What was happening in Europe that so complicated foreign relations for the Lincoln government?

CHAPTER 2

ALLIANCES, WILD CARDS AND DON QUIOXTE

There are but two nations in the world of any real importance, the United States and Russia – everyone else is rotten and all other nations must, for their own safety, seek an alliance with one or the other of these Leviathans.

Pierre Soule, U.S. Minister to Spain, 1855

To understand the management of U.S. foreign policy during the American Civil War, it is essential to know some of the basics of the Crimean War, 1853–1856. It is significant that Britain and France cooperated to control the growing power of Russia.

England, France and Russia were all concerned about the declining strength of the Ottoman Empire in Turkey. The Ottomans threatened Russian egress out of the Black Sea through the straits of the Bosporus and Dardanelles to the Mediterranean and the Atlantic. The Black Sea was a tropical body of water that was part salt and part fresh water from the Sea of Azov. It never froze in the winter. Although heavily populated with indigenous Tatars, wealthy Russians began to build vacation homes in a climate that was more comfortable than St. Petersburg or Moscow. Strategically, Russia needed this warm-water sea to ensure open shipping lanes as well as access for her Black Sea fleet in winter when her northern ports were frozen. The warm winter temperatures found in all of the Crimean ports made control of the straits essential for Russian strength and growth. Russia also claimed that she was the rightful protector of the Orthodox Christians living in the Ottoman Empire, just across the Black Sea from Yalta and Sevastopol. She used this as the excuse to stand guard and ward off potential intruders. There were many greedy eyes watching the disintegrating Ottoman Empire and wondering when to strike and claim this strategic area for themselves. Austria-Hungary was interested. The Tsar was vitally interested. Serbia saw her chance to reclaim her ancient control over this area so close to her borders. When Tsar Alexander II made his move, the French and English knew they could not wait. However, the Russians fought hard to defend their interests in the area. There were few easy victories for England and France. They worked together, but lost many men in bloody battles. However, by the time of the Lincoln inauguration, England and France had learned to ignore enough of their traditional differences. The steamship and the telegraph had made the world a much smaller and accessible place. That uneasy alliance between Britain and France which frustrated and helped defeat the Confederate war effort was strengthened over Crimea. After this, Russia and the United States would emerge as prime movers in the world-wide balance of power – a balance they helped maintain for the next 150 years. The blockade, of which Britain and France bitterly complained and threatened to become a *casus belli* throughout the entire Civil War period, was also used by both Napoleon and the Aberdeen government during the Crimean War by blockading the Baltic Sea trapping the Russian Navy. For her part in the Crimean War, America wanted to be regarded as neutral so she could trade with any of the combatants.

America claimed that "free ships make free goods".[1] This was acceptable to England as long as Americans did not hire themselves out to the Russians as privateers. Although generally honored by the United States during the Crimean War, Britain was not as generous during the Civil War.[2] Many unemployed mill workers in Liverpool signed on as privateers helping to ship war material to the Confederacy in exchange for cotton. In 1853, England had a large navy, but Russia had only a small fleet. She would have benefitted from privateers of any source.

The British minister to Washington at this time was John F. Crampton. In addition to John Bright and Richard Cobden, Senator Charles Sumner of Massachusetts was also in contact with Crampton. The British representative heard rumors that Russian agents were attempting to have privateers built in American shipyards and manned by American crews. Crampton wrote to his Foreign Office that, "With regards to the reports of the proceedings of Russian Agents here for building vessels of war and securing the services of privateers, I think that on the whole (tho I may be wrong in this) that they have been greatly exaggerated ..."[3] For this reason, some of Seward's and Adams' later "remonstrances" against the Palmerston government, for doing what Washington apparently refrained from doing during the Crimean conflict, may be better understood.

For more than 700 years, France ravaged England and England gave it back to France. They began a long history of warfare and friendship on October 14, 1066. Napoleon provided the biggest scare, however. By 1803, the English could observe new fortifications being constructed on the French coast near Boulogne. They knew something was going to happen. First Lord of the Admiralty, Lord Melville, immediately went into action and added 20,000 marines to an existing force of 100,000. The naval force was increased from 469 to 551 ships, and its budget increased from £12 million to £18 million. Before Napoleon could build and launch his armada, England found herself in a war with Spain. In October, 1804, Lord Cornwallis captured three Spanish treasure ships and sank one of them. Meanwhile, Napoleon was getting ready to crown himself emperor and launch his invasion fleet. "With God's help, I shall put an end to the destiny and very existence of England." He had assembled over 2,000 ships, carrying over 100,000 men and 15,000 horses. In order to launch a fleet of this size, the ships were parceled out to six different ports, from Ostend to Boulogne. French and Spanish forces were ultimately defeated by a smaller English force led by Lord Nelson. The battle off the Cape of Trafalgar was one of the greatest in British naval history. The Anglo-French theater of war changed to the colonies in America in 1757 and ended with an alliance during the Crimean War in 1854.

The nineteenth century was an age of Manifest Destiny for Europe, but America as well. America was destined to stretch "from sea to shining sea". After the war with England ended in 1783, the Louisiana Purchase was bought from France, from which 13 states were eventually carved out. One of them, Kansas, was a major factor in bringing the lawyer, Abraham Lincoln, off the ninth circuit and into the national debate.

That debate concerned popular sovereignty which, according to its champion, Senator Stephen Douglas, should allow states to decide for themselves whether they wanted to be free or allow slavery within their borders. Popular sovereignty was the fuse that ignited the powder keg in Kansas. While still a territory, free-soilers from northern Missouri would ride into Kansas towns and threaten the residents that when they became a state, they must vote to be free or they would come back and cause trouble. Slave owners from Southern Missouri, where Jesse and Frank James lived with their mother, would retaliate and ride into the same towns and threaten that if they did not vote slave, gangs would return and cause even more trouble.

In 1819, Florida was ceded by Spain to the growing country. The 1840s, under James K. Polk, saw the greatest growth. In 1845, Texas was annexed. In 1846, the Oregon Territory was acquired, and by 1848, Manifest Destiny was achieved with the acquisition from Mexico of territory which ultimately included California, Nevada, Utah, and Arizona. The United States were more interested in managing their own affairs than involving themselves in the problems of Europe or any other issue outside their own borders. George Washington had earlier warned about getting involved in European matters. The violence of the French Revolution impressed and terrified many in America. Americans were safe as long as they minded their own business.

In Europe, Russia had driven Napoleon from her frozen steppes. The Congress of Vienna had given Russia a sphere of influence which included Poland.[4] As Russia grew and prospered, Tsar Nicholas I helped the monarchies of Europe to maintain power and put down rebellion during the revolutions of 1848 that swept Western Europe. She became known as the "gendarme of Europe".

England and France formed an alliance in foreign policy for many reasons - including the United States. Although England and America had been bitter enemies at one time, France had generally been an ally. However, with the *coup d'état* in 1851 which elevated President Louis Napoleon to Emperor Napoleon III, Franco-American relations began to suffer. In terms of numbers, Napoleon had the largest army in Europe. It could march to Moscow and back, but it couldn't march to America. She didn't have the naval strength.[5] Having sold Louisiana to America to help the U.S. grow into a future counterweight against England, France now saw her stepchild on the high seas with three times the merchant tonnage than in France. Beyond the expansion of merchant shipping and the ironclad navies, the improvement in armament on board a ship or mounted in a fixed fortification, was threatening to change the balance of power as well. Protestant, democratic America was slowly becoming estranged from Catholic, dictatorial France. The growing strength of a democracy gave concern to many European monarchies and upstart dictators. Beginning with Alphonse Pageot and Bacourt Sartiges, French Ministers to the U.S. began urging closer ties with England. "Alphonse Pageot contended in the 1840s ... that unless American aggressiveness was contained, it's spirit of usurpation foreshadowed a world catastrophe."[6] Ten years later, Eugene Sartiges stated that America would "bow only to material force."[7] Fearing that the United States would ultimately control all of Central and South America, he urged greater cooperation with England to "resist the endless invasions of the North Americans."

Although England and France combined forces to control Russian expansion, neither partner in that alliance took their eyes off one another for long. England was an island nation that depended upon her navy and fixed fortifications for survival. If the navy could not keep her enemies out of the channel, then the huge smoothbore guns in her fixed fortifications on land would do the rest. The development of the steamship and rifled guns changed this equation. Crimea demonstrated that a conical projectile from a rifled gun could destroy wooden warships many times their size and number. Adding a steam-driven, converted warship with 4.5 inches of rolled iron plate bolted onto 18 inches of teak added a new dimension to national security. France and England were in a naval arms race that taxed their budgets and patience – both home and abroad. Britain was rapidly converting wooden ships to ironclads with protected, retractable screw propellers. France was experimenting with all metal ships and cheaper floating batteries whose sole purpose was to slowly steam or be towed into place where they could batter an enemy fort into submission. Crimea was the great proving grounds for all of this new and terrible weaponry. Britain was strapped for cash to maintain a global empire. Under Queen Victoria, the British Empire controlled 14 million square miles, and 450 million people in sixty-two countries.

So, in the face of a rapidly growing French navy, she decided to improve her land fortifications. But, Britain was nervous and frustrated because the great Russian port of Sevastopol took twelve months, not twelve weeks, to subdue. Although both sides complained that one or the other was not doing enough, Anglo-French cooperation eventually got the job done. "Not only were plans for floating batteries, mortar vessels and gunboats exchanged, but naval constructors of each power were permitted to inspect the methods of the other. The French sought with success the plans for the famous British 68-pounder gun. Napoleon III himself gave to Lord Cowley, for transmission to the Admiralty, a project he had devised for transforming wooden ships of the line into ironclads capable of attacking coast defenses. The British Ambassador deemed particularly gratifying the readiness with which his majesty imparts plans for rendering more efficient a branch of our service, of which France might, almost without causing surprise retain feelings of jealousy and caution."[8] While war was raging in Crimea, the U.S. secretary of war under President Franklin Pierce sent Major Alfred Mordecai on a commission for six months to observe the battle. In addition to weapons, he was also instructed to look at the army command structure. The secretary of war was Jefferson Davis.

After the election of Abraham Lincoln, Richard Lyons of the British legation in Washington was convinced that the Lincoln government still regarded England as an enemy. France looked more and more like a necessary ally. Seward tried to ensure that France was treated well, but he also believed that England and France had wounded each other in previous wars to the extent that any new alliance would probably not last. He believed that he knew his enemy. Lyons was sure that Lincoln and Seward would use this presumed hostility to gain a free hand in subduing the Confederate "sugar-coated rebellion" without interference from Europe. In Dispatch No. 206, May 20, 1861, Lyons wrote to Russell, "The Cabinet of Washington no doubt hope that the state of Europe may be such as to render both England and France unable or unwilling to send a naval or military force across the Atlantic; above all it trusts that England and France may be at war with each other."[9] Lyons goes on to state the goal of the Anglo-French alliance is to be "absolutely inflexible of purpose." He recommended that the Foreign Office remain calm regardless of taunts from Seward. Unruffled, focused and hardworking, this philosophy worked well for a man like Lyons. Russell and Palmerston were different personalities. However, Lyons worked well with Mercier, Thouvanel, de Lhuys and Charles Francis Adams. He strove to secure control of Union foreign policy from Seward in the early stages of the Lincoln administration. There was a great deal at stake.

The Anglo-French alliance, as it concerned the United States, served many purposes. Among them were: to secure adequate cotton and grain supplies; to block an anticipated seizure of British and French colonial interests in Canada and the Caribbean; to keep North and South diverted so as to be able to deal with pressing problems in Europe without any interference from either side; and to deal with the perceived Seward plan to unite North and South by fighting a greater enemy, that Anglo-French alliance. In Dispatch No.569, October 18, 1861, Lyons wrote to Russell, "A noisy dispute if not war with a Foreign Power would, it is thought, answer this purpose, and have the additional advantage of consolidating the restored Union by joining North and South in common efforts against a foreign foe".[10] Both Lyons and Russell knew that Seward was initially against any hostile action against the South. He wanted peace first. However, they weren't sure if the secretary was rash enough to force the United States into a foreign war in order to unify the country and avoid civil war at home.

By the time Abraham Lincoln became president of the United States on March 4, 1861, England and France knew that they needed to continue to work together. Although they were both locked in a naval arms race, and neither trusted the other, working together was safer than war. There were checks and balances in place in Europe to maintain a peaceful balance of power in the short term. They were concerned, however, that there was no check or balance to the growing power of the United States. U.S. industrial and commercial growth also demanded a growing network of legations and consulates all over the world. Through his work as secretary of state, William Henry Seward was in regular contact with his representatives from Paris to St. Petersburg. His information on foreign affairs came from his ministers, consular representatives, spies, detectives and special purchasing agents. Consular officials ultimately proved to be invaluable in securing the intelligence data necessary to more effectively manage the affairs of the State Department. Some of Seward's information about affairs in Western Europe came from many sources including John Lothrop Motley in Vienna and Cassius Clay in St. Petersburg. Motley was more measured and careful with his words than Clay. His dispatches were read with care by the state department. After providing Seward with a detailed summary of the crisis between Germany, Denmark and the Duchies of Schleswig and Holstein, the secretary wrote in Dispatch No.52 on December 18, 1863, "Sir, I have received your dispatch of November 24, No.40, and I cannot too lavishly thank you for your careful and lucid exposition of the Schleswig-Holstein question."[11] The question was whether or not the Duchies of Schleswig and Holstein would become part of Denmark or Germany. Both provinces contained a predominantly German population. However, they had traditionally been part of Denmark. Prussia, under the leadership of Otto von Bismarck, flexed her muscles and saw this as a good opportunity to demonstrate her growing unity and strength. The sudden emergence of a new European power was unexpected and troubling to England, France and Russia. Perhaps the Franco-British alliance needed a new partner? Seward told Motley that if war broke out in Europe over this issue, nothing would prevent the United States from doing what Europe was then doing to the Union, i.e. supply arms and supplies to the combatants and make money.

Revolutions were toppling old monarchies and creating new countries in Europe. "In 1848 a violent storm of revolutions tore through Europe. With an astounding rapidity, crowds of working-class radicals and middle-class liberals in Paris, Milan, Venice, Naples, Palermo, Vienna, Prague, Budapest, Krakow and Berlin toppled the old regimes and began the task of forging a new, liberal order."[12] Belgium, Italy and Germany were the examples of this. Much of the correspondence between Napoleon III and Italy was over the exploits of Giuseppe Garibaldi and ensuring that Italy escaped the control of the Austrian Habsburgs. Napoleon wanted to placate the Catholic vote in France, and landed thousands of troops in Italy to secure the safety of the Pope and put down the rebellion brought about by Mazzini and Garibaldi.[13] Along with the French, British and the Russians, Garibaldi also believed in the future of the United States, and saw the U.S. as a player in the world balance of power. "America should increase rather than decrease in power, so that it might act as a check and counterpoise to the aristocratic and tyrannic (sic) powers of Europe."[14] This is precisely what "Napoleon the Little" feared.[15] Early in the Lincoln administration, Secretary Seward saw Garibaldi as someone who might energize the Union army. Battlefield victories would go a long way to ensuring successful foreign relations.

Victory went first to Jefferson Davis at Manassas on July 21, 1861. The normally confident Seward panicked and screamed at Lincoln's secretaries that all was lost. The secretary of state wrote to Henry Shelton Sanford, U.S. Minister at Brussels on July 27, 1861, Seward said, "I wish you to proceed at once and enter into communication with the distinguished Soldier of Freedom. Tell him that he will receive a Major-General's commission in the army of the United States."[16] If Irvin McDowell couldn't do it, maybe Garibaldi could. Although England and France were primarily concerned with issues in Europe, they never took their wary eyes off America. A member of the French Chamber of Deputies, Count Agenor de Gasparin, wrote *America Before Europe* in 1862.[17] He agreed with Garibaldi and was also prophetic in his observations of America and its relations with Europe. He foresaw the future alliance between the United States and Western Europe:

> "I believe in the frequent intervention of Europe in America and of America in Europe; I believe in the future entrance of the United States into the concert of great powers. Believe, in fine, that electricity and steam have overthrown many artificial distinctions, and that it will daily become more difficult to live in isolation. I believe at the same time that there should be neither European supremacy in America nor American supremacy in Europe."[18]

The large volume of correspondence between Lord Richard Lyons in Washington and Lord John Russell in London shed light on Union relations with the British. Likewise, dispatches between Baron Mercier and Foreign Secretaries Édouard Thouvanel and Drouyn de Lhuys provide valuable insight into the relations between Napoleon III and William Henry Seward. Shortly after Lincoln's inauguration and the initial stages of the blockade of Confederate ports, Lord Russell proposed to Palmerston that the English and French should act as mediators between the Union and Confederacy. Mediation was that type of interference that Lincoln had already warned about in his first address as president.

Mediation was one thing – war was another. Palmerston made it clear where he stood regarding war as a political tool. He wrote, "The love of quarreling and fighting is inherent in man, and to prevent its indulgence is to impose restraints on natural liberty. A state may so shackle its own subjects, but it is an infringement on national independence to restrain other nations."[19]

The British prime minister told his foreign secretary that war was a natural and desirable tool in the relations of nations to each other. He did not want war with America. However, he was not averse to using the threat and bluff of war as a tool to satisfy the British public and maintain his slim hold on the government. When discussing the faulty perception of British naval strength as it concerned America at this time, naval historian Howard Fuller notes, "Palmerston realized that British naval strength was more perception than reality. That's why he was often considered a master of 'bluff'."[20]

Lords Palmerston, Russell, Lyons and Mercier believed that the United States would probably not be reunited. The South was too big and independent-minded to give in. There was much discussion in London and Paris about whether or not a divided America was advantageous or not. Russell was advocating mediation to end the conflict and allow North and South to exist separately. He considered a plan whereby North and South would be separate for commercial purposes, but united for the common defense. Palmerston was sensitive to the fact that a mediation offer from Britain might be resisted by Seward just because it came from Britain. Seward feared that mediation would then lead to recognition and an inevitable war with the Union. Palmerston shared that fear. Writing to Russell, Palmerston believed that an offer of mediation from England would be refused by the Union, but he also believed that the war had dragged for a long time with no result, so maybe it was time to think about some form of intercession. Let's at least arrange an armistice, and then we'll talk about mediating the differences.

To complicate thoughts of mediation, Seward was always looking for ways to enhance his status as secretary of state. He always thought that Canada and the United States should be combined into one nation. He was not above recommending the invasion of Canada as compensation for the possible loss of the war to the Confederacy and permanent division of the nation. Canada was part of and allied to the British Empire. In Dispatch No.206 on May 20, 1861, Lyons wrote to Russell that he believed Seward would threaten to seize Canada in order to stall any possible interference in the Civil War from England. He was aware that during the presidential election, Seward had recommended the annexation of Canada as part of his platform. Canada was a constant issue throughout the war, but was more vulnerable than Seward may have known. Canada regarded America as a bully to be avoided. The *Toronto Leader* told its readers that the United States was "the Don Quixote of nations, always looking for some country to fight."[21] With Seward in mind, the *Toronto Leader* went on to say that, "they bluster furiously, they threaten fiercely, but they retreat judiciously."[22] By the time that Lincoln and Seward took office, however, England was financially weakened by her expenses in the Crimean War. Britain informed her colonies that as a result, they would be responsible for a greater share of the cost of their own defense. The cost of maintaining these alliances needed to be reconsidered. When Lincoln took the oath of office for the first time, Canada had only 2,436 British troops on her soil. Despite troop increases by May, 1861, Canada was primarily defended by local Sedentary and Active militia. No match for battle-hardened, fully-mobilized Union soldiers. Canada was extremely vulnerable, and there was little that Britain could have done about it.

In addition to annexation threats, Confederate raiders based in Canada, pillaged and burned towns across the border in Vermont.[23] Some of the letters burned by Judah Benjamin after the war were to special agent Jacob Thompson who was based in Canada. It is speculated that the letters contained a discussion of plans to burn Northern cities in order to draw Union troops away from Richmond. [24] Lyons knew that Seward initially believed that there would be no Civil War because there was strong Union sentiment throughout the South. Seward was wrong. Lyons also chided Seward for believing that there was strong Union feeling in Canada. He knew this to be a faulty assumption as well. Lyons knew his enemies. The British Foreign Office had long discussed what might happen in a war with the Union while the Civil War was still in progress. Initially, nobody in London thought this was realistic. The outcome would certainly favor Britain. However, as the ironclad navy grew and Union victories began to mount, Seward's threats of war and payback were suddenly taken seriously.

Seward's threats, the anticipated invasion of Canada, the cotton drain, a quasi-war already in progress as British-financed privateers ran through an ineffective blockade all made for strained relations between all nations involved. That Franco-British alliance was made more defensive with every taunt that Seward threw at them. The secretary's object was to frighten, confuse and thus cause disarray in any overt intervention plans then contemplated by London and Paris. Unfortunately, he was successful. Fear and confusion helped strengthen the alliance. France was anxious to see the war end and start the flow of cotton again. However, she would not take a step without the approval from England. Lyons wrote to Russell in Dispatch No.183 on May 6, 1861 and outlined the objectives of this young alliance. In discussing Confederate recognition, Lord Richard Lyons briefly outlined the scope of Anglo-French cooperation to Russell. He stated, "M. Mercier told me that if England and France acted in strict concert, he did not suppose the announcement (of Confederate recognition) would produce any other inconvenience that a boastful violent note from Mr. Seward; but that the most perfect understanding between the two powers was essential, otherwise it was not unlikely that this government might seek an opportunity to use one or the other as the scapegoat."[25]

Emphasizing mutual economic concerns, Lyons continues, "Mr. Mercier, the French Minister here, told me confidentially the day before yesterday, that he was very seriously thinking of writing to M. Thouvanel, that to recommend that he should concert measures with your Lordship, and if you assented, should say at once to the United States Minister at Paris, that France would not recognize the blockade of the Southern ports after the month of September next."

England and France were fearful that if the blockade were successful, and the war continued, then the Southern planters would abandon their cotton crops and plant wheat and other grains needed for home consumption. That might permanently eliminate that vital American cotton supply. Cotton from the South had proven to be of better quality than the cotton that was already being imported from India and Egypt. Lyons complained further that he believed that the war could not be won by the North. He was convinced that something had to be done to help bring the war to a close. By late 1862, the cotton drain was having an impact on British mills. The reserve supply had run out, and the mills in Liverpool, Manchester and Leeds were slowing down. Those still working were on half-time. Although England and France were acting in concert in dealing with America, the Anglo-French alliance had a serious threat from another far away source – Russia.

Lincoln's representative to St. Petersburg, Cassius Marcellus Clay, was an independent, pugnacious, vain character with an ego to match that of his boss, William Henry Seward. The first hint of Clay's vanity comes in the title of his 1886 autobiography, *"The Life of Cassius Marcellus Clay: memoirs, writings and speeches, showing his conduct in the overthrow of American Slavery, the Salvation of the Union, and the Restoration of the autonomy of the States."* Clay was from a slave-holding family in Kentucky who attended Yale University and came to believe that he alone saved the Union from dissolution. While at Yale, he heard William Lloyd Garrison speak. In his autobiography, Clay stated, "In plain, logical and sententious language he treated the 'divine institution' so as to burn like a branding iron into the most callous hide of the slave-holder and his defenders. This was a new revelation to me. I felt all the horrors of slavery; but my parents were slave-holders; all my known kindred in Kentucky were slave-holders; but Garrison dragged out the monster from all his citadels, and left him stabbed to the vitals, and dying at the feet of every logical and honest mind. As water to a thirsty wayfarer, were to me Garrison's arguments and sentiments."[26]

Clay's colorful prose is analogous to the way he lived. As a child, he said, "I am a believer in blood". This was just after his first fight with a neighbor who he defeated with his bowie knife. Hearing of the fight, he knew he would either need to face his disapproving and equally pugnacious mother or flee. He chose flight. However, he wasn't fast enough to outrun his mama. Faced with another caning, Clay momentarily considered fighting his mother as well. With the big bowie knife still in his hand, he had a decision to make. Ultimately, he submitted to a caning, to which his backside was fast becoming accustomed.

Clay's anti-slavery sentiments brought him into the Republican party and the friendship of Abraham Lincoln. The world for Clay was more black and white than the grey as seen by Henry Seward. Although politics ultimately brought Clay and Seward together, Clay ultimately decided that Seward was the enemy.

Senator Seward invited Clay to Washington for dinner. After the meal, Seward asked Clay to read the draft of a speech he was preparing to read in the senate chamber the next day. According to Clay, "In this speech, it will be seen that he was for Union slave or free … I read his speech very carefully, and said nothing. The truth is that it killed Seward with me forever."[27]

According to Clay, he was offered the position of representative to Spain, and secretary of war, but he refused, accepting the position of representative to Russia instead. His work in St. Petersburg was interrupted when Simon Cameron, secretary of war, was forced to resign due to graft, corruption and mismanagement of his department. Cameron was still powerful, however, and delivered Pennsylvania for Lincoln. The president needed to get him out of the way. Russia was far enough, and the court at St. Petersburg was thought sufficient to smooth his ruffled feathers.

Cameron was the first in Lincoln's cabinet to resign. He was not the last.[28] Confiding to his secretary, John George Nicolay, Lincoln said, "Cameron is incapable either of organizing details or conceiving and advising general plans".[29] There were reports that the secretary of war kept notes and government contracts on scraps of paper, written out with borrowed pencils, and then stuffed into his jacket pocket. Horses that were delivered blind, guns that wouldn't shoot and blankets that disintegrated in the rain were only part of the problem. On July 8, 1861, the House of Representatives convened the Select Committee on Government Contracts to look into the rumors of corruption in the war department. Eventually, thousands of pages from hundreds of witnesses told of ships that were bought for $18,000 and sold to the navy for $50,000. Cattle, guns and food supplies were sold by friends of Cameron at greatly inflated prices to the government. Cameron must go, but Clay had to be recalled.

Two months after arriving in St. Petersburg, Cameron complained that his wife was ill in the Russian capitol and maybe it was time to come home. Clay then returned to St. Petersburg and served the Lincoln administration for the remainder of the war. He worked hard to ensure that the entente that existed between the United States and Russia remained on track.

As with many who knew and worked with William Seward at this time, the personal letters and diary entries of Cassius Clay must be examined with care and put into proper perspective. Seward was a magnet for controversy. Just as care must be exercised when reading the diary entries of Gideon Welles, equal care must be used when reading the thoughts of Cassius Clay. His diary entries are in sharp contrast to his official dispatches to the state department. Knowing that all dispatches were now being published, Clay was careful with his language. Privately, however, he vented his anger at the secretary of state. Clay blamed Seward for mishandling a case of fraud between a New England arms merchant and the Russian government. He claimed, "But a very different Secretary of State from Lewis Cass had been put at the head of the cabinet of Mr. Lincoln – a man educated in the corrupt Albany School of politics; and who, for the first time, imported that execrable system into Washington; and which infested the whole Republican party with the virus of dishonor and death- that man was Wm. H. Seward."[30] Cassius Clay took exception to William Henry Seward, but that enmity probably did not influence the direction of relations between the Lincoln government and the policies of Alexander II. The dispatches of Clay and Seward as well as the diary entries of Clay make it clear that the Union State Department and the Tsar of Russia wanted an entente between the two countries to act as a restraint on the Anglo-French alliance. Seward's dispatches clearly state that he wished Clay to make sure that Alexander was aware of Lincoln's desire for good relations between the Union and Russia.

The Anglo-French alliance, and possibly the British Empire itself, was threatened by the position the Russian Tsar took on the American Civil War. When Abraham Lincoln became president-elect in 1860, Great Britain was at the height of its power. Her dominions, colonies, protectorates, mandates and territories afforded her control over at least 400 million people and one quarter of the Earth's land. At first, her only challenge appeared to be Russia in the east. As the Civil War progressed, however, she recognized that America was another threat, this time in the west. Finally, the most powerful nation on earth at that time was war-weary, financially strapped and over-extended. British prime minister Lord Palmerston used sheer bluff and bluster to maintain the fragile honor and security of Great Britain.

Honor was also important to France and her new emperor, Napoleon III. However, the desire to contain Russia was not the only reason for this unexpected alliance. Beyond the posturing of Seward and the threat of growing strength in Prussia, an increasingly dominant figure in international relations was flexing his muscles and influencing that "gouty crab", Napoleon. That figure was the minister of foreign affairs during both the Crimean War and the American Civil War. He was Édouard Drouyn de Lhuys. As the author of the 1856 Treaty of Paris, it has been suggested that Drouyn precipitated the Crimean War through his condescending attitude and conduct towards Russia and her ministers.[31] Cynically, Drouyn had hoped to draw Russia into an alliance with France and England to more effectively deal with an economically disruptive Civil War in America. With Russian cities still in ruins from the Crimean War, the Tsar didn't buy it. Nevertheless, Seward was up against a seasoned, skillful politician who was capable of minimizing a devastated Sevastopol in order to cut a deal.

Cassius Clay succeeded John Appleton as minister to Russia. Appleton first discussed Russian favoritism for the Union in Dispatch No. 16, April 8, 1861. Seward was immediately concerned with any European power who might be considering recognition of the Confederacy. He had a meeting with the Russian foreign minister, Prince Alexander Gorchakov. The prince reassured him. Appleton wrote, "Prince Gortchacow replied that the question of recognizing the Confederate States was not now before the emperor, and for the present he did not think it would be."[32] The first dispatches sent from Clay to Seward from St. Petersburg contained statements that Russia was very favorable to the position of the Union. The Tsar had freed his serfs as Lincoln and the Republicans wanted to do with the American slaves. As early as May 6, 1861, Dispatch No. 3, the secretary of state saw Russia as a counterweight to England. He flattered the Tsar, "Assure his Imperial Majesty that the President and the people of the United States have observed with admiration and sympathy the great and humane efforts he has so recently made for the material and moral improvement of his empire by the extension of telegraphs and railroads, and by removing the disabilities of slavery."[33]

All of Clay's personal correspondence with Seward as well as his autobiography show a sincere appreciation and love for Russia, the royal family and life in the capitol. One of the immediate problems he brought to the secretary of state was the rumor that privateers were being built in Russian shipyards for use by the Confederacy. By this time, the Laird rams were denied departure from the Birkenhead yards in England. Privateering had moved on to France. Napoleon was looking at all of his options. Clay, however, was in agreement that European non-intervention was not the result of diplomatic diplomacy by the Seward State Department, but by the gunboat diplomacy of the navy. Clay's conclusions are similar to those of British member of parliament, John Laird. According to Clay in dispatch to Seward, No.28, November 3, 1863, "It is now admitted on all sides that our success in ironclads and guns, has so far, saved us from European assault."[34] Clay sends Seward a clipping from The *Times* in which shipbuilder John Laird complains that Britain has wasted its money on big ships that are useless for close, offensive coastal operations in shallower U.S. waters. Laird was respected, and his speech on this subject in parliament was met with approval and "hear, hear". Laird preferred small ships like the *Monitor* for defensive purposes. He told his audience, "Our small ships, armed with a few heavy guns, as proved in the case of the *Monitor* and the *Merrimac*, and in the late victory of the *Weehawken* over the *Atlanta*, are a match for those leviathans of France and England which have cost so much time and money." Laird warns that the big ships that are fitted with 100 lb. Armstrong guns are not as effective as the smaller 68 lb. gun. He feared that the big, heavy ships now being built will put England at a disadvantage against France and America. He believed that the new ships, which drew from 25 to 28 feet of water, would not be able to get close enough to the most heavily fortified American and French cities. He warned, "If we went to war tomorrow, we should go into that war for the first year or two under most disadvantageous circumstances." When mentioning the Confederate privateers that were built in the Laird yards and sinking many tons of Union shipping, the parliamentary chamber erupted with cheers and laughter.

After Simon Cameron's departure and Clay's recall to St. Petersburg, Bayard Taylor, chargé d'affaires, temporarily took over Legation duties.[35] Taylor reported that Russia was anxious about lack of Union success on the battlefield, but was still loyal to the Lincoln government.

Britain and France were actively discussing mediation at this time. The Anglo-French alliance had reached out to Russia without success. The British Foreign Office realized that mediation would be resisted by the Seward State Department. Britain realized that an alliance with a broader base was required. With Russia unwilling to join, Palmerston tried to form an alliance with the Belgians. From King Leopold to John Russell on October 31, 1862, he wrote, "Lord Palmerston has written to me, without my having named the subject, that he thought the time had come to offer a mediation and to recognize the Southern states. That is not the feeling of the French who wish the North well as future enemies of England."[36] Anglo-French alliance and Crimea aside, building an alliance to help settle the American Civil War with mediation was not working. Seeking to strengthen the appearance of the Anglo-French alliance in Washington, Mercier and Lyons at one point requested a joint meeting with Seward. Officially, the Secretary declined. When Mercier and Lyons showed up at the State Department, Seward told one that he could remain and the other was invited to dinner. However, he would not see them together on any matter. Economics were taking their toll.

While alliances were central to maintaining relative peace and stability in Europe at this time, at least one Southern state, Georgia, was working hard to establish her own separate alliance with Europe. Before the war, mail and most commerce destined for the South, reached their destination through the port of New York. There were no direct mail or commercial shipping routes from any of the Southern ports to Europe. U.S. post offices were closed after Fort Sumter, and the mail routes to Europe were denied to the South. Incoming Confederate mail passed through Northern ports before being trans-shipped south to New Orleans and then to other cities like Charleston and Savanah. Having seceded from the Union, however, this arrangement presented a problem for all states joining the Confederacy. Recognizing that this immediately put the state of Georgia at a disadvantage, Governor Joseph E. Brown appointed a prominent plantation owner and former U.S. House of Representatives member, Thomas Butler King, to go to England and secure those vital mail routes and commercial contracts that would help sustain Georgia in her struggle for independence.[37] King arrived in London in March, 1861. Just to be on the safe side, Brown also asked King to buy 8,000 muskets before returning home. The state of Georgia acted on her own with no attempt to work with or through the emerging Confederate States of America. Like the rest of the South, Georgia sought relief from what they considered to be the heavy hand of central government. Direct trade with Europe had long been a concern for Georgia as well as many other Southern states. Without this capability, the South was further controlled by Northern interests.

The cotton and wheat shortage was beginning to have an impact on the economy in England and France. France was more anxious for the blockade to be lifted, however. If the Anglo-French alliance could be broadened to include Russia, that would be a formidable combination. The Tsar was not fooled, however. He realized that the United States, fully united, would act as a lever against the global power of England. After his return, Clay would attach clippings from The *Times* to his dispatches. Those clippings would clearly show that John Laird was keenly aware of the growing power of the American navy.

Before Clay returned to St. Petersburg, Bayard Taylor assured Seward that Russia would remain loyal to America, even in the face of military loses. In Dispatch No.16, October 29, 1862, he told Seward that Prince Gorchakov maintained, "Russia alone has stood by you from the first, and will continue to stand by you."[38] Expressing concern for the further break-up of a country that Russia needed to help her stand against England, he continued, "We are very, very anxious that some means should be adopted which will prevent the division that now seems inevitable. One separation will be followed by another; you will break into fragments." Regarding the invitation for intervention offered by the Anglo-French alliance to Russia, Gorchakov tells Taylor in the October dispatch, "There will be proposals for intervention. We believe that intervention could do no good at present. Proposals will be made to Russia to join in some plan of interference. She will refuse any invitation of the kind. Russia will occupy the same ground as at the beginning of the struggle. You may rely upon it, she will not change."

France and England tried without success to draw the Tsar into an alliance which would ultimately provide Britain with the breathing room necessary to maintain her global empire. Having failed with Russia and Belgium, the Anglo-French alliance tried to encourage Spain to join them in more productively managing relations with the Lincoln government. The issue of mutual concern wasn't cotton or wheat, however. The problem now was money. Mexico had placed a two-year moratorium on the interest payments to loans owned by England, France and Spain. Recognition of the Confederacy was being actively considered by England and France. Spain, on the other hand, by virtue of language and history, had always been looked upon as Mexico's closest relative. When France suggested more aggressive measures to force Mexico to pay up, England and Spain initially agreed. When those measures turned into invasion and occupation plans, Britain and Spain backed out. Napoleon III forged ahead without them. Her Catholic Majesty in Spain, Isabella II, was shocked and upset, but none of this directly involved the Union State Department. However, the privateering problem that Seward shared with England and France, he now shared with Spain. The problem was that Cuba often acted independently from Madrid. The ports at Havana, Bermuda, Matamoros and Nassau were used by privateers bringing supplies to the Confederacy. Cotton would go out on smaller blockade runners from Wilmington and Charleston to Nassau and Havana. From there, cotton from several ships would be loaded onto one larger vessel to proceed to Liverpool. Charleston was well-protected by shallow waters and narrow channels that forced blockade ships to stand guard further out to sea. A series of batteries and forts provided added protection that made her a valuable harbor for the Confederacy. After April, 1863, Wilmington took over from Charleston as the primary export harbor for the Confederacy.[39] Wilmington was also a shallow port that gave the small runners the space they needed to dash past the deep-draft union warships waiting offshore. Prevailing winds also helped. Confederate General William H.C. Whiting explained the conditions, "The prevalence of southeast weather at the main entrance, while it is very dangerous for vessels outside, forces them to the northward of the cape and gives easy access to vessels running the blockade ... in like manner the northeast gales drive the enemy to shelter to the southward of the cape and clears the New Inlet."[40] In addition to a friendly port in which to offload cotton and take on guns and saltpeter, Havana and Nassau served as vital coaling stations for steamers that needed fuel to make the return trip to England and France. Coal was as valuable as cotton.

This arrangement was not appreciated by the U.S. State Department. A letter from Seward to Gabriel Tessara, Minister from Spain, on July 15, 1861 outlined the problem. "Information has been received at this department that a piratical armed steamer called *Sumter*, on the 6 of July instant, entered that port (Cienfuegos) with seven vessels belonging to citizens of the United States, which she had captured with her officers, and also the officers and seamen of another such vessel which she had captured and burned on the high seas."[41] Lincoln and Seward could not afford to make any more enemies. This time, the ships taken as prizes were loaded with sugar. In another year, they would be packed with rifled muskets. In 1861, however, Minister Tessara was comfortable in telling Seward that the ships were illegally captured within the three-mile limit of Cuban waters. On September 3, 1861, Seward writes to Carl Schurz that because the prize ships had already been released, he would drop the matter. With the Anglo-French alliance always on the verge of war with the Union, Seward had to pick his battles. Russia did not recognize the Confederacy as a belligerent, but Spain did. Writing from the legation in Madrid on March 22, 1862, Horatio G. Perry protests Spanish recognition of Confederate belligerent status, but is quick to add that the Lincoln government only wishes friendship, not war. Minister of State, Calderon Collantes, received the Perry correspondence which stated, "I am therefore now instructed that, although the United States have continually protested against and do not now acquiesce in the decision of the Spanish government to treat the insurgents as belligerent, we have nevertheless not made this a cause for breaking ancient friendly relations with Spain."

The Anglo-French alliance remained intact. Unable to attract new members, the alliance remained a threat to Union security throughout this period. England was governed by those "hoary and shrewd men" who ultimately decided that war with the United States was not in their economic interests. They knew their enemy, and realized that William

Seward was probably bluffing. Prior to 1863, Palmerston could have called the secretary's bluff, but elected to retain control of Union foreign policy and refrain from provocation that could result in war. After 1863, Cassius Clay was correct in suggesting that Welles' navy was doing more to strengthen the U.S. foreign policy position than all of the dispatches from the Seward State Department.

CHAPTER 3

HOARY AND SHREWD MEN

[Judah] Benjamin was the only one in [Davis'] cabinet who was a true internationalist ... who knew both England and France intimately, and spoke fluent French and Spanish, and who could handle the press and diplomats with skill.

Eli N. Evans: *Judah Benjamin, The Jewish Confederate*

"The men in London who directed foreign policy were hoary and shrewd; they were not easily baffled."[1] While William Henry Seward and Judah Benjamin were learning on the job, the men who were really in charge of U.S. foreign policy were experienced professionals. The U.S. State Department believed that because they had the diplomatic infrastructure already in place, that this would give the Union an advantage in foreign relations. That infrastructure allowed the Lincoln administration to speak with one voice. Jefferson Davis' domestic and foreign policy was hindered by the fact that he initially spoke with seven voices, and ultimately with many more, some of whom did not agree. The preamble to the Confederate constitution began, "We the people of the Confederate States, each state acting in its sovereign and independent character, in order to form a permanent federal government ..." With each state sovereign and independent, Davis found it difficult to speak with one voice. Even if the infrastructure had been present, the message was unclear. The immediate, material needs of the Confederacy were clear, however. Fortunately, the Confederacy had resourceful men like Judah Benjamin,

Caleb Huse and James Bulloch operating as statesmen and purchasing agents in Europe.[2] They negotiated loans and bought tons of supplies for Robert E. Lee's army despite the best efforts of the Union spies and detectives who followed and noted their every move in London and Paris on an hourly basis. They were young and much less experienced than men like Palmerston and Russell. Yet these young men succeeded in forcing warriors like Ulysses Grant and George Thomas to fight for every bloody inch of ground they covered in four years of war.[3] Grant and Thomas were one thing, but Palmerston and Napoleon III were another. Those "hoary and shrewd men" with whom Seward had to deal included European as well as other Union representatives. Jefferson Davis considered himself as shrewd as Abraham Lincoln in appointing a "team of rivals" to his cabinet. Like Lincoln, Davis appointed a powerful rival to the second most powerful position in their respective governments. After Lincoln offered the job of secretary of state to William Henry Seward, Davis offered the job to one of his chief rivals for the presidency, Robert Toombs. Both Lincoln and Davis were harshly criticized during their tenure in office. Whereas his wisdom and insight have now made a historic celebrity of Lincoln, Davis is still generally considered to have been a "leader without a legend". Lincoln rose to the challenge, and Davis was crushed under its almighty weight. Nevertheless, after a cabinet shuffle, Davis was wise and shrewd enough to appoint a man to the critical job of secretary of state who, like Seward, was respected by some and reviled by others – Judah Philip Benjamin. The Confederate secretary of state, however, had a better knowledge of Europe and foreign policy than his Northern counterpart.

Nobody in Europe actively wanted a war with the United States, but Prime Minister Palmerston recognized the value of bluffing war in achieving Britain's goals. War with America might be economically and strategically counterproductive. England had a large, expensive empire to protect, so she tread carefully. France was a different matter. "Napoleon and his court loved intrigue and would rather be involved in a conspiracy than dance at a royal ball."[4] Although not always accurate relative to Napoleon, France was still trying to recapture the glory days of Napoleon Bonaparte when the rest of the world tread softly in her presence. Napoleon's court included his two foreign ministers, Antoine Édouard Touvenel and Édouard Drouyn de Lhuys. Thouvenel was a conservative politician who worked hard to keep the emperor out of trouble. That approach eventually wore out and he was replaced on October 15, 1862 by Drouyn de Lhuys. De Lhuys had "a cool head and a passionate heart – a heart full of love for his country."[5] Love of country suited the emperor who was looking to build an empire, not maintain one. This produced a potentially volatile situation for the United States. Europe had distracting issues, but America was too good an economic partner to be ignored. Slavery, however, was bad for business.

Prior to the Emancipation Proclamation, Abraham Lincoln made it clear that he was fighting to keep North and South together. Jefferson Davis had a much harder time explaining the reasons for secession. He couldn't offend England and France by stating that they were fighting to uphold slavery. England was especially concerned about appearing to support any aspect of servitude. President Lincoln confused matters somewhat by saying that he did not intend to interfere with slavery where it already existed. That didn't sit well with the British. The president preferred to think of the Civil War as a "sugar-coated rebellion". What made matters worse for the Confederacy, however, were the well-known speeches and writings of Vice President Alexander Stephens who said that slavery was the "cornerstone" of the Confederacy. Stephens made the job of the first Confederate Commissioners, Yancey, Rost and Mann, very difficult. Upon arrival in Europe, the Confederate commissioners avoided all mention of slavery, and stated that the war and secession was based on the injustice of the many tariff issues that had been festering between North and South for many years.[6]

The first "foreign policy" initiative on the part of the Confederacy, however, was not to the Foreign Office and the Tuileries, it was to Washington, and the offices of William Seward. Jefferson Davis thought that a friendly separation could be arranged, treaties signed, postal and property transfer arrangements made and all would be fine. That's not how it worked out. Seward had no choice but to officially refuse to meet with Davis' peace commissioners. Even unofficially, he refused to see them. Instead, he sent a written note to them stating that he wanted peace, and that Fort Sumter would not be resupplied. That remark he came to regret. The first "foreign relations" effort by the Confederacy ended in failure, and the commissioners went home.

In London, Henry John Temple, 3rd Viscount Palmerston was prime minister to Queen Victoria. He was a seasoned politician of long standing. He held many posts in British government including foreign secretary 1846–1851; home secretary 1852–1855; prime minister 1855–1858 and 1859–1865. "Henry John Temple, the third Viscount Palmerston, was one of the most fascinating men of his time."[7] Sometimes referred to as "a womanizer with ginger sideburns and a gunboat approach to diplomacy", his letters and dispatches, which made the six-week trip back and forth across the Atlantic from 1860–1865, give the historian an interesting look at the British conduct of foreign policy during this critical period. When Seward was secretary of state, Palmerston was close to the end of his life. That spare, laconic, controlled face and body had yielded to heavy eyelids and cheeks swollen with age and many years of struggle and ribald adventure. "Pam", as his friends called him, was convinced that the separation of North and South would be permanent and of great benefit to England as separate countries. On January 10, 1861, Russell wrote to Richard Lyons in Washington, "I do not see how the United States can be cobbled together again by any compromise ... I cannot see any mode of reconciling such parties as these. The best thing now would be that the right to secede should be acknowledged ... I hope sensible men will take this view ... But, above all I hope no force will be used."

Together, the United States were a potential future threat to the balance of world power still controlled by Britain, France, Spain and Russia. Prussia had not yet upset this combination. Divided, the states might be weaker and allow England and France to maintain better control. Cotton would continue to flow to the hungry mills of Manchester, Liverpool and Leeds. North and South would also remain lucrative markets for preferred European goods. Palmerston was an older man than Seward, but still sharp. "While competing actively on the hunting field and in the bedroom, Palmerston was emphatically not the average aristocratic ministerial drone. He had strength and vitality as well as intelligence ... "[8] During the Civil War, however, Seward dealt with a man who was more set in his ways and aristocratic outlook. His experiences in the Crimean War made him more cautious, and he preferred a divided, weaker America. Nevertheless, the United States, divided or united, was a market that had helped make England the wealthy powerhouse she had become. Pam had to be careful. His coalition government was also under threat. As an island nation, English budgets tended to favor defense over the riskier offensive posture. Palmerston and Queen Victoria preferred to stay safe with the construction and maintenance of fixed fortifications – not the new, experimental turret ironclads. Pam also had to deal with a secondary power behind the throne of Queen Victoria, Prince Albert. Lincoln's secretary of state never dealt directly with the Prince, but was the beneficiary of Albert's good judgment in the management of British foreign policy.

Prince Albert of Saxe-Coburg and Gotha, Germany, married Queen Victoria of England in February, 1840. Albert grew up in a comparatively poor, highly structured male dominated principality. He was bright, handsome, well-educated and raised to believe that women were incapable of understanding or dealing with matters outside of the home. "German misogyny was of a deeper dye than its English counterpart. England in the seventeenth century had produced Queen Elizabeth, the greatest ruler in its history. Part of the contempt for women that we shall find Prince Albert expressing throughout his life was due to the fact that he was a member of the atavistically sexist German aristocracy."[9] He enjoyed mathematics, science and order. Victoria, by contrast, grew up as the center of attention in a wealthy country which controlled the balance of political and military power in the world. She was also bright, self-centered, strong-willed and sometimes impulsive. She was her own woman, and in this she was in sharp contrast to her countrymen. "The English of the nineteenth century liked to hear of female weakness and submission ... If a woman married, her property, her earnings, her children, and her body legally belonged to her husband, to do with as he willed."[10]

Victoria was different. She enjoyed the power and influence that came with being Queen. She was a nationalist, so for her, England always came first. By contrast, Albert had an international perspective. He saw himself as a citizen of the world, and thought peace and prosperity were essential in maintaining Britain's place in the world. Unlike Palmerston, Albert was not concerned with a divided or united America; he just wanted the peace that helped ensure economic prosperity for England. Albert was German, however, and Palmerston saw him as a foreigner who had control over his Queen and thus over some of the conduct of foreign affairs. The other foreigner, U.S. minister Charles Francis Adams, helped to maintain balance and a reasoned approach to Anglo-American relations at this critical time.

In France, the political landscape was more complicated. William Lewis Dayton was the Union representative in Paris until his death in 1864.[11] He was succeeded by Paris consular representative John Bigelow. Dayton was a former senator from New Jersey as well as the first Republican vice presidential nominee in 1856 with John C. Fremont. Dayton replaced Charles James Faulkner in May, 1861. Faulkner was from Virginia, sympathetic to the Southern cause, and later served on the staff of "Stonewall" Jackson. Dayton didn't trust Faulkner and warned Seward immediately upon arrival in Paris. He complained that "London and Paris were swarming with Confederate emissaries."[12] Dayton didn't speak any French and exaggerated the extent of that Confederate flock. The Davis government had neither the money, the talent nor the basic inclination to try and control European public opinion at this early stage. King Cotton would do the trick.

Unfortunately for Seward, the new consul didn't think much of Dayton. He considered him to be just a political appointee. On his voyage to Paris on the *S.S. Persia*, Bigelow spent most of his time learning idiomatic French. His textbook language was good, but he wanted to be able to speak freely and with confidence to his French contacts. He knew the French would appreciate that. Writing about her subject, biographer Margaret Clapp asserts that Bigelow "did more than any other man to ward off dreaded French intervention on behalf of the Confederacy."[13] This is a very debatable conclusion because at this time, John Bigelow, was a consular rather than diplomatic representative. However, Seward and Dayton knew his real talent, and encouraged him to use his French to promote the Union cause through the French press. With Bigelow in the mix, France was about to become as volatile and interesting as the dance Seward was having with England. Between Bigelow and Napoleon III, Seward was working with kindred spirits.

Napoleon III is generally portrayed as quixotic and unpredictable as Seward. In both instances, perception became reality. Thus far, the 19th century had been hard on France. Ruled by dictators and Bourbon kings, revolution came back to France in 1848. Marx and Engels had published the *Communist Manifesto* in that year, and the populace of Europe was hungry for change. John Locke and Jean Jacques Rousseau had done their work well 100 years before. Democracy and universal suffrage was the battle cry. Many laborers in England and France related to and sympathized with Northern attempts to abolish slavery – indeed, many in Europe thought of themselves as slaves to an aristocracy that made all of the rules. In this volatile turmoil, France was looking for a new hero, a new leader who would bring back the glory days of Napoleon Bonaparte. Imperialist expansion was on the minds of many European heads of state – whether they were kings, queens, princes or prime ministers. They all wanted to explore new lands and expand their wealth and power through the seizure of the resources found in conquered territory. Weakened by Civil War, the United States and the Americas were a prime target for England, France and Spain. Lincoln recognized this. In his annual message to Congress in 1861, the president warned, "Since, however, it is apparent that here, as in every other state, foreign dangers necessarily attend domestic difficulties, I recommend that adequate and ample measures be adopted for maintaining the public defenses on every side."[14] Lincoln recommended strengthening fortifications on the nation's sea coast, rivers and Great Lakes. The president thought it was important to stockpile guns and ammunition at American harbors. Navigation in and out of U.S. ports needed improvement so that gunboats and turret ironclads could keep foreign ships of war away from the coastline. This was especially important in places like Wilmington and Charleston where the channel markers could no longer be seen at night because the lighthouse beacons had all been removed by Confederate agents. It was also true of the most strategic city and harbor in the Union, New York.

In 1859, then governor of New York, William Seward, ordered a study of the defensive capabilities of New York harbor by Major J.G. Barnard of the Corps of Engineers.[15] The lessons of Crimea were still fresh in the minds of politicians all over the world. The port city of Sevastopol was pounded into submission by sea and land forces. Regardless of how many and how strong, fixed fortifications could not protect that city. Land fortifications were expensive, but could mount the heaviest guns and fire more rounds than ships at sea. The problem here was that ships could also pound those forts and land an army in some other unprotected place and join the navy in subduing those strongholds as the British and French did to Sevastopol. England already had a large navy, and both Palmerston and Queen Victoria were partial to fixed fortifications. They would protect the homeland, and the Royal Navy would protect the colonies. U.S. Commodore Matthew Perry mocked this approach, however, by stating that forts "are in truth like chained monsters, harmless beyond the reach of their manacles – not so with steam batteries". The study commissioned by Seward clearly advocated the benefits of a strong navy over the fixed fortifications that already guarded the narrow channels leading into New York Harbor. Hopefully, America's great port cities were safe from the grasp of armed alliances from Europe.

Napoleon was hungry to reclaim France's place as the leading power broker in Europe. Like Palmerston, Thouvanel and Mercier, he believed that a divided America was a *fait accompli*. His ill-considered "conquest" of Mexico was an attempt to stand over the shoulder of America and use Mexican proximity as a threat to help ensure that the United States did not get too cozy with Great Britain. In this situation, however, a divided America with two governments with which to deal was ultimately impractical and unpredictable. Unlike Great Britain, France did not have a great oversupply of cotton with which she could outlast the Union blockade of Confederate ports. The new emperor was willing to do anything to challenge and balance the power of Britain. He was also willing to do anything to restart the cotton gins and protect his economy. His offer of mediation was rejected by Seward. Mediation implied a diplomatic effort between two separate countries. Lincoln and Seward maintained that this was an internal rebellion, a family quarrel, not a war.

Seward believed correctly that mediation would ultimately lead to the recognition that he was charged with avoiding. Nevertheless, Napoleon III was less concerned with the definition of a rebellion versus a war. "The new emperor was a small, skinny man with a large head, an extraordinary mustache, and a libido to match. He had great charisma."[16] Except for the libido, Seward and Napoleon were a matched pair.

A FAMILY QUARREL.

'A Family Quarrel', Brady's National Photographic Portrait Galleries

Although the minister to France was William Lewis Dayton, the man to whom some of the Union looked to for answers was John Bigelow. As consul in Paris, Bigelow was at the center of the foreign policy drama. His letters to friends and colleagues as well as those written to him are a colorful source of information on the diplomacy of Édouard Antoine Thouvanel, Édouard Drouyn de Lhuys and Napoleon III. When Dayton arrived in Paris, he wrote to Seward on May 27, 1861. In his letter, Dayton informs Seward that the French press is hostile to the Union cause. He believes that if some extra money were spent to find a clever journalist who could challenge the press, that would be money well spent. Dayton knew that the French press was tightly controlled by the government. It was essential to find someone creative and resourceful. Dayton was right, and Secretary Seward knew the right man for the job. Money was soon expended to secure the literary talents of John Bigelow, editor and co-owner of the *New York Evening Post*.

Writing later in his *Retrospectives of an Active Life*, Bigelow claimed: "Mr. Seward said that the Government had selected me for the Paris consulate not primarily for the discharge of consular duties, which were then trifling and every day diminishing, but to look after the press in France. Our legations and consulates had been filled largely, not to say exclusively, during the Administration of President [James] Buchanan, with men of more or less doubtful loyalty, and London and Paris were swarming with Confederate emissaries."

Bigelow was told that the French press regarded the Confederates as poor souls who were only fighting for the most basic rights, not for slavery. The press also picked up on what was commonly reported in the British papers that the disunion of North and South was permanent and could not be changed. Seward worked hard to stay on friendly terms with France, anxious that his new consul get to his post as soon as possible. Bigelow was a consular official who eventually got heavily involved in diplomacy.

Foremost among the "hoary and shrewd men" of the Lincoln administration foreign policy team was Abraham Lincoln himself. The president did not view himself as an expert on relations with Europe. He admitted that he would probably make mistakes. Charles Francis Adams was less charitable in claiming that Lincoln knew "absolutely nothing" about foreign relations. One member of his cabinet, however, consistently and firmly believed that Lincoln's good judgment was the single most important factor in maintaining stable and safe relations with Europe. That cabinet member and key player was Gideon Welles, navy secretary. Welles also kept a detailed diary of events at Lincoln's cabinet meetings. The navy secretary's observations and conclusions are important because his work brought him into direct contact with William Seward. Gideon Welles came from Glastonbury, Connecticut and worked in Hartford. He was the founder of the *Hartford Times*, and a member of the Connecticut General Assembly. He came to the attention of Abraham Lincoln because of his outspoken anti-slavery views and support of the new Republican Party. Welles' views were made known through his newspaper editorials. Seeking to geographically balance his cabinet, Lincoln offered the Navy Secretary post to Welles in 1861. Although William Howard Russell joked that Welles didn't know the stern from the bow of a ship, Welles was diligent, competent and forceful in advocating for the navy and ensuring that the blockade was as effective as it could be. Lincoln called Welles "Father Neptune". His personal ambition was exceeded only by that of Lincoln and Seward themselves. In 1861, he was fifty-nine years old, bald, and wore a light brown wig which contrasted with his snow-white beard, and had lived a sedentary lifestyle as a journalist and editor for many years. Yet he displayed passion, energy and loyalty to Abraham Lincoln that often brought him into conflict with the secretary of state.

At the State Department, Seward's first job was to ensure that England and France did not interfere in the rebellion. Interference could only be facilitated through the use of British and French vessels to either invade or blockade. They needed boats to steam across the ocean to do this. The British navy was the largest in the world at that stage in the Civil War. England was "neutral", however. International law allowed a neutral to deal in non-contraband goods without challenge – except for that troubling and lawful challenge of being searched first to determine if there was contraband aboard. Nothing was easy when dealing with sovereign nations eager to protect their own self interests. Even the definition of contraband goods upon which all could agree was a problem by itself. Were Confederate representatives as persons sailing to Europe for help contraband? Was the coal that fueled their steamships contraband? Was the iron plating on the new ironclad ships contraband?

Circumventing official neutrality were those privateers made in British ship yards and manned by English sailors who, upon arrival in North American waters, were confronted with the Union naval blockade, directed by Gideon Welles. Seward recommended the blockade that was a factor in causing England to accord belligerency status to the Confederacy. Treated as belligerents, the 1856 Treaty of Paris allowed Britain to trade with the South in non-contraband material. The Union blockade, as recommended by Seward, stood in the way, and the privateers and blockade runners quickly took up the slack. Welles was charged with maintaining the blockade in a manner and an extent to which Seward objected. Seward felt the need to threaten Great Britain, but not too strongly. He could not risk having his bluff called.

History has shown us that this was not necessary; Gideon Welles called Seward's bluff for him.

Welles considered Lincoln to have been fully in charge of all aspects of his administration, including foreign relations. Biased or not, Welles' conclusions are always supported by detailed factual data, good reasoning and a sequential presentation. Most historians consider Welles to have been a harsh, but very perceptive, judge of character. However, there are a few instances where his conclusions were incomplete. Regarding Lincoln and his managerial skills as president, Welles always had a quick defense. The opening paragraph of his rebuttal to Adams' eulogy of Seward set the tone for his entire response. He began, "It is to be regretted that Mr. Charles Francis Adams in his Memorial Address on the Life, Character and Services of William H. Seward should have permitted himself to do injustice to Abraham Lincoln. Any attempt to canonize Mr. Seward by detracting from the merits of his chief weakens the encomiums bestowed." Although it must be remembered that the jobs and objectives of Welles and Seward were connected through the blockade and its maintenance, the navy secretary's observations of Seward are similar to those expressed by legation and consular personnel all over Europe. Their opinions were generally consistent. Welles characterized Seward as possessing, "restless activity, unceasing labors, showy manifestations and sometimes incautious exercise of questionable authority".[17]

Working opposite Welles first in Montgomery and then Richmond was Confederate navy secretary Stephen Russell Mallory, from Key West, Florida. He was described as "a little round bellied man who looks like a prosperous shoemaker."[18] As a senator, he served on the Senate Naval Affairs Committee. Unfortunately for Mallory, he had the great misfortune to work with some of the Davis cabinet who were poorly suited to their work. Davis had little respect for foreign relations and less for the value of a navy. Mallory had diverse opinions on naval issues. On one hand, he favored flogging on board ship to maintain discipline. On the other, he was an early advocate of ironclad warships. While a U.S. senator and looking for data to help improve the navy, he compared it with the British Royal Navy. He presented his findings to the Senate in 1846, and clearly demonstrated that America had a lot of catching-up to do. Speaking in defense of the navy and demonstrating a real passion, love and respect for the service, he told the senators:

"But sir, in rising on this occasion to speak for the navy … I came here to speak of its soul, its spirit, by which the service moves and has its being; and for these – for the men who sustain your flag, and represent your spirit upon the sea, who hold their lives in their hands whenever her interests or the honor of their country demand their sacrifice … let me briefly remind you that, though inseparably connected, as it is, with national character, national rights and even national greatness, disclosing, as it does, so many heroic deeds and memorable examples of devotion to country, it has received less attention from the fostering congress than any other branch of the public service."[19]

Mallory advocated ironclad frigates, not the vulnerable steam paddle-wheel ships then being produced. He also made enemies as the author of the 1855 Naval Reform Act which sought to promote officers based upon merit, not longevity.[20] Mallory was responsible for the forced retirement of many older officers who had not been to sea in many years. The Retirement Board, which was a product of the Naval Reform Act, became known as the "plucking board." Welles would have appreciated and enjoyed Mallory's passionate words in defense of the navy and his proactive interest in reform. Unfortunately, he was at the mercy of Confederate treasury secretary, Christopher Memminger. At the start of the war, when the small Confederate navy needed help, Memminger turned down an offer from a British company to buy six ironclad frigates for ten million dollars. The ships were worth twice that, but Memminger was new to the job, and didn't think that the Confederacy could afford it.

Back in Washington, Edward Bates had been a serious rival for the Republican nomination in 1860. Newspapers at the time of the Chicago Convention in the Wigwam show Bates at the top of the list and Lincoln at the bottom. News accounts discuss Bates in detail, but hardly mention Lincoln. Bates was already sixty-seven years old and retired from public life when he was asked to serve as attorney general in the Lincoln administration. According to Bates, Lincoln considered him for secretary of state, but finally concluded that William Seward was too powerful a rival to deny him that important post. In his diary, he gives us Lincoln's reaction to Seward:

"The actual appointment of Mr. Seward to be Secretary of State would be dangerous in two ways – 1. It would exasperate the feelings of the South, and make conciliation impossible, because they consider Mr. Seward the embodiment of all they hold odious in the Republican party – and 2. That it would alarm and dissatisfy that large section of the part which opposed Mr. Seward's nomination."

Bates kept a diary throughout the Civil War. His reflections are both personal and political. Right after mentioning his daffodils coming up earlier than expected that spring, he will then comment on the latest crisis confronted by the cabinet.

John George Nicolay and John Milton Hay were secretaries to Lincoln throughout the war. They had easy access to Lincoln and were keen observers of the drama unfolding on the second floor of the Executive Mansion. Both men knew and revered Lincoln. Their 1890 biography of the president consumed ten volumes and was the most complete and detailed record of the Lincoln administration at that time.[21] Both men were used by Lincoln to act as eyes and ears in different parts of the country during the war. Nicolay provides a vivid picture of Fredericksburg right after the battle. He was sent by Lincoln to gather information on what went wrong. Like Welles, Nicolay and Hay are partisan observers of this historic period. However, they often provide insight and detail that cannot be found in any other source. Many of their conclusions agree with those of many of the key players and other observers of the Lincoln government at this time.

Nicolay and Hay talk about Seward's talents and plans for the new government and the nation:

"Seward naturally took a leading part in the new cabinet. This was largely warranted by his prominence as a party manager; his experience in the New York governorship and in the United States Senate; the quieting and mediating attitude he had maintained during the winter; the influence he was supposed to wield over the less violent Southerners; the information he had gained from the Buchanan cabinet; his intimacy with General Scott; his acknowledged ability and talent; his optimism which always breathed hope and imparted confidence. During the whole of March, he had been busy with various measures of administration … All this activity, however, did not appear to satisfy his desires and ambition. His philosophic vision took a yet wider range. He was eager to enlarge the field of his diplomacy beyond the boundaries of the Republic. Regarding partisanship as a mere secondary motive, he was ready to grapple with international politics. He would heal a provincial quarrel in the zeal and fervor of a continental crusade. He would smother a domestic insurrection in the blaze and glory of a war which must logically be a war of conquest. He would supplant the slavery question with the Monroe Doctrine. And who shall say that these imperial dreams did not contemplate the possibility of changing a threatened dismemberment of the Union into the triumphant annexation of Canada, Mexico and the West Indies."[22]

This perception of Seward at this early stage is interesting and consistent with the perceptions of other observers of the Lincoln government. Most agreed that he had great energy, but often tried to take on too much and had to work in haste to catch up. It is also important to note that Nicolay and Hay considered the secretary to be optimistic, hopeful and confident. This was also an ever-present part of the man's personality since his youngest days. Lincoln needed this around him.

Senator Charles Sumner of Massachusetts was also an important figure in the Lincoln foreign policy effort. Hoary and shrewd, he was chair of the Senate Foreign Relations Committee, had traveled extensively in Europe and was a regular correspondent with two influential members of the English parliament, Richard Cobden and John Bright. At the time of Seward's April 1, 1861 memo, *Some Thoughts for the President's Consideration*, Lincoln was already concerned about his secretary's judgment. Seward had resigned his office two days before the inauguration, only to rescind this resignation three days later. Lincoln was forearmed and responded quickly and firmly to Seward's recommendation that a war with England might help unite North and South in the secession movement then underway. It sounded crazy – Lincoln was horrified and turned to Charles Sumner for advice. The president had no background in foreign relations, but he knew that Sumner was more experienced in such matters. According to David Herbert Donald, "Quietly burying Seward's fantastic proposal in the files, the President began looking for a more reliable advisor in foreign affairs. It was inevitable that he should turn to Sumner."

May, 1861 was not a good month for Seward, because it was then that he drafted the infamous Dispatch No.10 to Charles Francis Adams in England, in which he threatened war with the most powerful military force at that time. Lincoln showed the dispatch to Sumner, who recommended changes. Most of the final changes were those of

Lincoln alone. However, he listened carefully to Sumner who suggested conciliatory language. Some historians have suggested that Sumner and Seward were operating separate state departments. According to David Herbert Donald, "Lincoln gave Sumner a virtual veto power over foreign policy. Before Congress assembled in July he authorized the Senator to go through all of the foreign correspondence since the Inauguration; he asked Sumner's advice on that part of his message to Congress dealing with foreign affairs."[23] Some believed that Sumner's influence continued only through the first year of the Lincoln administration. Correspondence with Richard Cobden, John Bright and the Duke and Duchess of Argyll clearly shows that this was not the case. Although Sumner was singularly focused on slave emancipation, he remained a close advisor to Lincoln on matters of foreign relations and international law throughout the war.

Charles Sumner's counterpart in the House was Henry Winter Davis, from the border state of Maryland. Davis had been a slave holder who became a Republican and rejected the vice presidential nomination in 1860. His impulsivity rivaled that of Seward. Davis served as chair of the House Committee on Foreign Relations. The Confederacy was not well equipped and prepared to deal with this mix of hoary and shrewd men.

While Georgia and other secession states sent their own representatives to Europe to secure arms and credit, the only Confederate government purchasing agent seeking help from London and Paris was Massachusetts-born Major Caleb Huse.[24] Huse graduated from West Point and had accepted a teaching position at the University of Alabama when the war broke out on April 12, 1861, the day Fort Sumter was bombarded. Remaining in Alabama, he was commissioned in the Confederate army and immediately sent to Europe. He was ordered to buy as many Enfield-style rifles and artillery pieces that he could find. Arriving in London on May 10, 1861, Huse immediately went to the offices of the London Armory Company. Walking into the director's office to place his order, he was stunned to find a Union purchasing agent already there to buy all that the company could produce and sell.[25]

Lincoln and Seward had ministers plenipotentiary and consuls in all of the important cities of Europe working their small army of spies and purchasing agents to buy the war material needed to supplement

'Arms of ye Confederacey', G.H. Heap Inv., 1862.

what the Northern factories were already producing. The factories at Springfield and the Colt facility in Hartford were already working at peak capacity. Jefferson Davis needed skilled craftsmen and gun smiths, not cotton and sugar cane farmers.

He couldn't rely on the Tredegar Iron Works in Richmond for everything. So, while Seward worked through Charles Francis Adams, who in turn relied on Thomas Haines Dudley and a well-financed group of purchasing agents from London, Paris, Hamburg, Vienna, Rome, St. Petersburg and many other cities, the Confederate States of America initially relied on one man, Caleb Huse. "The temporary (Confederate) plan, a hand-to-mouth affair, imperfect as it was, cannot be labeled as a failure."[26] It didn't fail initially because Caleb Huse successfully and resourcefully represented the War, Ordinance, Quartermaster, Medical and Navy departments. In 1862, he arranged for the purchase and shipment of 100,000 rifled guns from Austria to be shipped to Charleston through the port of Hamburg. Austria had decided to switch from gunpowder to gun cotton as a propellant for their weapons. Unable to retrofit existing rifles, they decided to manufacture new ones designed to use gun cotton. As a result, they had a large surplus of rifled guns ready for sale and delivery. Unfortunately, success quickly went to Huse's head. When the Davis government realized that they needed to specialize their operations, other purchasing agents were sent to Europe. This didn't sit well with Huse, who actively tried to frustrate the activities and contracts of several of the new Confederate agents. Particularly upset was Alexander Collie of Alex Collie and Company.[27] Collie was making substantial profits from their work with the Confederacy. When Huse questioned some of their contract language, Collie complained to Secretary of State Judah Benjamin that, "Huse is not only unbusiness-like, but discreditable and disgraceful in the highest degree."[28] Collie took huge profits from their commercial work with the Confederacy, but they claimed that they were also taking a big risk. The blockade had tightened. In the end, Huse had been so productive that nobody in Richmond dared to fire him. In 1862, Major J.B. Fergusson arrived to take over purchasing for the quartermaster and James D. Bulloch for the Navy Department. Unfortunately for a slowly-organizing Confederacy, this may have been too late. By late 1862, the war had already seen Forts Henry and Donaldson as well as the vital port of New Orleans fall. If this wasn't enough, the "victory" at Antietam and the subsequent issuing of the Emancipation Proclamation gave Britain the pause that Lincoln needed. Ultimately, Jefferson Davis learned a hard lesson and appointed Alabama businessman Colin J. McRae to supervise and coordinate all purchasing agents and their activities in Europe. McRae did an excellent job, but like too many Confederate initiatives, it was too little, too late.

In addition to "hoary and shrewd men", the Lincoln and Palmerston governments were both heavily influenced by public opinion. Print media played a significant role in foreign relations at this time. Sometimes referred to as Black Republicans, Lincoln and many of his cabinet were regularly vilified through editorial and political cartoons in the newspapers in America and Europe. Lincoln, however, was elected for a four-year term. He had time. Jefferson Davis was "elected" to a six-year term that could not be renewed, while Lord Palmerston headed a shaky Whig coalition that was always cautious of the opposition. Palmerston was a much older man than Lincoln and did not necessarily have a four-year term of office left to him at the start of the American Civil War. Both parties read the newspapers and were sensitive to public pressure. Jefferson Davis, by contrast, was not elected. He was selected by a small group of wealthy planters who wanted someone with a military background who would uphold the "cornerstone" of the Confederacy. The editor of the *Richmond Examiner*, Edward Alfred Pollard, made it his mission in life to take Davis to task in the newspapers for every issue and battlefield loss that occurred. He continued to pursue Davis in print long after the war ended. He would not give up. "Jefferson Davis was not the man to act as leader of a cause so broad and august ... Mr. Davis was to a great degree an accident of the war; he added nothing to its inspiration, and he mixed with a great cause a game of selfishness and an experiment of vanity."

Public opinion in London was often influenced by news accounts in the influential *Times, Telegraph, Standard, Punch* and the *Illustrated London News*. The *Times* got its information from Lyons dispatches as well as the stories written by one of the *Times'* correspondents, William Howard Russell. Abraham Lincoln acknowledged the power and influence of the *Times* when he met Russell for the first time at a dinner party at the home of Secretary Seward. According to Russell, "Mr. Seward then took me by the hand and said 'Mr. President, allow me to present to you Mr. Russell of the *Times*'. On which Mr. Lincoln put out his hand in a very friendly manner, and said, 'Mr. Russell, I am very glad to make your acquaintance and to see you in this country. The *London Times* is one of the greatest powers in the world. In fact, I don't know anything which has more power – excepting perhaps the Mississippi.'"[118]

William Howard Russell was an influential journalist, a Southern sympathizer, and a colorful man who traveled the world writing about foreign wars and foreign relations. In 1854, on the island of Malta during the Crimean War, a British soldier described him as "a vulgar, low Irishman, [who] sings a good song, drinks anyone's brandy and water and smokes as many cigars as a Jolly Good Fellow."[29] Wherever there was a good fight, Russell was there to write about it. With an intense but patient look, jowls dimpled and fattened with hard living, Russell was aware of his influence and the mistrust of his pen in the North. Russell approached the first secretary of war, Simon Cameron, about being allowed to draw food and supplies from the department commissary. Writing constantly from the battlefield, Russell had few sources of ready support to sustain him. Although he realized that what Cameron might do for him, the secretary would be required to do for any other newspaper correspondent seeking assistance. Russell rationalized Cameron's position, but also acknowledged the power exercised by him and his paper. Russell kept a diary in which he wrote colorful and detailed observations of his activities, North and South, during the first two years of the Civil War. He had easy access to all of the key players on both sides involved in the foreign relations drama at this time. On March 28, 1861 Russell tells us that he "was honored today by visits from a great number of members of Congress, journalists and others." On Easter Sunday, March 31, Russell had lunch with Lord Lyons and dinner in the evening with Baron de Stockel, Russian representative in Washington. On April 3rd, he met with a confederate contingency at their hotel in Washington. In attendance was Charles Sumner, chair of the senate foreign relations committee. His access brought him information. That information reached British leaders and mill workers alike. If William Henry Seward spoke ill of England after a glass of brandy, John Bull heard about it.

The British population was split in its sympathy with North and South. European aristocracy hoped that democracy would fail and their dominant position in politics made secure. The mill workers of the cities related to the gritty, hard-toiling men of the North. However, many of the journalists and artists writing for the English papers were in sympathy with the South. In addition to Russell, journalists Francis Charles Lawley and Percy Greg wrote columns sympathetic to the Confederate cause. More influential than Lawley or Greg was a talented artist named Frank Vizetelly. The artist contributed to the *Illustrated London News*, which by 1863 had a circulation of 300,000 copies compared to 70,000 for the *London News*. Russell and Vizetelly were similar in personality and politics. Vizetelly was a big man with sandy hair and a bushy red beard. He enjoyed being with people, and had fun telling stories about his travels. He knew and admired Giuseppe Garibaldi, another big man adored by crowds in Europe and America.

Like Russell, Vizetelly pushed his heavy body forward with a determination that took him to many of the most critical battles of the Civil War. He became close friends with J.E.B. Stuart and was made an honorary captain by James Longstreet. Both Vizetelly and Russell witnessed and wrote about the Northern defeat at First Bull Run. Russell's column spared no detail as Union troops threw down their weapons and fled in retreat. The Vizetelly drawing, which entertained and influenced thousands of British readers, shows Northern troops in a chaotic panic and running with arms and legs flung far ahead of them as they sprinted back to Washington. In some ways, a Vizetelly picture was worth a thousand words from Russell.

Nevertheless, the Russell column and the Vizetelly drawing angered the secretary of war, Edwin Stanton, to the point that he refused to give either man a pass to travel with the Union army. Their vital access was denied. Russell temporarily went back to England, but Vizetelly went south, and met Jefferson Davis and Robert E. Lee. From 1861 until 1864, Vizetelly wrote sympathetically about the Confederacy. Writing about his new cause, he states, "The more I see of the Southern Army the more I am lost in admiration of its splendid patriotism, at its wonderful endurances, at its utter disregard of hardships ... "[31] Although the Union blockade sometimes made it difficult to get his pictures to the London papers, Vizetelly still managed to have 133 engravings published on everything from the death of Elmer Ellsworth to the final days of Jefferson Davis. The key players in the Civil War drama were diverse in talent and impact.

The job of maintaining effective foreign relations for Lincoln was a complex business. Jefferson Davis realized the complexity of this later in the war. Lincoln himself was more involved in foreign policy than generally thought. Davis, at first, deferred to King Cotton. Charles Sumner is described by modern historians as the alternate secretary of state who advised Lincoln on the more serious aspects of foreign relations. Judah Benjamin actually served Davis in this capacity when the president was so burdened with depression. All of these men were dealing with experienced politicians in London and Paris who were "not easily baffled." Lord Palmerston and the dying Prince Albert were actively taking part in foreign diplomacy. The prince may have averted war between England

and the Union by allowing Lincoln to save face over the *Tent* Affair. On both sides of the ocean, public opinion was always influenced by the press. This was particularly so in England. In the end, however, those hoary and shrewd men in London and Paris controlled much in the foreign relations battle at this time.

CHAPTER 4

WHISTLING IN THE WIND

There is evidence that Mr. Seward is an ogre, resolved to eat all
Englishmen raw.

Charles Francis Adams Sr., December 20, 1861

As already established, Lord Palmerston, the British prime minister, referred to Seward as a "vaporing, blustering, ignorant man." Palmerston had been in politics long enough to know himself, and he thought he knew his enemy. More critical was the opinion of Lord Richard Lyons, the British representative in Washington, who complained that Seward "hoped to excite the American Mob against European powers by blustering words which might well lead to violent deeds." Lyons also knew himself, and he worked hard to understand Seward and what he considered to be the "mob mentality" of American politics. Republican party stalwart Francis P. Blair wrote John Bigelow, Union consul in Paris on October 26, 1861. Lincoln and Seward had been in office for seven months. Blair complained:

"Your friend, Seward, has been a nightmare to the administration. Let me mark the steps he has taken in frustration of the President. When the President put his foot on the car for Washington, he announced his mission to be the restoration of the Govt., and to retake all that had been taken from it by secession. He had proclaimed his purpose to make Seward his Premier in advance; and the first step of this minister was to prepare to frustrate the policy declared by the President."

The man who was initially considered for the position of secretary of state over Seward was Charles Francis Adams. He and Lyons may be considered part of that British team which ultimately came to include people like John Bright, Richard Cobden and Edward Forster. This team was essential in mitigating the impact of possible English and French incursion into the Civil War, as well as the early missteps of William Seward. England may have been the more critical player at this early stage because France was reluctant to take action without England taking the first step. Although a qualified ally of the Union and a diplomatic wild card, Russia decided to stay out of the conflict.

Adams and Lyons were a matched pair. Adams' father was president, as was his grandfather. Charles Francis has been described as "reserved and austere, he lacked the arts of popularity and shunned their acquisition; having little natural charm or personal magnetism, he discourages familiarity or bonhomie ... A stark personality was coupled with orthodox values." Lyons was cut from the same bolt of cloth. He was a 41-year-old bachelor who hated the hot summers in Washington. Sitting for a picture at Matthew Brady's studio, Lyons stared quietly past Brady as if he were trying to anticipate Seward's next move. He had a youthful round face with dark hair quickly combed right to left by hand. He was quietly correct, right down to his well-tailored new suit.

Lyons was not a noisy creature. An endearing description of him is left by one of his young secretaries, Edward Malet. Believing that he knew his boss as a man of hard work, dedication and few words, Mallet was told to compose a response to a request for information from a British consul. The young secretary worked hard to create something that was brief, but to the point. He learned a hard lesson when the letter came back to him from Lyons. Entire sentences were stricken out and notes made in the margins. Lyons noted on the draft of the letter, "Brevity is the soul of wit, but I object to absolute nonsense – L."[1] Behind that quiet reserve was a mind that worked hard to analyze the motives, moods and moves of a man he initially considered his adversary, but later counted as a friend. Although not an enemy as per Sun Tsu, Lyons knew how Seward operated and how to deal with him. British diplomat and contemporary Henry Layard said of Lyons, "He was the type of what the modern English diplomatist must be – without initiative or views of his own … the qualities of caution, discretion, good temper, good sense and steadiness were displayed by Lyons to an uncommon degree during the tense and difficult years of his tenure in Washington."[2] Lyons took a dim view of Americans and their politics. "Lyons' letters from Washington reflect a vision of himself as a skillful diplomat successfully coping with irresponsible, half-educated semi-barbarians who constantly sought to trap or cow him and thus to injure his country through him."

Lyons was a diplomat and politician. His analysis of military strategy may not have been as accurate or perceptive as his assessment of the people in Lincoln's cabinet. Lyons admitted this deficiency and requested that a British military attaché be posted at his Legation to better report on the progress of the war. Lyons struggled to fully understand the complexities of the military aspect. To supplement this perceived deficiency, his dispatches frequently contained newspaper articles from the *National Intelligencer*, full of rich detail. However, the articles were as tainted as the back-slapping claims of Seward that the war would soon be settled by the next Union victory. The *National Intelligencer* was the official "mouthpiece" of the Republican party in Washington.[3]

It has been suggested that Richard Lyons was selected to represent Great Britain to the United States because he was a peer,[4] and England wanted to make a favorable impression on the U.S. However, it is clear that Lyons' success as representative to Washington was ultimately based on his wisdom and ability to remain cool in the face of great tension. By the time that war erupted over the resupply of Fort Sumter, Richard Lyons was an experienced veteran of Washington politics. Although at his post for only two years before Sumter, he quickly won the respect of the Buchanan administration and other members of Congress. He was the best possible choice to represent the interests of England at this critical time. His first letter was dated April 12, 1859 – the first issue was not the threat of war, but the problem of being able to read his illegible handwriting. His penmanship was as bad as Seward's. Lyons was promised an attaché to help him with his correspondence, but he had not yet arrived. Writing to Lord Malmesbury at the Foreign Office on May 24, 1859, he pleaded, "I should welcome anyone who was industrious and wrote a thoroughly good legible hand."

Lyons never enjoyed Washington. He particularly disliked the hot summers. At one point in the war, he asked for a leave, and returned to England for five months. One of his letters ended, "Commerce (Washington) has none. In fact, it is little more than a large village, and when Congress is not sitting it is a deserted village." In July, 1859, Palmerston replaced Lord Derby and John Russell took over from Malmesbury. The cast was now in place for the duration of the drama.

Before the election of Lincoln, one of the issues that confronted Lyons was Mexico. She was in a constant state of revolution, and the border with Mexico and the U.S. was a scene of mischief and murder. England was in a tight spot. She had loaned money to Mexico, and was concerned that the debt might not be repaid. Intervention was considered, but not at the expense of violating the Monroe Doctrine and upsetting the Buchanan administration. Lyons was always sensitive to the fact that relations between England and the United States had not always been amicable. He was careful in word and deed not to do anything to upset Washington. Lyons was critical to the success of British–American foreign relations at this time. But 1859 was destined to be a significant year in American history.

On October 16, 1859, John Brown attempted to seize government weapons at Harpers Ferry. From this point forward, many of Lyons' dispatches discuss concerns for the increasingly hostile relations between North and South. Regarding the Harper's Ferry raid, Lyons wrote to Russell on October 25, 1859: "The American public are absorbed by a foolish affair at a place called Harper's Ferry, where eighteen abolitionists contrived to obtain possession of the United States Armory."[5] The other issue that required patience and tact by Lyons was the disputed island of San Juan, off the northwest coast. The Oregon Treaty of 1846 made no mention of the island, so federal troops from Washington decided to occupy it. Lyons always treated the Buchanan administration with care, and caution. This was not an issue worth fighting for. Unfortunately, James Buchanan was a lame duck president who couldn't wait to hand his problems off to Abraham Lincoln. Lyons' attempts to settle the San Juan issue before March 4 were met with silence.

As the election of 1860 approached, Lyons was concerned about the split in the Democratic party, and the likelihood that this would provide victory for an anti-slavery Republican candidate. He was genuinely concerned about a possible Civil War. Very early, Lyons told Russell that England's cotton supply may be threatened. He recommended that an alternative supply be found. Lyons wrote to Russell on May 8, 1860, "It is all important to us to have the means of getting cotton from some other quarter, before abolition make any great progress."

Lyons was surprised by the nomination of Abraham Lincoln, and wrote to Russell on May 22, 1860, "The Republicans have thrown over the head of their party, Seward, and chosen for their candidate a Mr. Lincoln, a man unknown, a rough Westerner, of the lowest origin and little education."

Opinion of Lincoln aside, Charles Francis Adams and Lord Lyons both agreed on their opinion of Seward. On December 20, 1861, the senior Adams wrote to his son, Charles, Jr., who was in the Union army. Adams Sr. complained that:

> "The impression is general that Mr. Seward is resolved to insult England until she makes a war. He is the *bête noire* that frightens them out of all their properties. It is of no use to deny it and appeal to facts. They quote what he said to the Duke of Newcastle about insulting England as the only sure passport to popular favor in America, and a part of a speech in which he talked of annexing Canada as an offset to the loss of the slave states. This is the evidence that Mr. Seward is an ogre fully resolved to eat all Englishmen raw."[6]

Like Adams, Lyons ultimately came to see two sides of Henry Seward. As with Adams, first impressions were not positive. Lyons wrote to Russell on January 7, 1861, "With regard to Great Britain, I cannot help fearing that he (Seward) will be a dangerous foreign minister."[7] In a little over a year, however, Lyons and Seward were working together on a landmark treaty to end the slave trade by allowing for the search of each other's ships. Seward was slowly learning to pick his battles.

Richard Lyons was a critical element in the ability of the British Foreign Office to "manage" Seward and avert war. The situation and the outcome of the American Civil War might have been different if someone without Lyons' skills were British representative to Washington. Lyons may have been quiet, methodical and pedantic, but he was a shrewd judge of character. He knew his "enemy", what drove Seward, and what got him into trouble. Within a month of taking office, Lyons wrote to Russell of Seward's adaptable nature. Initially for peace with the South and the surrender of Fort Sumter, the secretary quickly became the fiercest hawk when his peace policy was rejected by the cabinet. However, Lyons also saw that Seward had painted himself into a corner with his bluster toward England. Lyons told Russell that Seward "sees himself in a very painful dilemma". If the secretary's bluff was called, and there was war with England at this early, vulnerable stage, Seward's authority and position would be in jeopardy.

Charles Francis and Henry Adams were educated men, father and son, who worked in the same office in London. Their views of Seward vacillated and dithered during the early years of the Lincoln administration. It is often difficult to believe that they were talking about the same man. This is further evidence of the fact that Seward confused those with whom he worked and communicated. Two months prior to Charles Francis' warning that Seward was "an ogre fully resolved to eat all Englishmen raw", his son Henry praised the secretary to his brother Charles on October 15, 1861. He stated "Never before for many years have we been so creditably represented in Europe or has the foreign policy of our country commanded more respect." Seward confused some of the U.S. legation personnel in Europe as well as those European representatives at home and abroad. This vacillation was a product of the confusion Seward projected through his public bluff and private caution.

The wavering reaction to Seward was a common theme in most of the diplomatic communication, public and private during the 1861–1865 period. Initially, however, Seward's foreign policy focused consistently on a strategy of bluff and bluster. Fortunately, the cooler heads maintained by hoary and shrewd men on both sides of the Atlantic helped to maintain relative stability. That stability allowed Lincoln the freedom and the time to focus almost exclusively on the war. Good relations with the United States were important to both England and France.

Napoleon's representative in Washington was Baron Henri Mercier. The Baron worked well with Lyons, but was a more provocative and independent personality than the British representative. He and Seward were kindred spirits. "Henri Mercier was a complicated man ... His tone and temperament were active, outgoing and generally optimistic, but his correspondence shows signs of sourness as well as laughter and wit."[8] Mercier was a physically active man who liked to ride, fence and swim. On February 22, 1862, Mercier and Lyons stared at the readers of *Harpers Weekly Magazine* with a look of silent determination.

As a true Frenchman, Mercier dressed in style and proudly wore his ample sideburns as if to announce his presence and clearly state his views. Both Mercier and Seward liked good brandy and Cuban cigars. Mercier, however, deplored the secretary's impulsive bluster and longed to go back to Paris. In a letter dated January 22, 1861, Henri Mercier expressed his concerns to Édouard Thouvanel. England and France believed that recognizing the Confederacy before war broke out would have been the best course of action. Fearful that recognition might immediately materialize, Seward reacted impulsively. According to Mercier: "Mr. Seward is definitely beside himself; there is no longer any way to talk sense to him. At heart, Seward is nothing but one of those demagogues who can sail only on the sea of popular emotion and who always tries to stir up passion in order to exploit it."

Early in his administration, Seward set the stage for the diplomacy of threat with England and France. Part of the issue was the blockade that he had recommended to Lincoln. Desiring to continue that symbiotic relationship with the North and South, but not risk war with the states, England declared herself neutral and accorded belligerent status, not outright recognition, to the Confederacy.[9] Neutrality, however, is difficult to define and harder to maintain. William Howard Russell of the *Times* said, "A neutral who tries to moderate the violence of either side is very like an ice between two hot plates."[10] According to accepted "international law" at that time, such status allowed the Confederacy access to foreign loans, as well as access to the sea ports of neutral nations. Their merchant ships and privateers could refuel with coal and provisions in the safety of foreign ports. Belligerency status would not allow them to officially buy armaments. Only full recognition as a sovereign nation would permit that. Frustrating the issue for Seward was the fact that Confederate privateers were protected by the accepted "one maritime league" from the shore of sovereign waters. This allowed the privateers and blockade runners space in which to maneuver and plan their escape to the open ocean. England recognized the South as a belligerent on May 13, 1861, Spain on June 17, 1861, France on June 30, 1861, and Portugal on

July 29, 1861. The Confederacy had no navy and thus issued Letters of Marque authorizing private ship owners to steal and burn as they wished. Confederate privateers now had a safe haven in the best ports of the Caribbean and Europe. Complicating this arrangement further was the fact that English neutrality dictated by default that she not provide prize courts in which captured Union vessels could be brought for adjudication and division of plunder. Under these circumstances, Confederate warships like the *Alabama* looted and then burned millions of dollars of worth of Union commercial shipping. The captured ship, or prize, could not be brought in to a neutral port without violating the existing laws of neutrality. The Atlantic Ocean was, therefore, a sea of burning hulls, sail cloth, steam engines and desperate men.

Although England had a cotton surplus at the outbreak of the war, eight months later, she was feeling the pinch. "At the time of the *Trent* Affair (November, 1861), mills that employed 172,257 hands now only had 64,393 employed. 15,572 laid off one day a week, 55,397 for two days and 28,832 for three days."[11] The English cared more about business than slavery. England had outlawed slavery in 1772. Charles Grenville, clerk of the Privy Council, stated that the Civil War would "be almost sure to interfere with the cotton crops, and this is really what affects us and what we care about." English restraint in dealing with Seward's blockade and threats under these adverse economic conditions is significant. A blockade that was as leaky as an old rowboat was yet respected as "effective" by a Palmerston government that did not want to get involved in another Crimea. Having recently spent £50 million to overhaul eight of the Southern British ports, and fearful of an overly aggressive posture that might endanger the coalition government, "The British government was very wary by the end of the Crimean War of grandstanding into another conflict which could spiral out of control again."[12]

The official dispatches between Lords Lyon and Russell throughout the war reveal much about Lincoln's policies, threats from the state department, and the subsequent European response. Partly as a result of threats from Seward, war was on the minds of many Englishmen. On November 1, 1861, Lyons wrote to Russell and told him that relations between England and the United States were so bad that war could erupt at any time and for any reason. Lyons was always aware that England was seen as the scapegoat for almost any problem in America. William Lewis Dayton, the U.S. representative in Paris had a meeting with his counterpart, Édouard Thouvanel, the day after he arrived in that city to head the Union Legation. After the exchange of credentials and welcoming comments, Thouvanel immediately raised the issue of cotton exports to France. Unlike England, she had no cotton reserves.

France had accorded belligerency status to the Confederacy on June 30, 1861. The Seward reaction to the belligerency recognition issue was dangerous. In an attempt to keep England and France out of the "rebellion", Seward threatened war against the most powerful armies and navies of Europe. In frustration, Lord Lyons' Dispatch No.206 on May 20, 1861 to Lord Russell in London stated:

"Mr. Seward's personal and immediate objects in taking this rash course are plain to all. Since his peace policy was overruled in the cabinet, he has devoted himself to making a strong effort to recover his lost popularity. He has endeavored to place himself at the head of the War Party. He has ever regarded the foreign relations of the country as safe material from which to make (to use his own phrase) political capital at home ... The President is, of course, wholly ignorant of foreign countries and of foreign affairs."

Was Seward "crazy like a fox?" Was his threat a successfully deliberate ploy to confuse, unbalance and thus control English and French foreign policy? Did he know himself and his enemy well enough to mold foreign policy on a foundation of threat and bluster? Seward was bluffing, but did the British prime minister Lord Palmerston and members of parliament know this? Lords Lyons and Russell both knew that Seward's bluster had more to do with personal gain than a serious desire to go to war with England. Incorrectly, however, Lyons and Russell believed that Seward was positioning himself with the public to take the presidency from Lincoln in 1864. Lyons was perceptive in observing that Seward's failed attempt as peacemaker prior to Fort Sumter was replaced by the face of a warrior in deference to public opinion. Dispatch No.206, from Lyons to Russell on May 20, 1861 confirmed that he was fully aware that Seward abused England for personal gain. However, he saw through Seward and realized that public bluster was sometimes balanced with private caution. Both men ultimately came to believe that Seward had no intention of pushing for war with England. Further in Dispatch No.206, Lyons confirmed "Mr. Seward and the part to whom he has now given himself up, really desire to plunge the country, at this crisis of its fate, into a war with England or France, seems impossible." They correctly believed that Seward was bluffing, and "whistling in the wind". They skillfully adjusted a foreign policy of cautious resolve accordingly. The situation was not as simple for Napoleon III. France was desperate for an end to the war and wanted to make a move to either recognize the Confederacy or arrange an armistice so that the issues could be worked out. Britain held firm, however. In Dispatch No.206 on November 20, 1861, Lyons clarified the recommended policy of England to Russell. "Inflexibility in conduct; firmness and conciliation in language; identity both in language and the conduct of England and France; and above all, manifest readiness on our part for war." England and France were ready to stand firm and call the secretary's bluff.

Seward's bluster also concerned Henry Adams, secretary to his father, Charles Francis Adams. He saw and heard the impact that Seward's inappropriate remarks had on the English workingman. He ends his letter to his brother with the statement that "Mr. Seward is the greatest criminal we've had yet." Counting coup against England was a dangerous game. In the midst of what may appear to be risky and unnecessary actions on the part of Henry Seward, it is well worth considering whether this really was nothing more than political "pandering to the mob", as suggested by Lyons.

Some have argued that the secretary threatened war with England and France as a means of uniting North and South against a common enemy. In 1861, this was an unrealistic and naive ploy at best. Lyons and Russell wisely restrained themselves. "Another possibility is that as a result of the enormous responsibilities that the war had heaped upon him, his bitter resentment at the attitude of England, his impulsive nature, and the psychological difficulty of reconciling himself to Lincoln's leadership, he simply lost his head and acted in hasty fashion."[13] Others have suggested that Seward wanted to appear strong so as to better facilitate his anticipated succession to the presidency after Lincoln. In Seward's own words, however, he tried to rationalize his erratic behavior. He held the general notion that threatening war with England and France would unsettle them enough to restrain their recognition efforts for a while at least. Henri Mercier recollected that Seward told him that his public bluff was just that. According to Mercier, "Mr. Seward added that if at the beginning of the crisis he had found it necessary to submit foreign governments to rather energetic language in order to reflect the feelings of the American people, he would nonetheless use every effort to keep peaceful and friendly relations with those governments."

When writing to the minister to Russia, Cassius M. Clay, Seward defends his threats by stating:

"However I may have at other times been understood, it has been an earnest and profound solicitude to avert foreign war that alone has prompted the emphatic and sometimes, perhaps, impassioned remonstrances [sic] I have hitherto made against any form or measure of recognition of the insurgents by the government of Great Britain."

Mercier frequently complained that Seward "pandered to the mob mentality" that he observed in American politics. At the least, however, Seward succeeded in further confusing the French representative. In the end, it may be argued that Seward had no consistent foreign policy plan. After Lincoln set him straight with threats to make war on England, Spain and France, Seward focused on just threatening England to make them mind their own business. When John Bull refused to cower under the threats, he wisely decided to try and work with the British, and not against them. His inconsistent behavior in the early stages of the Lincoln administration angered and confused foreign diplomats. "It is possible to argue that his [Seward's] unpredictability deterred the powers rather than any profundity of design." Under these circumstances, control was in the hands of those "key players" in the foreign relations drama, not the department of state. In theory, the Anglo-French alliance always had the option to call Seward's bluff, but Palmerston and his team did not allow Seward to provoke them – not an easy task for Palmerston.

Seward was bluffing. The prime minister knew it, but the citizens of England and France were left confused. "The combination of Seward's bluntness, resourcefulness and firmness puzzled and at times frightened them (the French) and annoyed the British. This is precisely the impression the secretary wanted to convey to them. When the news of his April 1 recommendation to the president was leaked, the very thought of an international war as a diversionary maneuver to prevent the outbreak of civil war seemed to border on sheer madness. But it was Seward's dramatic way of telling the Europeans not to trifle with the United States, now or in the future, or they would face complications of the upmost gravity, both of an economic and military nature. For the next four years, and particularly during the critically important first two years of his tenure as secretary of state, Seward tried to scare France and Britain enough to cause them at least to have second thoughts before deciding to intervene in the conflict on one way or another." If Seward's profound foreign policy design was to scare the British and French enough to give them pause relative to intervention in the Civil War, that design resulted in a stronger Anglo-French alliance, defiance of the blockade with ships built in British and French yards and manned by British crews; troops and guns being sent to Canada and invasion plans actively discussed by the prime minister. Secretary Seward could not have created a more hazardous situation with which the new Lincoln administration had to deal at this critical stage. Seward's bluff and threat might have caused so much fear and unrest in the English common man that they could have demanded action and tied the hands of those trying to defuse the situation and remain in office.

Had Lyons and Russell ever considered calling Seward's bluff? If so, what did they believe would be the result? What could they hope to accomplish by this? What action might Britain take to call the secretary's bluff? In Dispatch No.206, Lyons suggested that the Union would be crippled if England should turn the tables and blockade Northern ports. Without a federal income tax, Washington relied on duties placed on goods imported into the country. This was one of the reasons why Lincoln wanted to retain control over forts like Sumter and Pickens. They guarded busy, commercial harbors through which federal tax dollars flowed. Lyons declared that federal revenue would be "annihilated at one blow." In addition to lost revenue, the Union army would be deprived of the thousands of guns and ammunition then being imported from Europe. Lyons was perceptive and recognized that the spirit for war was high enough in the North to allow Lincoln to get away with introducing new taxes to make up for the lost income. Without this, the North would then be just as compromised as the South without import tax revenues. That would really cripple the Union war effort. In addition to a crippling blockade of Northern ports, Palmerston may have already discussed Northern invasion plans with Ambrose Dudley Mann of Georgia. Although Europe was absorbed in many issues including Poland, Italy and Schleswig-Holstein, all of the reigning monarchs still had their eye on the Civil War. England and France were allied. France had designs on Mexico. This was the age of aggressive imperialistic expansion by the nations of Europe. A weak and divided America was still a prime target.

If Seward's bluff was called, and war was to break out between the Union and Europe, with whom would the U.S. be in conflict, and over what circumstances? What was France up to now? Would she always follow England's lead? France was ruled by an ambitious nephew of the man who had terrorized Europe in the early 19th century. Napoleon III was a risk-taker whose primary agenda was to further the glory of France by whatever means was immediately at hand. Napoleon III was his own secretary of state and a wild card in this diplomatic drama. While France had been an ally in the American war for independence, England was the enemy in 1776. Complicating matters, the English Prime Minister, Lord Palmerston, held a view of war as a diplomatic tool that also put the situation at risk. Inherent though it may have been, Palmerston was bluffing to the same extent as Henry Seward. If war erupted in the period of 1861–1865, it would most likely be with England. She had provinces in Canada and throughout the Caribbean. Her island dominions would continue to be a potential *casus belli* because British companies shipped desperately-needed war material to Nassau and Bermuda for transfer to Lee's army in the South. Blockade runners purchased British guns and ammunition with cotton bales for the mills of Manchester and Leeds. Shots were being fired back and forth across the bows of privateer and Union navy gunboats. British neutrality didn't impact British business.

Although carefully watching events in America, England was still concerned with possible future conflict with France. Both countries were locked in an expensive, naval arms race. France was concerned with growing Prussian strength and unification under Bismarck. There was uncertainty over who would succeed to the throne in Denmark and who would absorb Schleswig-Holstein, as well as what action, if any, Prussia would take. Furthermore, the effects that the new *entente cordiale*

UNCLE SAM PROTECTING HIS PROPERTY AGAINST THE ENCROACHMENTS OF HIS COUSIN JOHN.

'Uncle Sam protecting his property against the encroachments of his cousin John', Edward Stauch.

between France and Russia on the balance of power in Europe were still to be seen. Although anxious to mediate the Civil War in America, it is clear from Monsieur Thouvanel that Napoleon III was more absorbed with the unification of Italy. France wanted to blunt Austria's drive to control northern Italy, as a unified Italy would help keep Austria in place. Thouvanel's letters to the French representative in Rome, Duc de Gramont, are much more voluminous than the few exchanges he had with the Comte de Flahault, the French representative in London. For every ten dispatches that went to Rome, one went to London. Charles Francis Adams outlined the issues which concerned Europe to his son Charles in the Union army, "There are clouds in the north and in the south, in the east and in the west, which keep England and France leaning against each other in order to stand up at all. The single event of the death of Napoleon, perhaps even that of Lord Palmerston, would set everything afloat, and make the direction of things in Europe almost impossible to foresee."[14] Nevertheless, nobody completely took their eyes off the war in America. On April 11, 1863, John Russell wrote to Richard Lyons and warned, "We think much about Poland, but the cases of the *Alabama* and *Peterhoff* prevent our forgetting America."[15] Although England wanted one war at a time, she also believed that she needed to control the expansion of Russia. For her part, Russia wanted a buffer between herself and Europe, and Poland served that purpose. After years of strict control from Russia, the new Tsar, Alexander II, loosened the grip. Martial law was lifted and censorship was relaxed. Unfortunately for the Tsar, this encouraged Polish rebels who fought to free Poland from Russian control. However, even the fear of a quickly growing Russian Empire could not force the British Foreign Office to take their eyes off the "American War".

What were the circumstances at this time which might have resulted in war between England and the Union? A list of conditions would include: full diplomatic recognition of the Confederacy; union invasion of Canada to offset possible loss of the South in the war; the damage being done to commercial shipping from the *Alabama, Florida* and others; the *Trent* Affair and other such forcible seizures after the original incident in 1861; continued blockade running; any attempt to force open Southern ports to secure cotton for English mills; continued threats and inconsistent foreign policy initiatives from Secretary Seward which confused the Foreign Office; the rapid growth of the Union ironclad navy which threatened English naval supremacy and the security of her Caribbean possessions; and possible Union alliances with Russia and other European nations which threatened the old balance of power and could leave England further vulnerable.

Two of the greatest possible causes of war with England included cotton, and the Confederate commerce raiders that were hurling men and commercial goods to the bottom of the sea. The cotton shortage critically impacted English mills and their workers. England's greatest concern was her economy. England desperately needed cotton, but she also needed to be careful of a rapidly growing Union ironclad navy, which could pose a serious challenge to an island nation. Although the new turret ironclads were only good for harbor defense, the Union navy had ironclad conversions as well as purpose-built ironclads that could have threatened the British homeland. Nevertheless, business was important, and the search was on for alternative suppliers of cotton. From London, Henry Adams wrote to his brother Charles in 1861. "Now is England's chance to free herself from what has been her terror for years. In India, in Egypt, in Abyssinia and in South America, there is an unlimited amount of cotton land of the finest quality and labor is abundant." Henry was ill-informed, however. Quantity and quality came from the American South. "In 1840 the supply received from the United States was 487,850,000 lbs. In 1858 it rose to 732,403,000 lbs. – the maximum quantity having reached in 1856, 780,040,000 lbs. ... In 1840 the supply of cotton from India was 77,011,000 lbs.;– in 1858 it had risen to 138,253,000 lbs."[16] Although Brazil and Egypt also supplied cotton to British mills, their quality and quantity were small compared to that coming from the seceding states. Labor was cheap in the alternate countries. However, poor roads and ports from which to ship were a handicap. Labor in India was cheap and abundant. Land was also cheap and the climate was very favorable to the growing of cotton. However, the rivers in the United States had always provided the best and fastest form of commercial transportation. Roads weren't good in America either. In the spring, most were so muddy that wagon wheels frequently sunk up to their axels. America's rivers, however, were well-charted and provided excellent transportation. If you could get your cotton to the Mississippi, you had no trouble shipping it to New Orleans. From there, it went to Europe on one of the many merchant ships waiting in the harbor.

Although the blockade got in the way, English economic concerns were partially alleviated by the Cobden-Chevalier treaty. The treaty was signed before the outbreak of the Civil War and reduced tariffs between England and France by as much as 30% on some goods. This free trade agreement helped to soften the economic pinch felt by the cotton shortage.

One of the most controversial and extensively argued issues of the American Civil War concerns the relative "success" of blockade runners and the amount of cotton that was ultimately smuggled out to England and France.[17]

By 1862, there were more blockade runners in service who

'The Blockade on the "Connecticut Plan"', Currier & Ives.

were more consistently penetrating the Union blockade. However, the shallow-draft of these vessels forced them to take on fewer bales of cotton. More runners got through with fewer bales of cotton on board. Faster engines, hulls painted a camouflage grey and travel by night enabled them to more successfully outrun Union patrol boats. Some argue that increased cotton supplies from China, Egypt and Brazil also helped ease the shortage by 1863. Contrasted with this is a pamphlet published in Richmond in 1864 by George McHenry, entitled *A Paper Containing a Statement of Facts Relating to the Approaching Cotton Crisis*. McHenry demonstrates that the amount of raw cotton in spinner's hands was in a sharp decline.

In addition to cotton and commerce raiders, the situation which quickly forced Kings, Queens, diplomats and cotton spinners alike to pay attention to the Civil War in America was the *Trent* Affair on November 8, 1861. Prior to this, the correspondence between diplomats in Europe focused primarily on continental issues. There was one exception, however. Before the *Trent* crisis, another issue of Seward's creation arose which placed Lincoln in a tight spot until wiser heads in England decided that

Table 1: McHenry Table on British Cotton Supply

Date	Raw Cotton in Warehouse	Raw Cotton in Spinners' Hands	Yarns and Goods on Hand	Total
January 1858	155,007,301	85,900,000	400,000,000	640,907,301
January 1859	96,865,677	95,000,000	415,000,000	600,865,677
January 1860	168,014,154	105,000,000	465,000,000	738,014,154
January 1861	206,486,450	135,000,000	510,000,000	851,486,450
January 1862	218,755,837	80,000,000	460,000,000	758,755,837
January 1863	107,041,247	35,000,000	270,000,000	412,041,871
January 1864	74,186,871	15,000,000	100,000,000	189,186,871

it was not a battle they wished to fight. Seward's threats still confused and angered the diplomats of England and France. Unfortunately, this posturing sometimes clouded more of the secretary's work than was always warranted. Seward's bad-boy reputation continued to compromise his effectiveness. The issue was the 1856 Declaration of Paris. In 1856, those nations involved in the Crimean War decided that some maritime rules of war needed to be developed and agreed upon by all. On April 16, 1856, over 40 major powers in Europe signed an agreement which declared that: privateering is abolished; the neutral flag covers enemy's goods with the exception of contraband of war; neutral goods, with the exception of contraband of war, are not liable to capture under an enemy's flag; and blockades, in order to be binding, must be effective.

The United States declined to sign the Declaration in 1856. The U.S. Navy at that time was small, and depended on privateers to keep the coast and merchant ships safe. It was not in the best interest of the country then. All that changed by 1861. Jefferson Davis issued Letters of Marque on April 17 which turned armed privateers loose on Union shipping which made the work potentially very profitable and attractive. Armed with a Letter of Marque, a ship owner or captain could man and arm his ship and capture "enemy" ships and keep the plunder. The key word here was "enemy". An enemy was another sovereign nation that was threatening you. Seward and Lincoln were adamant that the seceding states did not constitute a separate nation.

Through privateering, a captured ship or "prize" could be taken to a port where a neutral prize court would decide who would get what. The Confederacy, with a small navy, relied on privateers to serve as their commercial fleet as well as their navy. Partly in retaliation, and on recommendation from Seward, Lincoln ordered a blockade of all the key Southern ports. It was impossible to blockade the entire Southern coast, which measures some 3,500 miles long. To add strength to a blockade that initially had little in the way of "teeth", Lincoln mistakenly declared that privateers would be treated as pirates and hanged if caught. The 1856 Declaration of Paris and accepted international law clarified that pirates came from opposing, sovereign nations at war with each other. The matter got complicated because Seward now believed that the Declaration would benefit the Union cause by outlawing the privateers. Impulsively, he sought help in the Declaration of Paris. On April 24, he urged all appropriate legation personnel to begin discussions with their counterparts about signing onto the Declaration. Almost simultaneously, Russell had advised Lyons to begin similar discussions with Seward. Their dispatches were crossing the Atlantic at the same time in the opposite directions. Lyons wrote to Russell in Dispatch No.251, June 4, 1861 "I had the day before yesterday the honour (sic) to receive Your Lordship's Dispatch No.136 and No.139 both of the 18th ultimo, directing me to make proposals to the Government of the United States to adhere to the principles respecting maritime law laid down by the Congress of Paris." It is clear that the complex and possibly counterproductive recommendation that the Declaration of Paris be adhered to was not that of William Seward alone, as some contemporary historians have claimed. England and France were thinking along the same lines and taking action at the same time. The problem again, however, was that the Declaration was intended to bind sovereign nations at war. The blockade as recommended by Seward was an additional problem because one could blockade an enemy nation, but not your own states within the same nation. Seward and Lincoln both claimed that there was no war in America, but a rebellion. However, it can't work both ways.

After the Confederate victory at First Bull Run on July 21, 1861, Europe believed that the separation of North and South was likely to be permanent. The Confederacy was recognized as a Belligerent entity, a quasi-independent nation. Seward saw the Confederacy as a rebellious partner that would eventually be compelled to come back to the union. When this happened, the Declaration would not apply. Yet on April 24, he urged Adams and Dayton to probe adherence to the Declaration with Thouvanel and Russell. What should Adams and Dayton do? Britain was confused because regarding the Southern privateers as pirates would not be seen as a neutral act on the part of a nation that wanted to remain neutral so as to maintain a business relationship that was now vital to their economic health and political stability. They also saw the confusing conflict in which Seward had caught himself. Lincoln realized that he had been boxed into a corner. "When Lincoln investigated the full meaning of the blockade that Seward had got him to declare, he realized that the situation was worse than it appeared at first. At Seward's suggestion Lincoln had declared the blockade "in pursuance … of the law of nations". The law of nations in this case was the Declaration of Paris. Seward told Lyons that the Declaration would legalize the Union blockade and outlaw the Confederate privateers as pirates. "Lyons was almost as slow to think as Lincoln himself. He was also devastatingly logical." Having recognized the South as a belligerent on May 14, 1861, Lyons pointed out that the North may well sign the Declaration, but the South might not be so bound if she is not a sovereign nation as Lincoln and Seward claimed. Seward and Lincoln were caught in a trap of the secretary's design. Lyons went on to state that if the North and South were not separate countries as Seward claimed, then they were not legally enemies as per the Declaration and the blockade could not thus be recognized by the European signatories. Only a sovereign nation could blockade another nation and expect that other countries would honor the blockade – if effectively maintained. "Lincoln pondered in his slow sure way over the blockade-privateer proposition. Seward had led him into a bad complication this time – one of the worst for international amity in his administration … Seward's colleagues in the cabinet accused him of getting the nation into this predicament because he was ignorant of international law." Ultimately, however, cooler heads in London prevailed. "Negotiations over the Declaration of 1856 lagged, and eventually came to naught; the idea of treating the Confederate privateers as pirates met stubborn English resistance." In this manner and in this particular instance, control of U.S. foreign policy remained in the hands of the English, not the American secretary of state. How much of this impacted Lincoln foreign policy? As navy secretary, what was the reaction of Gideon Wells? In view of the fact that this issue impacted England more than France, what were the opinions of Adams, Lyons, Russell and Palmerston?

Gideon Welles took a dim view of Seward. We should expect that the impact on his department *vis-à-vis* Seward's advocacy of the 1856 Declaration would be considerable, and that he would react in his diary. The Welles diary at this point in the Lincoln administration contains no reference to the issue with the Declaration. We know that Seward advocated adherence to the Declaration of 1856. We also know that he recommended a blockade to Lincoln. However, the conflict of interest presented by the Declaration apparently did not bother Gideon Welles. Nevertheless, Seward's reputation continued to impact his legacy as interpreted by some historians today. It is important to provide a balanced view where it is warranted. The answer to a lack of response in Welles' diary may be that the navy secretary recognized, as did Seward and Lincoln, that blockading the ports, as opposed to "closing" them on paper, would be more effective. Closing the ports would be an unenforceable piece of paperwork that would probably just further encourage the Anglo-French alliance to defy and create a true threat of war. Only a blockade, contrary to the language of the Treaty of Paris, would be successful and deter England and France. Although caught in his own trap, Seward was accidentally correct in recommending the blockade.

What do we know from Adams, Lyons or Russell concerning the Declaration issue? Adams' official correspondence is generally professional and impersonal. He avoided subjective complaints until after the war. In his private correspondence to his wife and son in Massachusetts, his language was more colorful. One would expect that this private correspondence would contain Seward invective if Adams was concerned about the issues found in the Declaration of Paris. Between May 12, 1861 and the incident with the *Trent* on November 8, 1861, there is no mention of the Declaration in Adams' private correspondence. Lyons and Russell, however, had much more to say. Nevertheless, neither man went so far as to suggest that this was a serious situation as claimed by some current historians. Dispatch No.251 on June 4, 1861, Lyons to Russell, tells us that the greatest concern was the reaction Seward might have regarding whether or not England and France would adhere to the Declaration concerning the abolishment of privateers. They were more concerned with a Seward reaction than international law. Lyons wrote "I found that Mercier was not without apprehension that the proposals, unless communicated with much tact and caution, might occasion an outbreak of anger from Mr. Seward and even lead to some violent proceedings on the part of the government."

Richard Lyons, Henri Mercier, Richard Russell and Lord Palmerston thought Seward was bluffing, but sufficiently unstable as to warrant special care. There was fallout on the domestic as well as the international front. The secretary of state had recommended a blockade of major Southern ports to Lincoln as well as signing on to the 1856 Treaty of Paris. The blockade caused Britain to recognize the Confederacy as Belligerents. The Queen declared neutrality so that she could officially still trade in non-contraband goods with North and South. However, the blockade prevented this. The solution was the use of privateers by Jefferson Davis and blockade runners by private individuals in Great Britain. The stage for possible war with England was now set. Not only had Seward disappointed Lincoln with his memo on *Some Thoughts* and Dispatch No.10, he caused some confusion again with the recommendation to sign on to the Treaty of Paris. The treaty outlawed privateers, but it only recognized this position as between two sovereign nations, not two sections of the same country in an internal rebellion. Lincoln was frustrated, and began to turn increasingly to Senator Charles Sumner of Massachusetts for advice on foreign relations.

Seward was the *bête noire* of foreign relations in the Lincoln administration. Lincoln was losing trust in and patience with his secretary. Seward's posture was a deliberate ploy to try and control the direction of foreign relation with England and France. The ploy backfired. The politicians of England and France realized that Seward's threats were "whistling in the wind". The Anglo-French alliance retained control of Union foreign relations and elected not to call that bluff.

CHAPTER 5

AMERICAN BRAGGADOCIO

Neutral nations are those who, in time of war, do not take any part in the
contest, but remain common friends to both parties without favoring the arms of
the one to the prejudice of the other.

Emmerich de Vattel, *The Law of Nations*, 1758

"I have not yet succeeded in plumbing the depths of American brag-gadocio." These words Henri Mercier, French minister to the United States, wrote to his boss, Édouard Thouvanel, the French minister of for-eign affairs, regarding the difficulty in dealing with Americans in general and the U.S. secretary of state in particular. Throughout most of the Civil War, the issue of neutral rights was a problem. Diplomatic bluff, bluster and braggadocio were usually loudest over issues surrounding neutrality and Confederate recognition.

Henri Mercier was a well-dressed, outgoing yet introspective man who didn't enjoy meeting with Seward. He was born in Baltimore, Maryland, but preferred Paris. Mercier and Thouvanel were separated by 3,000 miles of ocean, as well as ideology. They lived and worked in two very different worlds.

Mercier and his British counterpart, Richard Lyons, considered Americans to be a dirty mob of people whose opinions were easily mold-ed and influenced like those of a child. In the Department of Foreign Affairs in Paris, Édouard Thouvanel and Édouard Drouyn de Lhuys were similar to the team of Russell and Palmerston. Each one worked for the other at different times and through different crises in the mid-nineteenth century. Thouvanel was pragmatic while Drouyn de Lhuys was much more ideological and doctrinaire. During the Crimean War, for example, Thouvanel wanted to work with Russia and not against her as found in the policies of Drouyn de Lhuys. During the American Civil war, both men worked with Napoleon III to protect French interests and end the war.

Representatives of all foreign legations, along with members of the Lincoln cabinet, lived in a city that didn't compare to the sophistication of London, Paris or St. Petersburg. Washington was a city of primarily small, wooden houses and shops. Amid an endless low profile of outhouses and kitchen gardens, suddenly hoisted up the unfinished dome of the capitol and the State and War Departments near the Executive Mansion. Pennsylvania Avenue was very wide, and very dusty. In the spring, it was a sea of mud that made travel to the capitol or Executive Mansion difficult. In an attempt to connect downtown with the Potomac River and provide faster commercial transit, a canal was dug. By the time the Lords of London and Paris arrived, however, the canal was a stagnant, green pool that was full of dead rats and a few stray cats. The mall in front of the capitol was littered with small shacks and the tools required to complete the work on the capitol dome. Both Mercier and Lyons thought the unfinished capitol looked like a Roman ruin. In sharp contrast, the best hotel and restaurant in town, Willard's Hotel,[1] was a real center of power in Washington. Situated on the corner of East and 14th Streets, this was where meetings were held, strategy and scheming planned, and plots hatched. According to Lincoln secretary, John Hay, the halls of Willard's were crowded with, " … Generals, and Colonels, and Majors, and captains, governors, senators, honorables; all chew tobacco; all spit; a good many swear, and not a few make a merit of being able to keep two cocktails in the air at once."

Secretary of State Seward lived in a rented house that bordered Lafayette Park. It was three stories, and filled with some furnishings from Auburn. Seward used the house to promote his agenda through an extensive entertainment schedule. In addition to Seward's house, the secretary also used his neighbor's house for secret meetings that would be otherwise detected by the guest list. Seward's letters to and from his neighbor Samuel Cutler Ward during the critical 1861–1862 period, are extensive. They corresponded every week. Ward also acted as a spy for Seward because he sometimes traveled south with his friend, William Howard Russell. Everyone enjoyed Seward's company and the many parties he hosted. Oysters and Cuban cigars mixed easily with talk of the blockade, John Bull and Napoleon's designs on Mexico. Lincoln preferred to come to Seward's house for an informal atmosphere that the East Room of the White House did not provide. Mary Lincoln did not come with him on these occasions, which made the evening that much more relaxing.

The White House had been redecorated at great expense by Mrs. Lincoln.[2] Stewart's and the new Lord and Taylor in New York contributed much to the renovation. Nevertheless, the White House had problems which made entertainment difficult. The house was always damp, which caused paint to peel and woodwork to rot. When the house was quiet, the president could hear rats running about underneath the floor boards. Soldiers quartered in the basement relieved themselves where they could. Clearly, they weren't concerned with diplomacy.

In view of the fact that Abraham Lincoln was preoccupied with the Civil War, serious questions arise regarding his foreign policy during this critical period. It was during this time that England and France debated whether or not to recognize and officially aid the Confederacy and thus likely provoke a conflict with a potential Union-Russian alliance. Seward claimed that the Union could subdue the South and England at the same time; a *de facto* war on the sea already being waged.

The first foreign relations issues faced by the Lincoln State Department were: neutrality, belligerent rights and the 1856 Treaty of Paris. During the first four years of the Lincoln administration, war between the Anglo-French alliance and the Union was realistic. By this time, there were long-standing issues between England and America that were not of Seward's creation. Neither American braggadocio nor Britain-bashing began with Seward. In fact, the visit of the Prince of Wales in 1860 was so successful, and the prince so well-received, one would think that relations between the United States and Great Britain had always been good. The Prince arrived in New York on October 11, 1860. The arrival was recorded by the *Times*, a paper that later took many opportunities to criticize the Lincoln government and William Seward. This was not the case when the *Times* reported that the Prince arrived in New York to "an ovation such as seldom been offered to any monarch in ancient or modern times. It was not a reception, it was the grand impressive welcome of mighty people. It was such a mingling of fervent, intense enthusiasm, of perfect good order, of warmth and yet of kind respect, that I am fairly at a loss how to convey in words any adequate idea of this most memorable event."[3]

The secretary of state enjoyed interacting with people and diplomats on his terms, and had many face-to-face meetings with foreign representatives in Washington. He wasn't a loner, but had no intimate friends, with the exception of Thurlow Weed. He shared brandy and cigars with anyone who wanted to talk politics.

At this early stage of the Lincoln administration, Seward had little skill, and took little time to plan. He had to save a bruised political ego and the Union at the same time. He was the *de facto* president who was going to either preserve the peace or effectively prosecute the war through the channels available to him as secretary of state. Using England as a political scapegoat and punching bag had a long history in the United States, and Seward often used threat and bluster against England as a means of diverting attention from battlefield failures. He also wanted to mollify that conservative element who felt injured by a British self-serving policy regarding neutrality rights, privateering and the preservation of the English economy. England was an old enemy. When America was a young country with few traditions in place to help unify her, it was easier to create that unity through the public hatred of an enemy. England served this purpose well. "A hatred of the despotism whose chains they had broken supplied Americans with a national identity and a patriotic rallying point".[4]

America was then, and still remains, a nation of immigrants. It was thought that a large number of Irish immigrants living in America, fighting for the Union and also hating England didn't help. Many believe that the mob mentality that both Lyons and Mercier condemned was aggravated by Irish immigrants having fled British rule. However, immigrants from Germany and Great Britain made up the largest portion of the foreign-born population in America. In addition to the German newspaper Lincoln purchased to help with his first campaign, the first German-American elected to the U.S. Senate, Carl Schurz, worked hard to secure Lincoln's election. The president's only official secretary, John George Nicolay, was a German immigrant. While hoping to win the Republican nomination himself, William Seward said, "The German spirit is the spirit of tolerance and freedom. It fights oppression everywhere."[5] The potato famine in Ireland and the 1848 revolution in Germany helped to drive many immigrants to America. Most of the Irish were city-dwellers who settled in the Northern cities, not the agricultural South, while many highly skilled Germans settled in New York. It was possible to become an American citizen in five years. For those who had no vote in their native country, they enjoyed being able to participate in the political process. Initially, statistics were not kept on foreign-born volunteers in the Union army, but John Slidell and others pushing the Confederate cause in Europe often claimed that the percentage of Irish and other immigrants in the Union army was "at least half". This helped them to claim that they were being invaded by a bunch of guerillas and mercenaries. More recent and responsible estimates of immigrant enlistments in the Union army come in at less 20%.

Britain-bashing enabled American politicians, led by Senator Stephen Douglas, to play a dangerous game of trying to check the growth of British power and influence by suggesting that a Russian-American alliance might be in the works. Before Richard Lyons, John Crampton assured his Foreign Office that the United States was honoring its neutrality by not allowing the construction of privateers in U.S. shipyards for Russia or anyone else.[6] England sheathed her sword. From Crampton to Clarendon, October 16, 1854 we learn that war between England and the United States was always a possibility. William Henry Seward is rarely mentioned in the Crampton dispatches. President Franklin Pierce, Senator Stephen Douglas, Secretary of State William Marcy, Attorney General Caleb Cushing and presidential hopeful James Buchanan were the key American players in this earlier drama. All found it profitable to divert attention from difficult domestic issues to foreign relations problems. England was far away and easy to blame. The alliance that England and France had formed to deal with Russia in Crimea was of concern to Americans. They felt threatened by the combined power of the two countries. Crampton's dispatch of October 16 continued, "Hence, the Alliance of England and France is gall and wormwood here. It upsets the old established policy of the country playing them against each other … It is in vain that they affect to feel and try to get up a sympathy with Russia in order to counteract it."[7] Problems with Great Britain aside, how did the Lincoln State Department plan to communicate with and influence those foreign nations they hoped would stay out of the Civil War?

Abraham Lincoln and Henry Seward had help in selecting men to represent the United States in Europe. Thurlow Weed and Charles Sumner both made suggestions. Some of the selections were politically-motivated, but most of the representatives chosen were intelligent, educated and generally competent. By contrast, Jefferson Davis initially sent emissaries to Europe who were strongly identified with slavery. That was a mistake. It has been suggested that Davis did not initially value good foreign relations; King Cotton would best represent the interests of the Confederacy. In the belief that the war would be quick, Davis' first representatives to Europe were a poor choice. In addition, Davis did not have an established diplomatic network already in place to enable King Cotton to do its work. Seward had the advantage of a well-developed, professional state department. The secretaries, couriers and consuls needed to make things work were already in place. He also had the advantage of having established credit at Barings Bank in London and the Bank of Belgium in Brussels. From these accounts, the spies and detectives who kept close watch on every Confederate move in Europe were paid. From these same accounts, thousands of guns and hundreds of tons of saltpeter were secured through purchasing agents like W.S. Bailey in Hamburg for shipment to New York. Without an established foreign relations apparatus, Davis started from the beginning. His first problem was how to pay for the goods and services he desperately needed from Europe. Virginia farmers weren't the skilled craftsmen needed to rifle gun barrels. Without established credit, the Confederacy was forced to send her representatives abroad with gold coins in their pockets and bars in their luggage. Through the goodwill of Charles Prioleau, CEO of Fraser Trenholm and Company of Liverpool, an unsecured line of credit was opened for the Davis government.[8] When that ran out, Judah Benjamin suggested using cotton for barter. Beyond credit, the primary issue was that Davis didn't believe that he really needed a foreign policy. According to James L. Orr, chairman of the House Committee on Foreign Affairs of the Confederate Congress, the Davis administration "never had a foreign policy, nor did [it] ever consent to attempt a high diplomacy with European Powers."[9] The Davis cabinet believed that cotton was king, and that France and England would recognize and intervene on behalf of the South in order to secure uninterrupted cotton shipments. The seceding states did not give sufficient credit to the anti-slavery sentiment in Britain.

Davis' first representatives to London and Paris were Ambrose Dudley Mann, William Lowndes Yancey and Pierre Rost. Ambrose Dudley Mann was an experienced diplomat having served as consul in Germany, Hungary and Switzerland. He was caught in the middle, however, between Jefferson Davis and the then secretary of war, Judah Benjamin.[10] Mann was a friend of Davis, but no match for the cunning and sharp mind of Benjamin. He simply ignored Benjamin and went straight to Davis with matters that were already beyond the scope of the Confederate president. The problem was that Mann preferred to send unrealistic and pretty pictures of the issues in Europe to a president under so much stress that he initially preferred to believe Mann. Benjamin knew better. "At times frustrated, at times full of drive with a pompous sense of exaggeration, Mann pursued his mission without glory until the twilight of the Southern adventure."[11] Rost was born and raised in France. That was his primary qualification. The only member of the first team of Confederate representatives without any foreign experience was Yancey. That was unfortunate because Yancey was "a firey Southern rights politician from Alabama with a marvelous reputation for oratory, a man who could hold a crowd for hours. Yancey was entirely out of his depth amid the intrigue of European diplomatic courts. He was ignorant of the world and by his own admission, wholly unsuited by experience and personality to the gentle art of diplomacy." [12]

The Confederate secretary of state during the short provisional government period in Montgomery was Robert Toombs. His instructions to the three representatives were primarily a statement as to why the South had seceded, and why cotton was king. This was a tricky declaration because he needed to avoid the word "slavery". However, the first act of foreign diplomacy to Europe by Jefferson Davis was a disaster from the start. He rejected a proposal by Secretary of State Robert Toombs that would have provided specific instructions relative to the *quid pro quo* that would result from an alliance between the countries of Europe and the Confederacy. Before the move to Richmond, the Confederate Provisional Government conducted business at the Exchange Hotel in Montgomery, Alabama. Robert Barnwell Rhett was an ardent secessionist and a member of the Confederate Constitutional Committee. Coming downstairs from a meeting at the hotel, Rhett saw William Yancey in the lobby and asked him about his impending mission to Europe. Rhett was amazed and upset when he learned that Toombs' proposal for detailed instructions had been vetoed. He told Yancey that without specific instructions as to what to say and negotiate with those in London and Paris, he shouldn't go. His mission was doomed to failure from the start. Rhett told Yancey:

> "Sir, you have no business in Europe. You carry no argument which Europe cares to hear. Unless you shall have it in your power to arrest attention there by some great and lasting offer of practical advantage to the governments and peoples there, to compensate them for the risks they must incur in receiving you and recognizing your government, you can do nothing worthy of your time … My counsel to you as a friend is, if you value your reputation, to stay at home or go prepared to conciliate Europe by irresistible offers of trade."[13]

Toombs had proposed a three-part plan to encourage European recognition with something specific and "irresistible". Palmerston was fond of saying that Britain had no permanent friends, no permanent enemies, only permanent interests. Rhett was right. An appeal to British permanent interests might work. An early biographer of Yancey, John Witherspoon Du Bose faults Davis for believing that cotton was all that was needed to convince Europe of the benefits of recognition. "(Davis) devoted his labors, almost exclusively, to the minor, perfunctory tasks of his office. He was … ignorant of the real state of affairs into a fatal self-contentment."[14] Toombs proposed to: lower the import tax to 20% (compared with 26% Morrill Tariff); create an alliance for a minimum of twenty years and agree to support Britain and France in the defense of their colonies in the Caribbean and the Americas; charge 30% import duty on anyone not agreeing to Confederate import rules

'The Southern Confederacy a fact!!!', L. Hough Publ., 1861.

and regulations. All of this would be in exchange for recognition of the Confederacy.

Instead of the specifics which might have helped at this early and critical stage, the commissioners were simply instructed to avoid any mention of slavery and remind London and Paris that the South had been invaded by a gang that had been taxing them to death through a series of protective tariffs for many years. Toombs was forced to end his general instructions of March 16, 1861, "With each of these countries you will propose to negotiate treaties of friendship, commerce and navigation, similar to that which you will propose to Great Britain ... You will correspond as frequently as you may require, with this Department, transmitting your dispatches by conveyances as you may deem the most safe and expeditious".[15] Poorly armed, the Confederate commissioners arrived in Europe having paid their own travel expenses. They were given no funds to defray the additional cost of sustaining themselves in

London and Paris while they lobbied the men in power as best they could. They immediately complained of the well-financed Union effort to influence public opinion in Europe, but strangely received no reply from Montgomery. Yancey, Rost and Mann weren't aware of it, but safely sending their dispatches back to Montgomery would prove to be almost as difficult as convincing the British Foreign Office that secession had nothing to do with slavery. The Confederate representatives were no match for those representing the Lincoln administration. They were much less of a match for the men of the British Foreign Office. Nevertheless, the U.S. State Department and the British Foreign Office faced a unique difficulty that didn't trouble either Jefferson Davis or Napoleon III.

Much of the official correspondence between Washington and London was made public through the established British *Blue Book* and the new *Papers Relating to the Foreign Relations of the United States* publication by Seward.[16] Although private and confidential correspondence was not published, Seward had an uncomfortable habit of selectively publishing private letters to and from both Charles Francis Adams and William Lewis Dayton. Both complained, and both were ignored. Publication of the *Blue Book* gave concern to Richard Lyons who was methodical in his thinking and worried constantly over how his actions would be evaluated in London. For this reason, we only learn from the official, published dispatches what these politicians were willing to share with the public. A Foreign Office circular clearly advises foreign representatives to only write what they can defend in public. "In drafting your ordinary dispatches upon current affairs … you will insert nothing which, in your opinion, it would be unwise to publish, or which could not be published without serious injury to your own usefulness as a Public Officer."[17] We know that Secretary Seward published his State Department dispatches in an attempt to blunt the negative opinions that were circulating about him and his work. He was also following a precedent already established by the British Foreign Office. This frustrated many in public service. The U.S. minister to Austria, John Lothrop Motley,[18] complained to James Russell Lowell, "Since Secretary of State Seward instituted this system (which between you and me I don't at all fancy) of publishing annually the dispatches to and from the State Department, one is obliged to write the most perfectly circumspect and idiotic trash". Under these circumstances, the historian is immediately drawn to those Lyons, Russell and Seward dispatches which are marked *Confidential* and *Secret*. From February 12, 1863 to November 3, 1863, those dispatches from Lyons to Russell marked *Confidential* contain the most sensitive and revealing information about the hopes and fears of British diplomacy with the Lincoln government. Lyons is clearly concerned about the future of British authority internationally in the face of growing Union naval strength. He was not alone in that concern, and he feared a war that England might not win. He also talks about pay-offs and bribes to American spies who try to sell detailed plans of New York and Boston harbor defenses to England in the event of what appeared to be imminent war between the two countries. During the Civil War, it was up to the dispatch recipient to determine whether or not to make them available for publication.

The official as well as private correspondence of those key players clearly indicate that, in their opinion, the secretary of state was learning on the job. Seward was a man who got some things wrong, but some things right. Unfortunately, when problems arose, Seward often got the blame – whether guilty or not. Judah Benjamin also shared this unfortunate gift with Seward. Perception became a harmful, controlling reality for both men. Both were polarizing figures throughout their public life, and were a magnet for controversy. This was especially so during the Civil War. Benjamin, however, had the added problem of being Jewish in a Christian, anti-Semitic world. If Seward was the *bête noire*, Benjamin was Judas Iscariot. Stephen Vincent Benet accurately captured the public perception of Benjamin in his 1928 poem, *John Brown's Body.* Many in the South saw Benjamin as, "The dapper Jew, Seal-Sleek, black-eyed, lawyer and epicure, able, well-hated … " Apart from the *Blue Book* and the *Foreign Relations of the United States,* political figures were severely criticized in the press. Seward was often censured by Horace Greeley in the *New York Tribune.* The *Richmond Examiner* was edited by Edward Pollard.[19] He didn't discriminate in his hate for politicians, Northern or Southern. Although particularly critical of Jefferson Davis, Pollard also took on William Henry Seward and Judah Philip Benjamin. At one point during the war, the *Richmond Examiner* offered a $50,000 reward for Seward's head – with or without the cigar.

Due to the controversy Seward and Benjamin generated, great care must be exercised when reading the diaries and letters of the key players at this time when the subject of these men arises. Seward began work in the Lincoln administration with the belief that he was the *de facto* president. This immediately put him at odds with many of Lincoln's cabinet. Gideon Welles' disapproval is clear: "[Seward's] claquers and supporters busied themselves in representing that Mr. Seward was *de facto* President ... Mr. Seward gave encouragement to these representations."[20] The diary, letters and post-war writings of many, including Gideon Welles, are an important asset in analyzing Lincoln foreign policy. However, many were deeply partisan observers who often clashed with William Seward. For this reason, Welles' conclusions must be examined carefully. It is also important to balance some critical issues where Seward was right and his critics wrong. Ironically, where Seward imagined himself as the *de facto* president, Judah Benjamin actually functioned as the *de facto* president as Davis' fragile health deteriorated under the terrible weight of war. "Judah P. Benjamin acted in Davis' name, wrote speeches and dispatches for him, and presided over an occasional Cabinet meeting. Generally, Benjamin acted as his alter ego."[21] In this, Benjamin was different from Seward. Lincoln's secretary of state gained strength by acting through an alter ego such as Thurlow Weed and even Lincoln. Acting on his own, he lacked the strength to act as he could through others. By contrast, Judah Benjamin was quiet, self-assured and his own man to the end.

In Washington, there were others who knew Lincoln and Seward and had some interesting and amusing observations of their work. Some were more critical than Greeley and Pollard. An example of this would be Polish immigrant "Count" Adam de Gurowski. An abolitionist with a tongue sharper than that of Charles Francis Adams, de Gurowski was fired from his job as a translator at the State Department for highly critical views of Seward and Lincoln. He told freelance journalist Robert Carter that, "Seward is an assish, asinine ass." This is unfortunate because de Gurowski kept a detailed diary during the first two years of the war that provides humor and some insight into the political scene in Washington. He was, however, the only man from whom Lincoln feared assassination. In addition to Gurowski, the secretary of the London legation was

Benjamin Moran. Nobody was in a better position to accurately report on the diplomatic activities of the most important U.S. Ministry in
Europe. Moran's diaries, however, contain more social information than
political. He thought Charles Francis Adams lazy and commented that,
"Mr. Adams is very civil, but it is the smile of the ogre." Unfortunately,
Moran paid more attention to what he had for dinner than the latest
intelligence from the U.S. consul in Liverpool, Thomas Haines Dudley. It
has also been suggested by some that the empty chair in the Carpenter
portrait of the first reading of the Emancipation Proclamation was that
of a lesser-known, but influential advisor to Lincoln, Anna Ella Carroll. A
pamphleteer who successfully argued in favor of the emergency powers
exercised by a president in time of war, some credit her with successfully
arguing for the Union assault on Tennessee, which many historians consider to have been the state that controlled the success or failure of the
Union war effort. Carroll, however, had little or no impact on the State
Department and foreign relations. The letters of even these more marginal
people all contain a consistently common theme, however. That theme is
that the ego and personal ambition of William Henry Seward drove him
to try and control Abraham Lincoln and the direction of all government
policy, foreign and domestic. Senator Charles Sumner, writing to John Jay
on October 4, 1861, writes that, "Unless the Secy of State has changed,
he will not hearken to suggestion. He is too strong in egotism."[22] The job
of secretary of state is demanding and complex. Some of that complexity
during the Civil War came from the fact that there was little in international law to provide guidance. Vattel and Wheaton were relied upon for
help on both sides of the ocean. The rights of neutral countries, seeking
to profit from war, have been an issue for centuries.

Neutrality issues were always a *casus belli* to countries which were economically dependent on their ability to trade in both non-contraband
and contraband material with other nations at war. England and France
were especially sensitive to the issue of neutrality rights and responsibilities. Attempts were made by the U.S. Congress to deal with pirates and
privateers in 1794, 1797 and 1800. However, in addition to the search
and seizure issues of the War of 1812, U.S. Neutrality Acts of 1818 and
the Treaty of Paris which arose from issues during the Crimean War of
1854, Seward and the Crown law officers relied on Vattel, Wheaton and

the Admiralty decisions of Lord Stowell.[23] The Neutrality Act of 1818 was similar to the Foreign Enlistment Act of Great Britain, and the Code Napoleon in France. Section 1 of the Neutrality Act of 1818 states, "That any citizen of the United States shall, within the territory or jurisdiction thereof, accept and exercise a commission to serve a foreign prince, state, colony, district or people in war, by land or by sea, by any prince, state, colony, district or people with whom the United States are at peace, the person so offending shall be deemed guilty of a high misdemeanor, and shall be fined not more than two thousand dollars and shall be imprisoned not exceeding three years." In view of the fact that private yards in both England and France were building and outfitting privateers and war ships for use by the Confederacy against Northern shipping, it's unclear as to what Secretary Seward was thinking at this time. The secretary of state was a polarizing figure whose actions were sometimes intemperate and counterproductive. Nevertheless, he acted with some justification in view of the privateering by England and France.

Vattel and Wheaton, writing almost 100 years apart, define the term "nation" in almost identical language. It is important to remember that both men refer to nations as established, sovereign, independent bodies. Seward considered the Confederacy an enemy within the common, unified border of the United States of America, not a separate, sovereign entity. So, the first issue of legal guidance was already in dispute even before the first shots were fired. According to Vattel, a nation or a state is a "body politic, or a society of men united for the purpose of promoting their mutual safety and advantage by their combined strength." The American legal expert, Henry Wheaton, made a distinction between a nation and a state. He defined a State as, " … a body politic, or society of men, united together for the purpose of promoting their mutual safety and advantage by their combined strength." Any Southern slave owner who hated the Black Republicans of the North could easily conclude from this that the so-called Confederate States of America was united for mutual safety as the Yankee army marched south. As such, they might rightfully consider themselves a state. If they were still unsure as to their status, Wheaton tells us that a nation, " … implies community of race, which is generally shown by community of language, manners, and customs." Again, the slave-owning elite as well as the subsistence farmer would both agree that they had language, manners and customs in common. Therefore, they may also consider themselves a nation. Lincoln and Seward disagreed. Wheaton, however, added some clarifications to his definition of a state. Not included in states would be "associations of robbers or pirates ... A state is also distinguishable from the unsettled horde of wandering savages not yet formed into a civil society."

The real issue, however, concerned the rights and obligations of neutral nations in time of war. First, what is the nature and scope of the new relationship between the neutral and the warring parties with whom they have done business? Second, should the neutral nation also suffer along with the warring parties and have her commerce and livelihood threatened? England wanted it both ways, and Wheaton gave her the answer. Unfortunately, William Seward didn't have a background in international law as did Charles Sumner and Judah Benjamin.

Despite this shortcoming, many historians consider Seward to have been an effective secretary during the Lincoln administration. Doris Kearns Goodwin states that "History would later give Secretary of State Seward high marks for his role in preventing Britain and France from intervening in the war." Goodwin's praise may be justified to a degree when we look at Seward's subsequent accomplishments during the later years of the war. This is especially true in his continuing capacity as secretary of State under Andrew Johnson.

Walter Stahr's book is entitled *Seward: Lincoln's Indispensable Man.*[24] Stahr says that for him, "Seward was not only important: he was fascinating."[25] Goodwin and Stahr notwithstanding, Seward contemporaries on both sides of the Atlantic still took a negative view. He was still the *bête noire*. Lord Richard Lyons complained that "Seward's ridiculous pretentions to a knowledge of Europe were totally unfounded." Lack of a knowledge of international law and European politics put Seward at a disadvantage. His plan to keep France and England out of the Civil War was to threaten them with war if they intervened. That was risky business. What was Seward thinking? Could he successfully bluff one country with the largest navy in the world and the other with the biggest army and get away with it?

The secretary of state was a product of this particular era in America. That time was a period of adolescent growth that contributed to the

aggressiveness observed in Seward. The secretary was often support-
ed in his bluster by others like Cassius Clay, Union representative to
Russia. On January 24, 1862, Clay tells Seward, "You think you can trust
England. I do not. So I would prepare at once for a war with that power,
as an inevitable result of any reverses which would prevent a subjection
of the South before the first of April next." This, however, was typical of
Clay who never had anything positive to say about John Bull. Somehow,
England still needed to be checked.

In order to restrain Britain from recognizing the Confederacy, Seward
threatened war. Internal correspondence between officials in England
indicate that they were confused and felt genuinely offended by Seward's
approach. War between the Anglo-French coalition and the Union at this
early stage of the war was ultimately averted by the diplomatic skills of
European politician and diplomats, not that of William Henry Seward.
Lincoln said he wanted "one war at a time." Could a two-front war
with the Confederacy and Europe have crippled the Union war effort
and result in a permanent division of America? Long after the war, the
son of Judge Dudley Mann of Georgia later told John Bigelow about
invasion plans he overheard discussed between his father and British
Prime Minister, Lord Palmerston. Mann was a Confederate envoy to
Belgium who preceded Mason and Slidell. Immediately after this alleged
discussion, however, a confidential dispatch from Lord Richard Lyons
to Lord Russell provided specific details about the strength of potential
Union forces capable of invading an admittedly poorly-defended
Canada. Seward considered Canada as possible compensation for the loss
of the Southern states. Invasion of Canada was part of the diplomacy of
threat. Those specifics from Lyons included an assessment of rifled and
smooth bore guns that the British would face in the defense of Canada,
likely jump-off ports for Union forces as well as the number of ammunition rounds each gun was expected to be supplied with. Lyons included
a description of the velocity with which large shot must be discharged
in order to destroy Union ironclads.[26]

Although Europe was absorbed in many issues including Italy, Poland
and Schleswig-Holstein, all of the reigning monarchs still had their eye
on the Civil War. England and France were allied. France had designs
on Mexico. Spain had already annexed Santo Domingo (modern-day

Dominican Republic) and was interested in Cuba and the rest of the Caribbean. This was the age of aggressive, mercantilist expansion by the nations of Europe. A weak and divided America was a prime target. In Europe, some old divisions were slowly healing. Italy was agitating for unification. Protestant Prussia was now led by Kaiser Wilhelm I and his aggressive prime minister, Otto von Bismarck,[27] who sought to unify Germany. What else was happening in Europe or on the high seas?

By late 1862, Charles Francis Adams complained to British foreign secretary Lord Russell that America was already at war with Britain on the ocean. Attempting to break what was considered an ineffective blockade, Britain allowed the Confederacy to contract privately for warships, smaller privateers and shallow-draft blockade runners in British shipyards. She looked away when she allowed English seamen to violate the Foreign Enlistment Act to man those ships and give battle at sea to Union commercial shipping. If enough commercial tonnage could be sunk, then maybe those Union ships blockading Southern ports would be pulled off duty and sent to sea to protect unarmed merchants. A blockade that was already full of holes would crumble and allow cotton to become king again.[28] The Foreign Enlistment Act not only forbade the enlistment of British citizens on foreign vessels, it also dictated that ships built in British yards for foreign countries must not have any fittings for war. They not only could not have cannon on board, they could not even have the hardware necessary to secure a gun carriage. The problem faced by Lord Russell was that the ships being built in British yards for the Confederacy were not fitted for war in Britain. They were installed later at sea or in another friendly port, usually Nassau, Bahamas. The foreign secretary initially felt that both he and the Crown law officers were correct when they fended off both Adams and Seward complaints about these ships being built at the Birkenhead yard in Liverpool. However, we know that Russell spoke to others that he was suspicious as to a large order that had been placed with Laird for two new warships. He told Seward that the Foreign Enlistment Act had not been violated, but expressed his doubts in private to others. The issue was the damage done by the *Alabama* and other armed vessels. Adams stated that England built this warship, outfitted it with guns and manned it with British crews flying the English flag. Thousands of tons of Union commercial shipping were being sunk. A *de facto* state of war already existed. In addition to the armed privateers, British yards also built shallow-draft ships that were steam-driven for the speed necessary to outrun Union warships in the blockade. The Confederacy needed war materiel. As she ran low on gold supplies to pay for it, Davis began to ship cotton out of shallow ports like Wilmington, North Carolina to Nassau where it was combined with other cotton shipments and sent to England. The reefs and shoals surrounding the entrance to the Cape Fear River leading to Wilmington made it easy for the shallow-draft ships to enter the river in safety. The reefs and two narrow river inlets made it impossible for the deep-draft Union warships to get close. Deep-draft Union blockaders had to stay far off Frying Pan Shoals. The cotton coming out of Wilmington was bartered for guns. Some of the so-called blockade runners were paddle wheel ships and some were screw-driven. The paddle wheelers proved ineffective because the propulsion system, the side paddle wheels and their engines, were vulnerable to cannon fire.[29] Ultimately, Wilmington and Charleston, Mobile and Matamoros became the primary ports for blockade running. Some blockade runners realized substantial profits and some notoriety as well.

Born aboard ship and raised in Fayetteville, North Carolina, John Newland Maffitt became known to the Confederacy as the "Prince of Privateers". Joining the navy at 13, he was later posted to the United States Coast Survey, which allowed him to survey and become familiar with much of the U.S. east coast. He was particularly knowledgeable of the waters and coastline from Florida to Virginia. This prompted him to recommend unguarded ports like Mosquito Inlet at New Smyrna, and Fernandina, Florida.[30] The shallow waters of the inlets led to the St. John's river whose depths of six to eight feet prohibited Union warships from chasing Confederate privateers and blockade runners laden with guns and ammunition for Robert E. Lee's army. Even the new 90-day Union gunboats with shallow draft were unable to navigate in shallow inlets and intercostal waterways like that.[31] George Trenholm of Fraser Trenholm relied on Maffitt to help his privateers safely into protected harbors. Before the fall of New Smyrna to federal troops in March, 1862, Trenholm wired Judah Benjamin "We took the liberty of telegraphing you this morning in relation to Captain Maffitt. It is important that we should command his services without delay."[32]

During the critical 1862 period, the cotton surplus in England was gone, and the Palmerston government was giving serious consideration to Confederate recognition. Maffitt and the blockade runners could not keep up with the demand for supplies. Also by this time, complaints of the Seward approach to foreign relations got more serious. The sentiment of some in Congress was that the Secretary should either resign or be removed from office and replaced. Opposition was also manifested in Lincoln cabinet meetings, in the newspapers and in the minds of diplomats, foreign and domestic. Much of this damage was self-inflicted. Immediately after taking office, Gideon Wells tells us that few cabinet meetings were held. At Seward's suggestion, the secretary called those cabinet members to separate meetings with Lincoln as needed. Seward was always present, and kept a close watch on the activities of all government departments. He quickly made enemies. Salmon Chase objected to the excessive control that Seward was attempting to exercise. Lincoln realized that he was being pushed into a corner and instituted regular cabinet meetings, twice a week, with all members who could attend. Initially, if Seward came late or did not attend, serious discussion was delayed until his arrival. That didn't last long, however. Powerful men in Congress had powerful friends.

Senator Charles Sumner was chairman of the Senate Foreign Relations Committee and friend to two members of the British parliament, John Bright and Richard Cobden. The intimate detail which Sumner shared with his English friends about the inner workings of the Lincoln government is surprising. Knowing Seward in this vicarious manner may have helped solidify English governmental resolve to stand up to the secretary and turn his bluster against him. This unique insight provided by Sumner may have enabled the British Foreign Office to better control the U.S. State Department. Sumner wrote to Bright on November 18, 1862 regarding Seward opposition to the Emancipation Proclamation. He characterized the secretary of state, "Seward has talent and prodigious industry, but little forecast and a want of seriousness."[33] If your opponents believe that you are not serious about your motives, they may be emboldened to stand firm and call your bluff. Threats of war may have been interpreted as the kind of bluff that Prime Minister Palmerston well understood. As late as 1863, Sumner told Bright that,

"A difficulty, amounting almost to calamity, is the want of confidence in Mr. Seward."[34] Having Charles Sumner tell an influential member of the British parliament that there is little confidence in the secretary of state cannot help but ensure some resistance to the bluster that had become central to Lincoln foreign policy at this time.

The foreign relations of the Lincoln government during the American Civil War involved a large and diverse group of representatives and consular officials all over the world. Some of these representatives were experienced professionals like Charles Francis Adams in London. Others, like William Lewis Dayton in Paris, were political appointees. At this time, the Seward State Department was primarily charged with ensuring that Europe did not interfere with the Union war effort and divert the administration from reunifying the country. The world was a dangerous place that was undergoing much change. Europe initially took little notice of the Civil War in America. However, the enigmatic and pugnacious personality of the secretary of state along with the rapid growth of an ironclad navy forced a change in European attitude and interest. Was Seward crazy like a fox or just plain crazy?

CHAPTER 6

DISPATCH NO.10

Regarding the case of neutral nations resorting to my enemy's country for commercial purposes, it is certain that, as they have no part in my quarrel, they are under no obligation to renounce their commerce for the sake of avoiding to supply my enemy with the means of carrying on the war against me.

Emmerich de Vattel, *The Law of Nations*, 1758

Abraham Lincoln's knowledge and control of foreign relations and international law is a matter of subjective interpretation. The president himself stated that he had little knowledge in this area. Charles Francis Adams, U.S. representative to Great Britain during the Civil War, was a tart critic of Lincoln's lack of foreign policy knowledge. Adams and Navy Secretary Gideon Welles spoke and published their opposing viewpoints of the respective skills, foreign and domestic, of Lincoln and Seward. Welles was as critical of Seward as Adams was of Lincoln. Seward's job was to manage the foreign affairs of the United States. In this, he inevitably clashed with the navy secretary whose ships in turn clashed with Confederate privateers and commerce raiders financed and built in Britain. Seward was frustrated with British and French violations of neutrality as he understood it. Unfortunately, the secretary of state had little knowledge of international law and less inclination to study it. Fleet Admiral Sir Alexander Milne read significant passages of Vattel to his officers while patrolling the waters of the North Atlantic.[1] He wanted to honor British neutrality, and used Vattel to guide him. According to Charles Francis

Adams, later champion of Seward, "Long retired from public practice, [Seward] had never given any particular attention to the problems and collection of usages which make up the body of what is denominated international law. He now also freely admitted to his cabinet colleagues, that almost daily called upon to deal with novel and intricate international issues, he never opened the treatises and that he was too old to study."[2] Adams later learned that Seward relied on his chief clerk at the State Department, William Hunter, for guidance on international law.[3] Under these circumstances, the secretary's frustration is understandable.

While delivering the eulogy at Seward's funeral, Charles Francis Adams made it clear that Lincoln knew "absolutely nothing" about foreign relations. True or not, others have claimed that the *de facto* secretary of state, upon whom Lincoln placed great trust, was Senator Charles Sumner of Massachusetts. Many in government at that time considered Sumner to be an expert in international law. Reliance on the advice of others was necessary because the president was distracted by the war. Gideon Welles was one of only two cabinet members to serve Lincoln throughout his presidency. He was a keen observer of the inner workings of the Lincoln administration. He kept a detailed diary, often disagreed with Secretary Seward and took issue with Adams' assessment of Lincoln in a paper entitled, *Lincoln and Seward, Remarks upon the memorial address of Charles Francis Adams*. Welles stated, "In an important dispatch of the secretary of state to Mr. Adams, who was then our minister at London, Mr. Lincoln took the document, which he considered in some respects exceptional, criticized, modified and with his own hand expurgated, modified and improved it, and changed its character. This paper related to the recognition of belligerent rights ... There were other marked cases of intelligent supervision of our foreign affairs and their management by the President."[4] There were significant instances where Lincoln's intervention had a controlling impact on foreign policy and its influence on the war. As already referenced by Gideon Welles, one of these instances was that "important dispatch" – the infamous Dispatch No.10.

In his first message to the thirty-seventh Congress in its second session, December, 1861, Abraham Lincoln stated that he was aware that France and England were actively considering recognition of the

Confederacy as an independent, sovereign nation. He knew that America was vulnerable and that cotton was an issue for England and France. Sounding more like Seward now, Lincoln stated, "Nations thus tempted to interfere, are not always able to resist the counsels of seeming expediency and ungenerous ambition, although measures adopted under such influences seldom fail to be unfortunate and injurious to those adopting them." He pointed out that "injury" would be the reward for those who interfered. Up to this point, the man always thought quick to threaten injury was Seward. Dispatch No. 10 would show Lincoln and Seward beginning to form an alliance in a matter of strategic national importance. The dispatch is significant for what Lincoln left in as well as what he took out. The process of editing the initial dispatch, communicating it to Representative Adams and the subsequent publishing in 1862 of the entire original document was important in allowing the relationship between Lincoln and Seward to develop and mature.

Up to this point, Seward had been the *bête noire* of the Lincoln government. People in and out of the administration were calling for his resignation. English and French legation representatives thought him dangerous. Unfortunately, this impression was confirmed with some unnecessary help from Charles Sumner. Sumner was Chair of the Senate Foreign Relations committee and friend of some powerful members of parliament in London. He was critical of almost everyone but himself. He was particularly disparaging of Seward to his friends in England. Seward didn't help himself, however. As confirmed by Gideon Wells, "Mr. Seward entered upon his duties with the impression, undoubtedly, which Mr. Adams seems to have imbibed, that he was to be *de facto* President, and, as the premier in the British government, to direct the affairs of the nation in the name of another." The detailed but sometimes partisan account of Gideon Welles claims that Abraham Lincoln was in control of the war and his secretary of state at all times. Welles portrays Lincoln as shrewd and careful, and Seward as careless and dangerous. Welles was one of the first to see and commit to writing that Seward attempted to inject himself into the government as *alternate* President.

Foreign relations for the Confederacy began when Jefferson Davis sent a commission to Washington to discuss peace between two sovereign nations. Lincoln's intentions at this time were not to interfere with

slavery where it existed in the South; maintain control of federal property throughout the United States, and ensure that the U.S. remained
united. Under these circumstances, the peace which Seward initially
sought could not be reconciled with his official refusal to meet with
the Confederate commission. "Foreign relations" with the South was
incompatible with the unity Lincoln sought.

Henry Seward believed that one way to unite the country was to
fight a common enemy. Although any enemy would do, England was
always his favorite target. Lincoln disagreed and put Seward in his place
by stating that he, the president, would decide how to deal with those
foreign nations that threatened to interfere. Lincoln forced Seward to
cool down, but in the end did not disagree with Seward's blustering
posture towards England. Lincoln was always seen as the voice of moderation and Seward that of impatience and war with England. By allowing
an edited Dispatch No.10 to be sent, Lincoln and Seward were acting
more in concert. Lincoln was in control of his own foreign policy to a
greater extent than previously believed. Significant changes were made
by Lincoln, but the aggressive dispatch was sent. England was warned
that any action on her part that compromised the Union effort to quell
the "rebellion" would result in war. Full recognition of the Confederacy
was such a compromise.

"Recognition" of the Confederate States as a sovereign nation was
a complex and potentially dangerous move.[5] The concept of secession
was as old as the nation itself. This was the age of John Locke and Jean
Jacques Rousseau in which the common man felt empowered to hold
his leaders accountable for their actions as administrators acting with
the public trust. The idea of making changes to the existing governing
structure was new. In America, the separate states were held together
during the revolution by the Articles of Confederation. Historians argue that when the Articles were replaced by a Constitution in 1787, all
states were bound by it in perpetuity. No state could withdraw or secede.
Alexander Hamilton argued for a strong federal government, and Jefferson
for the ultimate sovereignty of individual states. Temporarily, Hamilton
won. Significant for foreign relations during the Civil War was the fear
by Federalists that without a strong Union from which states could not
withdraw, Europe would intervene and take advantage of disunion.

'The Dis-United States. Or the Southern Confederacy', Currier & Ives.

Although South Carolina fired the first shot that began the Civil War, one of the first serious threats of secession came from New England, not the South. In 1814, the New England states gathered at Hartford to complain about the war of 1812, and the domination of the federal government by the Virginia aristocracy. After tempers cooled in Hartford, they ignited in South Carolina over the Nullification Crisis of 1832. South Carolinians were upset over the high tariffs intended to encourage the purchase of domestic over foreign goods. Northern factories and artisans were producing those goods. The state legislature declared the tariffs null and void within South Carolina. By 1856, Southern congressmen approached G.P.R. James, the British consul resident in Norfolk, Virginia, and asked whether or not England would support the South in the event of disunion. Part of the complexity resulted from terminology. By 1861, the Lincoln administration argued that this was not a war but a rebellion on the part of some of the Southern states. Wars were conducted by sovereign nations. A rebellion was an internal conflict which other nations were expected to respect by not making treaties or other obligations with the rebels. This is an important distinction because the head of the British Foreign Office was Lord John Russell. Russell read and relied on Vattel to guide and provide justification for the actions of the Foreign Office at this critical time. Vattel spoke about independent, sovereign nations, not warring factions of the same nation. Seward wanted Lord John to remember this so that when he read Vattel next time, he would be more careful about violating neutrality and recognition.

Recognition had practical consequences, however. The commercial benefits were considerable. In lieu of full recognition, "belligerency" status also allowed a country to "solicit loans, contract for arms and enlist men abroad, except when forbidden to do so by neutrality laws; to send commissioned cruisers to sea, exercise belligerent rights of search and seizure, and make use of prize courts; and to have the Southern banner and commissioners recognized as representing a quasi-political community." Ultimately, belligerency allowed the Confederacy to satisfy some of these needs and be able to stand against the wealthier Union. Neutrality, however, would not permit England to admit captured Confederate prizes to be adjudicated in her "neutral" prize courts. That would be a violation of neutrality that even John Bull could not get away with. "Out of deference to the state against which the rebellion is aimed and because of uncertainty about the probable success of the rebellion, foreign countries are inclined to delay their decision on recognition for a considerable time." Lord John and Pam wanted it both ways, however.

One of the most respected theorists on international law at this time was an American, Henry Wheaton. Russell felt justified when he read in Wheaton, "When countries are intimately connected with each other, through situation or commerce, a revolt of any magnitude in one materially affects the rights of the others, and entails upon them the necessity of pursuing some definite course of conduct recognizing the insurgents as belligerents, or by acknowledging them to be independent."[6] Lord John could not have asked for more support – and from an American no less. France also had an interest in the belligerency and recognition issue.

French foreign secretary, Édouard Thouvanel wrote to French representative in Washington, Henri Mercier, on May 11, 1861 to provide a French definition of belligerency which allowed Napoleon III the latitude he required. Thouvanel wrote:

> "... to be called belligerent, it is enough that a portion of a people in revolt have possession of only enough force to create, in the eyes of neutrals, a doubt as to the final outcome. In such a case modern international law required that foreign powers, without prejudice to the final results of the clash of forces, keep an attitude of impartiality toward the two contestants."[7]

Through the French rationale, if they wanted to trade with the enemy and maintain business as usual, make sure that the enemy has just enough strength to allow you to claim that you can't predict who will win the contest. This would not compromise your neutrality status by appearing to favor one side over the other. If that failed, just fall back on Wheaton. Uncertainty as to who would win the contest continued for much longer than anyone anticipated.

England and France wanted cotton, grain and access to those lucrative American markets which had proven so profitable to both countries. Before Charles Francis Adams arrived in England to represent the Lincoln administration, Queen Victoria proclaimed that England was to remain neutral in the Civil War. Neutrality allowed her to treat Union and Confederacy as equal belligerents. She should be allowed through the blockade unmolested. England's economy was more important than any other consideration. Belligerency status was not recognition as a sovereign nation. It represented a tentative, quasi-recognition that she hoped would not anger the Union and still protect her rights via the 1856 Treaty of Paris. Full recognition would have to wait. England wanted to see if the South could maintain her independence from the North in the face of Lincoln's outspoken insistence that the nation must remain united, not separated.

The issue of neutrality and how neutral nations were expected to act when their allies were at war was a subject of much controversy since 1793. On February 1st of that year, war broke out between England and France. This created serious problems for the United States. Thomas Jefferson argued strongly for French support – France, after all, had spent much to support the American revolutionary effort. She also sent Rochambeau to help Washington, and show him how a proper siege operation works. That siege and the French navy resulted in the surrender of Cornwallis at Yorktown in 1781. America was free from control by England. The British, however, were strongly tied to America by blood, common language and common law. They were successful trading partners. George Washington sided with Alexander Hamilton and generally favored England. Jefferson favored France. Washington wanted to remain neutral and ignored Congress in declaring American neutrality. The matter quickly became complicated when the new French representative, Edmond-Charles Genet, arrived in Philadelphia. His purpose was to ensure American support for the French war effort. Citizen Genet created issues that were later reflected in the neutrality issue of 1861. With bright red hair and an outgoing personality to match, Genet arrived in Philadelphia determined to go over the head of George Washington if necessary to secure support for France.

Herein lay the problem as it related to 1861: Genet encouraged French privateers to capture British commercial ships, and bring them into American prize courts to then be converted into French warships to further prey on British shipping on the high seas. Just as in 1861, Washington declared neutrality which thus disallowed the use of prize courts. One can't be neutral and then sit in judgment on one side or the other. Genet ignored the neutrality proclamation and brought captured British ships into American ports anyway.[8] In addition to this, Genet organized the outfitting of American privateers manned by American and French crews to continue pillaging British commercial shipping. Although initially cheered and supported by Jefferson, Genet constantly crossed the line. Jefferson finally characterized Genet as "hot-headed, all imagination, no judgment, passionate, disrespectful and even indecent toward the president."[9] Washington ordered a halt to the arming of privateers in American ports. However, just as the *Alabama* "slipped" out of a British dock in 1861 to devastate Union shipping for years, some of Genet's privateers also "slipped" away from their moorings in Charleston and sank many tons of British commercial shipping during this period. The entire issue of neutrality, belligerency and the rules governing neutral and belligerent nations was just as uncertain in 1861 as it was in 1793. England, France and the United States had a long history of working neutrality to their own advantage.

Charles Francis Adams and William Lewis Dayton represented the Union to Great Britain and France respectively. The U.S. State Department was more structured and proactive in managing relations with foreign countries than was the Davis government. In the belief that cotton and free trade with the South would secure Confederate recognition from Europe, Robert Toombs sent emissaries to London, Paris, St. Petersburg and Brussels. Arriving first in London, the group of Rost, Mann and Yancey met with Foreign Secretary Russell on May 3 and May 9. The meeting was unofficial because the Confederacy was not an independent nation. The meetings were sympathetic, but unproductive. England wanted to wait and see how the situation in America would develop before taking a position. Just before the arrival of the Confederate commissioners, England had declared her neutrality in the matter. Arriving in Paris, the commissioners also saw Foreign Minister Édouard Thouvanel unofficially. The Confederates initially believed that this meeting was more productive because they knew that France did not have as large a cotton reserve as did England. In fact, the first words from Thouvanel concerned cotton and when could France expect shipments to be resumed. Ultimately, however, France and England had already agreed to act in concert regarding the issues in America. The Confederate commissioners were disappointed again. Returning home empty-handed, they were replaced by more experienced politicians, James Mason and John Slidell.

Mason had been a long-standing member of the Senate Foreign Relations Committee, and Slidell had helped negotiate the treaty that ended the war with Mexico in 1848. Both were ultimately compromised choices to represent the Confederacy, however. Mann believed that the war department should handle foreign relations in war time. During peace time, the job could then be managed by the state department. Slidell was a slick politician from New Orleans. He had befriended Judah Benjamin and helped him quickly rise through the political ranks in the South. Even beyond the city limits, the term for trickery and fraud was "Slidellian." It was at this critical time that William Seward wrote Dispatch No. 10 to Charles Francis Adams, who had just arrived in London. "(Seward's) notorious Dispatch Number 10 (May 21) proposed breaking off relations with Britain if it continued to communicate – officially or otherwise – with Davis' commissioners. He spoke in provocative terms of being forced into war with Britain if it recognized Confederate independence (a threat he had made before). Some historians claim that Seward's draft dispatch provoked Lincoln into one of his rare interventions into foreign policy. The President countermanded Seward's order that the message be read to Lord Russell, and blue-penciled the Secretary's more warlike phrases."

Some historians claim that the decision to modify the Seward draft was that of Charles Sumner. According to David Herbert Donald, "When Lincoln received this bellicose document, he showed it to Sumner. In shocked outrage the Senator read the dispatch, and he enthusiastically approved Lincoln's proposal to excise the more offensive passages and to mark the entire document as being for Adams' information only, not to be read or presented at the British Foreign Office."[10] The diary of Edward Everett from August 31, 1861 later records Sumner as warning Lincoln about Seward, "You must watch him and overrule him."[11] The dispatch was not to be shown or read to Lord Russell. Adams was to summarize it and be guided by the spirit of the message when meeting with Russell. This was wise advice. When reading the dispatch, and looking at the sentences removed by Lincoln, it is clear that the president was more the voice of moderation. Nevertheless, even as edited, Lincoln approved of a strong message against Confederate recognition by England. Before approval, he exercised better judgment and removed enough of Seward's language so as not to foreclose other options. It is also interesting and significant to note that Lincoln allowed Seward to publish selected dispatches from the state department in a volume entitled *Papers Relating to the Foreign Relations of the United States.*[12] Again, Lincoln didn't disagree with the basics of what Seward was saying to the British, he objected to some of the language, and the way in which it was originally to be presented.

Although dreaded by diplomats, publishing State Department papers, however, was in the same tradition as already found in the publication of the parliamentary *Blue Books.* The first State Department volume was published in 1862, one year after the original Dispatch No. 10 was sent and one year before the watershed year 1863 when Vicksburg and Gettysburg helped to convince London and Paris that Union victory was likely and

Confederate recognition would be disadvantageous. The dispatch published in 1862 was in the original, aggressive Seward form. It contained all of the original language leveled by the secretary against England which Lincoln considered unwise in 1861. In 1862, England believed that the South could still win the war. Shiloh, Antietam and Fredericksburg were fought at great cost to the North. Due to Union battlefield losses, the possibility of Confederate recognition seemed greater now. Europe wanted to be on the side of a winner. The publication of *Papers Relating to the Foreign Relations of the United States* continues to suggest that Lincoln was not always the voice of moderation trying to calm a "vaporing, blustering, ignorant" Seward. Whether or not Lincoln was directly involved in the decision to publish the State Department dispatches is not known. However, we may reasonably believe that the president at least tacitly allowed publication of something that he was in a position to stop. If Seward was so bold and the President so unaware of the publication of the first volume, Lincoln would certainly have been in a position to be aware and then stop publication of subsequent volumes. This did not happen.

Lincoln is known to have wanted "one war at a time". To calm himself down, he often wrote strongly-worded letters to those who disagreed with him, but then put the letter in his desk drawer unsent. He did this to relieve stress and clarify his options. However, after some modifications, Lincoln allowed Secretary Seward to send Dispatch No. 10 to Minister Adams. It didn't go into the desk drawer. The dispatch is quoted here to show Lincoln's revisions and intentions. Material removed by Lincoln is in square brackets and bolded.

"No. 10

Department of State. Washington, May 21, 1861
SIR:–Mr. Dallas, in a brief dispatch of May 2d (No.333), tells us that Lord John Russell recently requested an interview with him on account of the solicitude which his lordship felt concerning the effect of certain measures represented as likely to be adopted by the President.[13] In that conversation the British secretary told Mr. Dallas that the three representatives of the Southern Confederacy were then in London, that Lord John Russell had not yet seen them, but that he was not unwilling to see them unofficially. He further informed Mr. Dallas that an understanding exists between the British and French governments which would lead both to take one and the same course as to recognition. His lordship then referred to the rumor of a meditated blockade by us of Southern ports, and a

discontinuance of them as ports of entry. Mr. Dallas answered that he knew nothing on those topics, and therefore could say nothing. He added that you were expected to arrive in two weeks. Upon this statement Lord John Russell acquiesced in the expediency of waiting for the full knowledge you were expected to bring. Mr. Dallas transmitted to us some newspaper reports of ministerial explanations made in parliament. You will base no proceedings on parliamentary debates further than to seek explanations when necessary and communicate them to this department. **[We intend to have a clear and simple record of whatever issue may arise between us and Great Britain.]**

The President **[is surprised and grieved]** regrets that Mr. Dallas did not protest against the proposed unofficial intercourse between the British Government and the missionaries of the insurgents **[as well as against the demand for explanations made by the British Government]**. It is due, however, to Mr. Dallas to say that our instructions had been given only to you and not to him, and that his loyalty and fidelity, too rare in these times, (among our late representatives abroad, are confessed and) are appreciated.

Intercourse of any kind with the so-called commissioners is liable to be construed as a recognition of the authority which appointed them. Such intercourse would be none the less **[wrongful]** hurtful to us for being called unofficial, and it might be even more injurious, because we should have no means of knowing what points might be resolved by it.[14] Moreover, unofficial intercourse is useless and meaningless if it is not expected to ripen into official intercourse and direct recognition. It is left doubtful here whether the proposed unofficial intercourse has yet actually begun. Your own **[present]** antecedent instructions are deemed explicit enough, and it is hoped that you have not misunderstood them. You will in any event desist from all intercourse whatever, unofficial as well as official, with the British Government, so long as it shall continue intercourse of either kind with the domestic enemies of this country **[confining yourself to a delivery of a copy of this paper to the Secretary of State after doing this]**. When intercourse shall have been arrested for this cause, you will communicate with this department and receive further directions.

Lord John Russell has informed us of an understanding between the British and French governments that they will act together in regard to our affairs. This communication, however, loses something of its value from the circumstance that the communication was withheld until after knowledge of the fact had been acquired by us from other sources. We know also another fact that has not yet been officially communicated to us – namely, that other European States are apprised by France and England of their agreement, and are expected to concur with or follow them in whatever measures they adopt on the subject of recognition. The United States have been impartial and just in all their conduct toward the several nations of Europe. They will not complain, however, of the combination now announced by the two leading powers, although they think they had a right to expect a more independent, if not a more friendly, course from each of them.

You will take no notice of that or any other alliance. Whenever the European governments shall see fit to communicate directly with us, we shall be, as heretofore, frank and explicit in our reply.

As to the blockade, you will say that by **[the]** our own laws **[of nature]**[15] and the laws of nature and the laws of nations, this Government has a clear right to suppress insurrection. An exclusion of commerce from national ports which have been seized by the insurgents, in the equitable form of blockade, is the proper means to that end. You will **[admit]** not insist that our blockade is **[not]** to be respected if it be not maintained by a competent force; but passing by that question as not now a practical, or at least an urgent, one, you will add that **[it]** the blockade is now, and it will continue to be so maintained, and therefore we expect it to be respected by Great Britain. You will add that we have already revoked the exequatur of a Russian consul who had enlisted in the military service of the insurgents, and we shall dismiss or demand the recall of every foreign agent, consular or diplomatic, who shall either disobey the Federal laws or disown the Federal authority.

As to the recognition of the so-called Southern Confederacy, it is not to be made a subject of technical definition. It is, of course, **[quasi]** direct recognition to publish an acknowledgment of the sovereignty and independence of a new power. It is **[quasi]** direct recognition to receive its ambassadors, ministers, agents, or commissioners officially. A concession of belligerent rights is liable to be construed as a recognition of them. No one of these proceedings will **[be borne]** pass **[unnoticed]** unquestioned by the United States in this case.

Hitherto recognition has been moved only on the assumption that the so-called Confederate States are de facto a self-sustaining power. Now, after long forbearance, designed to soothe discontent and avert the need of civil war, the land and naval forces of the United States have been put in motion to repress the insurrection. The true character of the pretended new State is at once revealed. It is seen to be a power existing in pronunciamento only. It has never won a field. It has obtained no forts that were not virtually betrayed into its hands or seized in breach of trust. It commands not a single port on the coast nor any highway out from its pretended capital by land. Under these circumstances Great Britain is called upon to intervene and give it body and independence by resisting our measures of suppression. British recognition would be British intervention to create within our own territory a hostile state by overthrowing this republic itself. **[When this act of intervention is distinctly performed, we from that hour shall cease to be friends, and become once more, as we have twice before been forced to be, enemies of Great Britain.]**

As to the treatment of privateers in the insurgent service, you will say that this is a question exclusively our own. We treat them as pirates. They are our own citizens, or persons employed by our citizens, preying on the commerce of our country. If Great Britain shall choose to recognize them as lawful belligerents, and give them shelter from our pursuit and punishment, the laws of nations afford an adequate and proper remedy **[and we shall avail ourselves of it. And while you need not say this in advance, be sure that you say nothing inconsistent with it].**

Happily, however, her Britannic Majesty's government can avoid all these difficulties. It invited us in 1856 to accede to the declaration of the Congress of Paris, of which body Great Britain was herself a member, abolishing privateering everywhere in all cases and forever. You already have our authority to propose to her our accession to that declaration. If she refuse to receive it, it can only be because she is willing to become the patron of privateering when aimed at our devastation.

These positions are not elaborately defended now, because to vindicate them would imply a possibility of our waiving them.

1 We are not insensible of the grave importance of

1 **[Drop all from this line to the end, and in lieu of it write, "This paper is for your own guidance only, and not [sic] to be read or shown to anyone."]**

this occasion. We see how, upon the result of the debate in which we are engaged, a war may ensue between the United States and one, two, or even more European nations. War in any case is as exceptionable from the habits as it is revolting from the sentiments of the American people. But if it come, it will be fully seen that it results from the action of Great Britain, not our own; that Great Britain will have decided to fraternize with our domestic enemy, either without waiting to hear from you our remonstrances and our warnings, or after having heard them. War in defense of national life is not immoral, and war in defense of independence is an inevitable part of the discipline of nations.

The dispute will be between the European and the American branches of the British race.[16] All who belong to that race will especially deprecate it, as they ought. It may well be believed that men of every race and kindred will deplore it. A war not unlike it between the same parties occurred at the close of the last century. Europe atoned by 40 years of suffering for the error that Great Britain committed in provoking that contest. If that nation shall now repeat the same great error, the social convulsions which will follow may not be so long, but they will be more general. When they shall have ceased, it will, we think, be seen, whatever may have been the fortunes of other nations, that it is not the United States that will have come out of them with its precious Constitution altered or its honestly obtained dominion in any degree abridged. Great Britain has but to wait a few months and all her present inconveniences will cease with all our own troubles. If she takes a different course, she will calculate for herself the ultimate as well as the immediate consequences, and will consider what position she will hold when she shall have forever lost the sympathies and the affections of the only nation on whose sympathies and affections she has a natural claim. In making that calculation she will do well to remember that in the controversy she proposes to open we shall be actuated by neither pride, nor passion, nor cupidity, nor ambition; but

we shall stand simply on the principle of self-preservation, and that our cause will
involve the independence of nations and the rights of human nature.
I am, Sir, respectfully your obedient servant, W. H. S.
CHARLES FRANCIS ADAMS, Esq., etc,

Self-preservation, piracy and war are the themes of Dispatch No. 10. An
examination of the dispatch reveals 18 instances containing words and
sentences that were removed or changed. The document also contains
eight significant words or phrases that were left in place by Lincoln. Of
those 18 removed, 11 demonstrate Lincoln acting as the lawyer providing
clarification, not disapproval. Only three show the president softening
Seward's words. The president also removed two words/phrases that he
considered redundant and one area where he may have strengthened
Seward's words. Of the significant eight words or phrases left in by
Lincoln, three of these contain strong statements that were calculated to
command British attention. One instance left in by Lincoln may be considered very strong language that challenges the belief that Seward was
the rogue and the president the moderator holding the secretary back.
Belligerency status had already been granted the Confederacy. Lincoln
sent Dispatch No. 10 in order to foreclose the possibility of full recognition. Seward's threats might provoke Great Britain, but moderation could
also embolden the English and encourage full recognition.

An example of Lincoln's clarification occurs in the fourth paragraph beginning with "Intercourse of any kind". The president removed Seward's
word "wrongful" and inserted "hurtful". Lincoln correctly realized that
"wrongful" communication with the Confederate commissioners would
mean illegal or unlawful intercourse which technically could only happen
between one sovereign entity and another. The South was in rebellion,
not at war with the North. Therefore, Lincoln, the lawyer, substituted
"hurtful". This was a term which did not imply or involve the actions of
a sovereign nation. Anyone could be hurtful. Only an independent person, entity or nation could do something illegal, unlawful and wrongful.

Most significant, however, are the words that Lincoln elected to leave
in Dispatch No. 10. He told Adams to inform the British that he expected the blockade to be respected. England was dependent on cotton
and increasingly grain. Cotton imports from the South had increased
since 1840. "In 1840 the supply received from the United States was

487,850,000 lbs. Since that time, with some considerable fluctuations, it has steadily increased, until in 1858 it rose to 732,403,000 lbs. – the maximum quantity having reached in 1856, 780,040,000 lbs ... In 1840 the supply of cotton from India was 77,011,000 lbs.; – in 1858 it had risen to 138,253,000 lbs."[17] Although Brazil and Egypt also supplied cotton to British mills, their quality and quantity were small compared to that coming from the seceding states.[18] Although the Union blockade supposedly curtailed British cotton imports until 1863, data from an 1864 Richmond publication disputes this. Upon the request of F.S. Lyon, Chairman of the Confederate House Ways and Means Committee, George McHenry supplied data on available cotton in Britain (see Table 1, p.108).

In addition to the cotton issue, the activities of foreign representatives were also a problem in the South. Dispatch No.10 was received in London within three weeks of deposit in the diplomatic mail pouch. Jefferson Davis had a much harder time sending and receiving communication from Europe. When Davis was elected as provisional president of the Confederacy, he allowed the various foreign consuls to remain at their posts throughout the South. This was a difficult decision because these consuls had not been appointed or vetted by him. Many had been residents and consuls in locales for ten years and more. By 1861, some had been appointed by other presidents as far back as Zachary Taylor and Millard Fillmore. Davis didn't trust them all, but lacked the administrative machinery necessary to replace them at that time. So, how was the Confederate president to communicate with his newly-appointed representatives in London and Paris? Lord Lyons advised the consuls to send their dispatches and reports direct to London rather than go through him in Washington. He was concerned that his ability to remain neutral would be compromised by the perception of the Davis government that he was tampering with the mails. For Lyons at least, Admiral Milne of the North Atlantic Squadron came to the rescue. Lyons got permission to send his reports to London through Milne. In the initial stages of the blockade, Seward also allowed Milne to go into Southern ports and collect official dispatches. "In October, Lord Lyons secured permission for British consuls to have official intercourse with him and Lord Russell, by means of British men-of-war entering the blockaded ports, provided that such vessels should carry no passengers, except diplomatic or consulate agents, and none but official correspondence."[19]

Jefferson Davis and Judah Benjamin had a much harder time of communicating with their representatives in Europe as the blockade tightened. At first, the blockade was not as efficient as it soon became, and dispatches were able to get through. However, as the cordon of Union ships grew, Benjamin was reading about events in Europe and planning strategy based upon what he read about parliamentary debates in Northern newspapers. The original, problematic instructions given to Yancey, Rost and Mann could not be quickly or easily modified as suggested by Robert Toombs because it was difficult to communicate with them. "All (Benjamin's) communication with Europe until May, 1863 were (sic) so irregular and infrequent as to nullify to a large extent his efforts to control the Southern foreign policy."[20] Benjamin took over as secretary of state in March, 1862. Mason and Slidell had already taken over the duties of Yancey, Rost and Mann. However, Benjamin was unable to get his first dispatch through to Slidell until July 5, 1862-four months later. After this, dispatches arrived on October 25, December 31, February 6, 1863, February 27 and March 19. Originally, dispatches were sent by any ship available to run the blockade and carry them. In some cases, this was by a sailing sloop. These slow sailing craft were easily captured by the Union steam warships, and the Confederate mail bags captured. Seward ordered them printed in the *New York Times*. Soon, Benjamin was forced to write all of his notes and dispatches in cypher to avoid detection.[21] Benjamin had the same complaint with Mason. Dispatches sent in April, 1862 did not arrive until late June. On January 24, 1863, Benjamin complained to Fraser Trenholm in Charleston:

"It appears that Major Sanders, who was authorized by me to take charge of dispatches for Europe, and to whom I requested you to confide a bundle of dispatches has been guilty of the folly (if not worse) on taking them on board of a sailing vessel and allowing them to be captured to the detriment of the public interest. Major Sanders was especially instructed to go on one of your steamers. I write to beg that in the future you will not permit any dispatches to be taken by any other conveyance than by steamer even when a special messenger may be sent by the Department."[22]

Ultimately, those shallow-draft steam blockade runners were able to get Benjamin's dispatches to Europe in one month. However, much damage had been done by then. During the time it took the Confederate secretary of state to send a half dozen dispatches to Europe, William Seward was able to send hundreds in one month. Union dispatches not only went to London and Paris, but also to St. Petersburg, Vienna and all the way to Yeddo (Tokyo) Japan. The process of getting private mail from Richmond to Washington and other parts North was equally as difficult. John Beauchamp Jones, a clerk in Judah Benjamin's office, kept a diary in which he records the activities of letter-carriers who manage to sneak back and forth to Washington with as many as 300 letters stuffed in their saddlebags.[23] They average two trips per month at $1,000 per trip. An improvised Confederacy was up against an organized Union war machine. Many on both sides were learning on the job. However, Lincoln had the financial resources to create a degree of certainty that was far beyond the capability of even creative people like Judah Benjamin.

Benjamin left the war department and took over as secretary of state in March, 1862. By that fall, the politics in England were critical, and he needed to be able to quickly contact his representatives. By that fall, the cotton surplus had run out, and mill workers in Liverpool were working half-time. Gladstone made his Newcastle speech on October 7, stating that, "Jefferson Davis and other leaders of the South have made an army; they are making, it appears, a navy; and they have made what is more than either – they have made a nation." Also in October, the French were talking to the Governor of Texas to see if they would consider leaving the Confederacy. This was the time to strike.

Lack of effective communication was endangering Confederate foreign relations. Attempts to circumvent the few sanctioned avenues to Europe were immediately crushed by the Seward state department.

Great Britain and France maintained a diplomatic presence North and South. Lincoln made it clear that he would expel any foreign diplomat or consular official who did not obey federal laws. Any assistance to the Confederacy by a foreign official would result in their dismissal from official duties. Unfortunately, Lincoln was challenged by the British consul at Charleston, Robert Bunch. Bunch had been a consul of the United States since 1853. He served in New York, Philadelphia and after secession, in Charleston. So, his credentials were under the auspices of the United States, not the Confederacy.

The job of consular officials is to monitor the business and commercial interests of the country represented. They are not to be involved in diplomatic matters. Nevertheless, Bunch approved a passport for a cousin of the consul in New Orleans to travel to New York and then to London. The passport was issued to Robert Mure, who carried a mail bag with private letters to partners in England. Some of the bag contained letters and news clippings that were critical of the Lincoln government and congratulatory of the Confederacy for their success at Bull Run. Also contained in the bag were letters for the commissioners then in London discussing adherence to the Treaty of Paris and recognition of sovereignty. Seward requested that John Russell recall Bunch for this breach of security. Russell refused, so Seward recalled the consul's exequatur, or official permission to function as consul. Seward instructed Charles Francis Adams to inform Russell that Bunch acted beyond his capacity as consul, and was indirectly acting in a diplomatic capacity. He stated on November 21, 1861, "Mr. Bunch received from the government of the United States a recognition exclusively confined to the performance of consular duties." Adams and Russell quickly got into a discussion in which Adams complained that Bunch should have known of U.S. laws which prevent consuls from contacting foreign governments in matters diplomatic. Russell replied that the law actually referred to private citizens of the United States, not representatives of foreign nations. The exhausting series of dispatches that went back and forth across the Atlantic finally resulted in loss of patience on Seward's part and the revocation of the credentials accorded to Mr. Bunch. The matter is significant because of the great concern over possible Confederate recognition and the lack of cooperation by the British Foreign Office. It is also significant that although Mr. Bunch's credentials were revoked, Seward never enforced the revocation. So, Bunch stayed where he was. Seward was learning to pick his battles.

Seward's original Dispatch No. 10 stated that for the British government to receive the Confederate commissioners would be quasi-recognition of the Confederacy. Lincoln corrected him by inserting "direct" for "quasi". The President equated direct recognition of the Southern commissioners as an act that he considered "overthrowing this republic itself." Seward originally wrote that even "quasi" recognition would result in war with the Union. Lincoln elected to leave the overt threat of war out. He knew that the British would immediately equate any attempt to overthrow the Union government as an act of war. The situation, however, may already have been close to war with England.

Charles Francis Adams would write to British foreign secretary Lord John Russell that he believed that England was already at war with the Union. He stated that English sailors were serving as privateers on ships that were built in England and flew the British flag. One such privateer was built in a shipyard owned by a member of the House of Commons. Adams complained, "It now appears from a survey of all the evidence – first, that this vessel was built in a dockyard belonging to a commercial house in Liverpool, of which the chief member, down to October of last year, is a member of the House of Commons."[24] Lincoln decided to leave in a statement about privateers. He stated that "we treat them as pirates … the laws of nations afford adequate and proper remedy". The President was telling the Palmerston government that British citizens, serving as privateers, would be considered as pirates and adjudicated accordingly. In most countries in 1861, piracy was punishable by death. This was a strong statement that Lincoln elected to leave in the dispatch. Knowing that British citizens were serving on Confederate privateers, he was still willing to tell England that they would be treated as pirates and hung for their crimes.

Dispatch No.10 makes it clear that Lincoln expected Britain to respect the blockade. A so-called "paper blockade" was contrary to the Treaty of Paris, and technically could be lawfully ignored – if one dared to do so. Without an international force capable of enforcing either Vattel or Wheaton's laws, those decrees were potentially just "paper edicts". Seward wrote in his dispatch that, "The blockade is now, and it will continue to be so maintained, and therefore we expect it to be respected by Great Britain." If the Confederacy could not get supplies through the blockade, she would lose the war. She had cotton sitting in warehouses, and Europe was running low. Only a few Southern ports had the harbor facilities required to service ships which could slip past Union gunboats at night and race for the open sea and get to Nassau before being caught. Most of the Confederate seaports were deep-draft and well-guarded by Welles' ships. What Jefferson Davis needed were smaller ships that could

William Henry Seward

U.S. secretary of state

Judah Benjamin

Confederate attorney general, secretary of war and later of the Confederate State Department

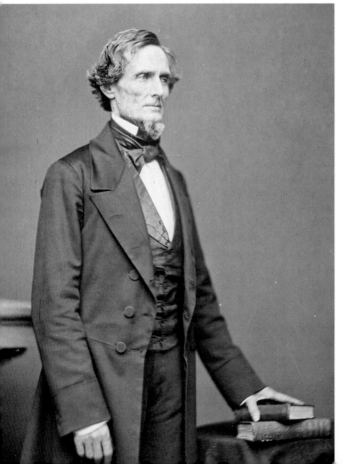

Jefferson Davis

President of the Confederate States of America

Abraham Lincoln

President of the
United States

Lord John
Russell

British foreign
secretary

Napoleon III

Emperor of France

Lord Richard
Lyons

*British minister to
Washington (1858–
1864). Left post
in 1864 due to ill
health. Succeeded by
Sir Frederick Bruce*

Henri Mercier

*French minister to
Washington*

Édouard
Thouvanel

*French minister for
foreign affairs
(1861–1862)*

*Lincoln with his
personal secretaries,*
John G. Nicolay
and John M. Hay

Benjamin
Disraeli

*Conservative
member of
parliament, later
prime minister*

William Ewart Gladstone

Chancellor of the exchequer during the American Civil War (later prime minister)

Charles Francis
Adams, Sr.

*Envoy extraordinary
and minister
plenipotentiary to
British Dominions/
England*

Charles Sumner

Senator from Massachusetts, chair of the Senate Foreign Relations Committee

Henry Shelton Sanford

U.S. minister resident to Belgium and unofficial head of U.S. Secret Service

William Lewis
Dayton

*Envoy extraordinary
and minister
plenipotentiary to
France, 1861–1864*

John Bigelow

*U.S. consul to Paris,
succeeded Dayton
upon his death in
1864 as minister*

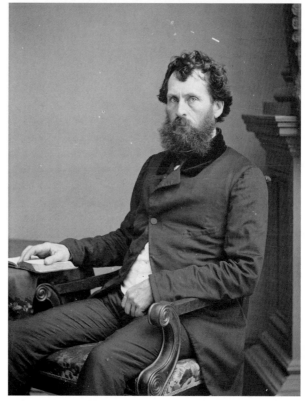

Gideon Welles

*Secretary of the
U.S. Navy*

W.H. Russell

*War correspondent
for The Times.*

Cassius
Marcellus Clay

*Envoy extraordinary
and minister
plenipotentiary
to Russia*

Stephen Mallory

*Confederate secretary
of the Navy*

William Loundes Yancey

Confederate Representative to England, France, Belgium and the Vatican

John Slidell

Confederate representative in Paris

James Mason

Confederate representative in London

Henry Winter Davis

Representative from Maryland, chair of the House Foreign Relations Committee

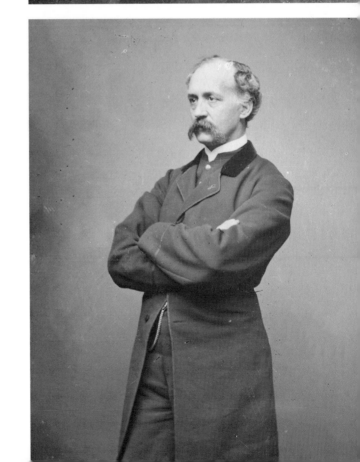

Varina Davis

*Wife of Confederate president,
Jefferson Davis*

John Bright

*Liberal member of parliament,
1843–1889*

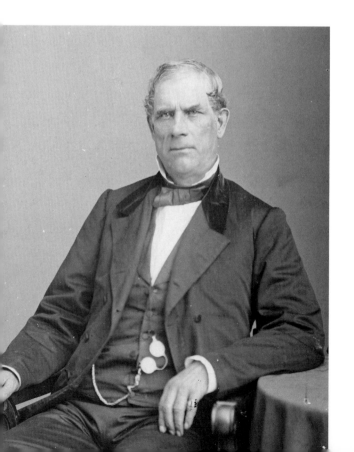

Thurlow Weed

*New York politician
and friend of
William Henry
Seward*

A Rebel Ram *designed to sink ships with an extended prow*

The White House *during the Civil War era*

The Department of State, *drawn by C. Burton, N.Y.*

A view of Washington, *which Lord Lyons considered to be*
"a dusty and dirty village"

get in and out of shallow-draft harbors and channels where the bigger gunboats couldn't go. A shallow harbor with narrow channels were ideally found in Wilmington, North Carolina. After the fall of Charleston, Wilmington took over the burden of supplying the Confederacy. There has been much research into the scope of blockade running and its relative success or failure.[25] Nevertheless, records on both sides show that in the early stages of the war at least, small blockade runners in large numbers made it past Union gunboats to Nassau, Bermuda and Havana where their cotton bales were loaded onto larger commerce steamers for shipment to Liverpool. There, the cotton was checked through the warehouses of Fraser, Trenholm and Company and exchanged for guns, saltpeter, uniforms, shoes and any other war materiel they could secure. Blockade running became very lucrative with some profits running as high as 700% after only three or four trips.[26]

Nassau, Bahamas was closer to the Southern coast than either Bermuda or Cuba, and suddenly became an active place. "The opening of the American Civil War in 1861 had the same electrifying effect on the Bahama Islands as the prince's kiss had on sleeping beauty. The islands suddenly shook off their lethargy of centuries and became the clearing house for trade, intrigue and high adventure."[27] In addition to Fraser Trenholm and Company, Alexander Collie and Company of London played a major role in the blockade running business.[28] Collie had every angle covered. They built runners for the Confederacy. Davis paid for 75% of the ship and Collie 25%. Collie then sold their interest back to the Confederacy, made commissions on the goods arranged for shipment on the boats, charged extra shipping rates to get the goods to the dock and in their spare time also sold cotton bonds at 7%. The blockade ship building business became so active that private contractors like Edward Pembroke paid £46,000 to shipbuilder George Thompson on the Clyde for a ship that the then sold to the Confederacy for over £51,000. Alexander Collie even went so far as to arrange for engravers to be contracted and sent on one of their ships to Richmond to design and print the Confederate currency.

Until the launch of the *Alabama,* Lincoln didn't have the same gun running issues that faced Jefferson Davis. Much historic publicity has been directed to the U.S. Consul based in Liverpool, Thomas

Haines Dudley.[29] The consul reported the results of his surveillance to Charles Francis Adams in London, but sometimes directly to Seward in Washington. Often overlooked, however, is the work done by U.S. minister resident to Belgium, Henry Shelton Sanford, who was responsible for paying and monitoring Dudley. Sanford was especially active during and immediately after the *Trent* Affair with securing guns and ammunition from Austria and shipping them through the port of Hamburg. He also maintained tight surveillance on Confederate purchasing agents in France, England and Belgium, and retained a line of credit at both Barings Bank in London and Bank of Belgium in Brussels. In addition, Sanford monitored the War Department account at the Bank of Belgium for Edwin Stanton. His work coordinating purchasing agents and spies came to the attention of Seward who wrote on May 22, 1862, "My Dear Sanford: I have your private note of the 30th. I cannot tell you how much I prize your courtesy and your energy . . ."[30] Sanford's papers contain a ledger entitled *Account of Disbursements for Secret Service*.[31] In addition to purchasing thousands of guns from Herman Boker, the New York firm with agents in Bonn and Hamburg, Germany, Sanford also paid private detective Ignatius Pollaky[32] to monitor the movements of the top Confederate purchasing agent in London, James Dunwoody Bulloch. Through Pollaky, Sanford knew Bulloch's movements right down to the number and color of the cab he took to various secret locations around London. People like Consul James H. Anderson in Hamburg and purchasing agents like James McDonald, W.S. Bailey and G.A. Smith are little known today. However, after the alarm was raised through Dispatch No.10, they worked hard to secure, insure and ship thousands of guns and tons of gunpowder to Union troops fighting on land and sea. In addition to managing and paying the purchasing agents, Sanford was also busy watching the purchases of Confederate agents. With a substantial line of credit at Barrings Brothers Bank, he was able to outbid and further frustrate Confederate agents who were trying to buy rifles, artillery and saltpeter. Writing to secretary of war Simon Cameron on November 1st, 1861, Sanford states, "Sir: I have the honor to inform you that I have succeeded in buying on account of the Govt. Retail contract for

72,000 stand of arms which were about going forward via (Le) Havre and Hamburg for the enemy."[33]

Sanford's favorite arms supplier was Herman Boker and Company. In addition to outbidding Confederate agents, Sanford also pushed his suppliers to speed up production and deliver their goods earlier than the contract date. November 14, 1861 to Simon Cameron, "Sir: In pursuance of your Instructions, I have agreed to advance to Herman Boker and Co. on condition of forwarding 60,000 guns at from 30 to 60 days earlier date than were otherwise possible."[34]

Simon Cameron was forced out as secretary of war on January 14, 1862. Lincoln didn't think he was up to the job, and Cameron was succeeded by Edwin Stanton. However, here is at least one instance where Cameron was willing to pay a $400 "incentive" to have his guns delivered sooner than originally contracted.

Lincoln ends Dispatch No. 10 by reminding the British that they signed the Treaty of Paris in 1856 which outlawed privateering. Business was business, however. Even members of parliament like William Shaw Lindsay, who was a shipbuilder, were making significant profits from the Civil War. The approval of Dispatch No. 10 and subsequent publication in 1862 of the original, unrevised dispatch suggest that Lincoln and Seward were not emperor and shogun, but more of the same mind regarding relations with England. Lincoln always chose his written words carefully. His edited Dispatch No. 10 and the published 1862 original show a president and secretary of state of like mind regarding the possible foreign relations threat to the successful prosecution of the Civil War. It is known that members of parliament read the unedited version of Dispatch No. 10 when it was published a year later. The difference between the two men lies in the fact that Lincoln conducted himself in a manner which left him room to maneuver. He didn't burn his bridges as Seward was quick to do. Both men were more like-minded than historians have formerly understood. They differed lay more in process and style, not in actual sentiment and intention. Dispatch No. 10 was sent on May 21, 1861. The winter of 1861–1862, however, would prove to be the first real test of the Lincoln/Seward foreign policy.

CHAPTER 7

ONE WAR AT A TIME

We cannot prevent the conveyance of contraband goods without searching
neutral vessels that we meet at sea: We have therefore a right to search them. If
we find an enemy's effects on board ship, we seize them by rights of war.

Emmerich de Vattel, *The Law of Nations*, 1758

On January 7, 1862, Minister to Russia, Cassius Marcellus Clay, wrote
to William Henry Seward about the extent to which he believed that
Europe was interested in the American Civil War. Clay wrote, "The
monarchies of Europe have always regarded our republic with jealousy
and distrust, because it was an ever-living protest against any other than
self-government. They are injured by us, because the immigration to us
of men, money, and the arts, is to them a great and increasing loss. They
have just cause to fear us because of our expansion by the acquisition of
territory."[1] Territorial acquisition involved the Louisiana Purchase from
France, the acquisition of Florida from Spain, and Seward's constant
threats to annex all or parts of Canada. European dominions in the
Caribbean were also seen as being vulnerable to the grasp of the State
Department. With the exception of Lords Russell and Lyons, the letters
and official dispatches of European heads of state and their Ministers
contain few references to the Civil War in the early stages. Most of
Europe was distracted by war, annexation and threat of impending war.
Prussia threatened to annex Schleswig-Holstein. She was led by a man
who believed that God needed him more than he needed God. The man

was Otto von Bismarck. He kept Lord John Russell busy at the Foreign Office because England feared the increasing German nationalism which grew stronger after the defeat of Napoleon Bonaparte. Prussia and Austria saw an opportunity when the Danish King was unable to produce an heir. Both Schleswig and Holstein contained large German populations which wanted to be part of the evolving German confederation. France was anxious to see that the Italian states became unified and out from under the control of Austria. That was to Louis Napoleon's benefit. In the middle of this, the Holy See wanted their independence as well. England and France were loosely allied as a result of their participation in the Crimean War, but neither one fully trusted the other. Russia was an exception to European politics, however. Clay was receiving his information from one of the most experienced and respected diplomats in Europe, Russian Prince Alexander Gorchakov.

Most historians believe that Europe was still more anxious about matters in their own backyard. Did Europe take serious notice of the war in America? There are those who say that democracy itself was on trial, and that aristocrats and the laborer both took notice, but for different reasons. The aristocracy hoped that their hold on the social order would be maintained by the failure of the democratic "experiment". They wanted to be able to say "I told you so." Others claim that the millworkers in Liverpool were very mindful of the turmoil in America because they considered themselves as slaves also. Freeing the slaves meant freeing them as well. Freedom through the suffrage movements that Russell championed and Palmerston vetoed. From a practical standpoint, few kings, queens or heads of state took their eyes off America, however. The United States was an excellent commercial partner, and she had an ironclad navy that was growing dangerously large. As a trading partner, the Southern states were very dependent on being able to import inexpensive goods from Europe, especially England. Ever since George Washington bought more than he could afford from Britain, Americans had been controlled by English merchants because of the massive debts accumulated from buying on credit. It was easier for the cotton planters of the South to buy what they needed from England with the high quality cotton that only came from the southern states. Northern manufacturers, however, wanted to be able to sell their products to those cotton planters and cut out the British. How to do this? Increase the tariffs on imported goods. In 1860, the tariff increased the price of imported products by 15%. On March 2, 1864, Congress passed a tariff that increased the price of imported goods to 35% by 1865. This hurt the South, which was so dependent on foreign imports. When seeking to convince the British Foreign Office that Confederate recognition was important, William Yancey stated that the reason for the split and Civil War was due to the long history of tariff issues between North and South – not slavery. England was sensitive to the tariff which hurt business. Palmerston was clear in stating that the British were upset with the tariff.[2] However, despite the duty, Napoleon III initially was much more concerned with Italy and Austria. This would soon change with his policy toward Mexico. England and France had a vested economic interest in a quick resolution to the Civil War. The question often arises, however, as to just how critical the Civil War was to the Western World at this time? Yes, Europe had serious issues. Although the economy of Britain and France was suffering due to the cotton situation, there were many who were making money from the war. The list of the companies who were making substantial war profits is long, but includes Alexander Collie and Company, Herman Boker and Company, Willoughbe, Willoughbe and Ponsonby as well as many others. Historian Alan Nevins has suggested that war with America would have serious long-term consequences.

> "It is hardly too much to say that the future of the world as we know it was at stake. A conflict between Great Britain and America would have crushed all hope of the mutual understanding and growing collaboration which led up to the practical alliance of 1917–18, and the outright alliance which began in 1941. Anglo-French intervention in the American conflict would probably have confirmed the splitting and consequent weakening of the United States; might have given French power in Mexico a long lease, with the ruin of the Monroe Doctrine; and would perhaps have led to the Northern conquest of Canada. The forces of political liberalism in the modern world would have received a disastrous setback. No battle, not Gettysburg, not the Wilderness, was more important than the context waged in the diplomatic arena and the forum of public opinion. The popular conception of this contest is at some points erroneous, and at a few grossly fallacious ...."[3]

The United States was occupied and distracted by a "rebellion" that made her appear vulnerable in the eyes of Europe. Two weeks after Lincoln took the oath of office, Spain forced the annexation of Santo Domingo (Dominican Republic) to her empire. Expansion was on the minds of many European nations at this time. The U.S. State Department took notice. In Dispatch No.19 on November 12, 1862, Bayard Taylor explains to Seward the real issue that Russia fears from the Civil War in America. He wrote, "What Russia evidently fears at present is the ultimate exhaustion of the two sections of the union, which will leave them either divided or united, helpless to resist the encroachments of hostile powers. The political equilibrium which she sees in the maintenance of the union in its original strength would thus be destroyed."[4] There were other threats to the Americas, however.

As Napoleon III was invading Mexico and ignoring the Monroe Doctrine, the rest of Europe paused over another matter and first took serious notice of events in North America. The concern was not the pillaging of men, money and the arts as claimed by Clay. The problem was that a Union captain, Charles Wilkes, forcibly removed two Confederate envoys from a British mail ship, the *RMS Trent*. The facts about the crisis and the ultimate resolution are important, but not as significant as it eventually was to the power and authority of the British Empire itself.

The basic facts of the *Trent* Affair are relatively simple and well-known. On November 8, 1861, Captain Charles Wilkes, aboard the *San Jacinto*, intercepted the *Trent* on the high seas off the coast of Cuba. On board were Confederate ministers James Mason, John Slidell, their secretaries and some members of their families. Mason and Slidell had evaded the Union Blockade of Charleston by slipping quietly out at 1am on the night of October 12. Blockade runners were often painted a dull grey so that they were harder to detect at night, and burned smokeless anthracite coal to help avoid detection. Many were equipped with powerful engines whose steam-driven paddle wheels could cruise at 26 revolutions per minute. When pursued by federal cruisers, they could sprint at 33 revolutions per minute. They were built for speed.

Before reaching England, brief accounts of the Mason and Slidell mission appeared in the Northern newspapers. It has been suggested that the mission was so well-publicized, that the publicity itself became an incentive for the captain of the *San Jacinto*, Charles Wilkes, to capture the ship and seize the Confederate envoys. This is unlikely. The *New York Times* of October 31, 1861 reprinted an article from the *Richmond Examiner* on October 29. The article read, in part, "By this time our able representatives abroad, Messrs. MASON and SLIDELL, are pretty well on their way over the briny deep towards the shores of Europe … The malice of our Yankee enemies will thus be foiled, and the attempt to capture them fail of success." Most of the *Times* articles in October, 1861 discussed generals, soldiers and battles. The cotton shortage in Europe and the work of privateers was occasionally mentioned. The Confederate mission to Europe was given little attention. This is not surprising because there were already three Southern representatives in England trying to secure assistance. William Loundes Yancey, Pierre Rost and Ambrose Dudley Mann had been wearing out their boots as well as their welcome since February. They found sympathy and encouragement among the British and French upper classes, but no practical result. Of the two new commissioners to Europe, John Slidell was the most skillful. "In John Slidell of Louisiana the Confederacy possessed its ablest diplomatic agent."[5] If the team of Slidell and Benjamin could not get help from Europe, nobody else on the Davis team could come close. John Slidell was posted to Paris and James Mason to London.[6]

Lords Russell and Palmerston were surprised at the publicity around the *Trent* because they didn't see that the presence of two more Confederate representatives would make any difference. The three already in England were ready to give up and go home. What difference could two more make? Nevertheless, there was immediate jubilation in both the North and the South. Jefferson Davis may have hoped that a dispute would arise between England and the Union which would give the Confederacy room to maneuver. His statement to his Congress in Richmond suggests as much. According to Davis, "The United States have thus claimed a general jurisdiction over the high seas, and entering a British ship, sailing under its country's flag, have violated the rights of embassy, for the most part held sacred even amongst barbarians, by seizing our ministers while under the protection and within the dominions of a neutral nation." It has been suggested that the publicity in the newspapers over the mission was done by Davis to encourage interception. Southern newspapers wrote that they hoped the *Trent* crisis would cause a war with England, and thus give the Confederacy a chance. The New Orleans *Daily Picayune* from January 3, 1862 told its readers that, "We may reasonably estimate the chances of a serious conflict between Great Britain and the United States as highly probable at an early day." Regardless of what may have prompted the Davis government, England was outraged at the seizure aboard one of her ships and demanded an apology and their immediate release. It didn't matter that Britain had used the same search and seizure tactics on American ships in 1812. For his part, Captain Wilkes was acting as he knew maritime relations to have been conducted for the past fifty years. Accepted international law allowed belligerent nations to search the ships of neutrals suspected of carrying contraband to the enemy. He believed that the Confederate commissioners were contraband as well as the dispatches they were carrying from Davis to the British Foreign Office. The persons of Mason and Slidell were thought of as "human dispatches" capable of remembering vital information which they could repeat to their agents and contacts in Europe. However, in 1812, the contraband Britain seized were sailors who sought to emigrate to America. Allegedly, Winston Churchill stated many years later that the Royal Navy was characterized by "rum, sodomy and the lash." By 1812, many English sailors decided to jump ship and start over in America. They enjoyed the rum, but hadn't bargained for sodomy and the lash. The original Russell note on the capture of the Confederate envoys was typically sharp and curt. It read:

> "Her Majesty's Government, having taken the facts into consideration, have arrived at the conclusion that the conduct of the Commander of the *San Jacinto* was not justified by international law. Certain individuals have been taken from on board a ship of a neutral Power, which was proceeding on a lawful and innocent voyage. Her Majesty's Government are unwilling to imagine that the United States Government will not of their own accord be anxious to afford ample reparation for this act of violence committed by an officer of the United States Navy against a neutral and friendly nation. The reparation which Her Majesty's Government expect and with which they would be satisfied would be: 1. The liberation of the four gentlemen captured, and their delivery to your lordship, with a view to their being again placed under British protection. 2. An apology for the insult offered to the British flag."

Albert, the Prince Consort, husband of Queen Victoria, was dying. He had sufficient strength and good sense, however, to realize the unnecessary danger in which Russell had placed England. He wrote an alternative note and requested that this be sent to Seward via Richard Lyons. It read:

> "Her Majesty's Government, bearing in mind the friendly relations which have long subsisted between Great Britain and the United States, are willing to believe that the United States naval officer who committed this aggression was not acting in compliance with any authority from his Government, or that, if he conceived himself to be so authorized, he greatly misunderstood the instructions which he had received. For the Government of the United States must be fully aware that the British Government could not allow such an affront to the national honour to pass without full reparation; and Her Majesty's Government are unwilling to believe that it could be the deliberate intention of the Government of the United States unnecessarily to force into discussion between the two Governments a question of so grave a character, and with regard to which the whole British Nation would be sure to entertain such unanimity of feeling. Her Majesty's Government therefore trust that, when this matter shall have been brought under the consideration of the United States, that Government will of its own accord offer to the British Government such redress as alone could satisfy the British nation, namely, the liberation of the four gentlemen, and their delivery to your Lordship, in order that they may again be placed under British protection, and a suitable apology for the aggression which has been committed. Should these terms not be offered by Mr. Seward you will propose them to him."

It has always been suggested by historians that the dying Prince was the hero who saw the needless danger in the Russell note, and recommended changes to the Queen. Subsequent research, however, has shown that the Queen herself was also in favor of modifying the note. Any such diplomatic communication would normally have come to her from her prime minister – not her husband. Victoria was sufficiently concerned that this matter might get out of control that she wrote a note in her own hand to Palmerston expressing her concern. Further confirmation of the Queen's proactive role comes from Seward's eyes and ears in Europe, Thurlow Weed. Having lunch with Russell at his estate, Lord John recommended that Weed take a walk in the garden and enjoy the view. Lady Russell accompanied him and took him aside and commented that, "Ladies you know are not supposed to have any knowledge of public affairs. But, we have eyes and ears, and sometimes use them.

In these troubles about the taking of some men from under the protection of our flag, it may be some encouragement to you to know that the Queen is distressed at what she hears, and is deeply anxious for an amicable settlement."[7] Palmerston and Russell displayed a lack of good judgment at this stage. Victoria and Prince Albert wanted to give Lincoln a way out. Whether or not the seizure of the *Trent* was approved by the Union government was not important. Albert's words generously suggested that Lincoln did not have previous knowledge of or authorize the seizure of the commissioners.

History has shown that Secretary Seward wrote a conciliatory note stating that Wilkes acted on his own. That note was written after the dying prince consort personally toned down an otherwise harsh note originally drafted by Richard Russell. This new dispatch allowed the Lincoln government to save face by allowing them to proclaim that the only fault lay in not taking the ship, with commissioners aboard, to a neutral prize court for adjudication. The closest prize court, however, was in Key West. Some historians have given Seward credit for averting war with Britain. Seward's note stated that the Union had not broken international law. He conceded that Wilkes acted on his own, and made his only mistake by not taking the *Trent* to port for adjudication in the appropriate prize court. Mason and Slidell were released and war was averted.

Years after the fact, Charles Francis Adams believed that Seward was the hero who saved the Union. Yet, in this critical early period of the Civil War, Adams was highly critical of Seward. In a letter dated December 20, 1861 to his son Charles Jr., the senior Adams referred to Seward as the "... *bête noire* ... who would eat all Englishmen raw." Yet, later in 1873, he changed his mind and praised Seward for his work as secretary of state and separately for his handling of the *Trent* Affair. As secretary of state, Adams stated, "The marvelous fertility of his pen spread itself at once over every important point on the globe... The effect of this was that, from a state of utter demoralization at the outset, the foreign service rapidly became the most energetic and united organization thus far made abroad." Regarding the *Trent* Affair specifically, Adams credited Seward with averting war. He stated in 1873, "In my firm belief, that act (*Trent* note to Russell) saved the unity of the nation. It was like the fable of the Roman Curtius, who leaped into the abyss which could have been closed in no other way." Adams correctly praised Seward for that "marvelous fertility" in his written communication. There is no doubt that the final note to Lord Lyons releasing the Confederate commissioners was well-written and ultimately satisfied the Foreign Office. Seward may take credit for writing the note, but whether or not the original proposal to release Mason and Slidell came from him is a matter for some discussion.

When the Lincoln cabinet met to discuss the *Trent* crisis and determine a course of action, historians are divided as to the recommendations of individual cabinet members. There is also much dispute as to the position taken by Lincoln. Some say that he didn't want to give them up, and others say that he realized that they were a liability to his ultimate goal of restoring the Union without interference from Europe. Nicolay and Hay were not sure. They knew there was an initial meeting between only Lincoln and Seward on the matter, of which they noted, "Of the first confidential interview between the Secretary of State and the President on this important topic, there is no record."[8] Lincoln's December 3, 1861 message to Congress contained no direct reference to the *Trent* crisis. However, Lincoln indirectly stated how he felt about the matter. He stated in his message, "I venture to hope it will appear that we have practiced prudence and liberality towards foreign powers averting causes of irritation; and with firmness, maintaining our own rights and honor." In Dispatch No.735, Lyons to Russell on December 3, 1861, Lyons did not see Lincoln's words as those of conciliation and possible release of the Confederate commissioners. He may not have had adequate time to analyze and reflect on the message. Lyons tells Russell that he is sending him four copies of Lincoln's message to Congress. He admits he has not had time to read the message, but was told that it contained no mention of the *Trent*.

This was a very difficult time for England. Prince Albert died on December 14, 1861. Lord John Russell wrote to Lord Cowley on December 16 that the queen was doing the best she could under the circumstances. She was strong, but Russell thought her strength was nothing more than a quick rebound from the shock of the death of her husband. With her husband gone, Queen Victoria was in no position to help or recommend a course of action in the *Trent* matter. Writing back to Russell in the third person on December 25, "The Queen feels the kindness of Lord Russell's expressions. She is bowed to the earth-utterly broken-hearted and desolate . . ."

In Washington, the president asked his secretary of state to write what he thought should be the response to England, while Lincoln proposed to write his own. The president wrote his memorandum in the person of the secretary of state. Ultimately, any note would go out in Seward's name, regardless of the true author. Lincoln's memo is dated December, 1861 (no day). In this memo, Lincoln did not recommend the release of Mason and Slidell. He wanted to use the situation to complain about Britain's neutrality proclamation which had encouraged the privateers attempting to break the blockade, pillage and sink Union commercial shipping, and otherwise evade the blockade through Mexico. Finally, he ended the memo with an offer to submit the issue to arbitration. He stated that, ". . . the government of the United States will, if agreed to by Her Majesty's government, go to such friendly arbitration as is usual among nations, and will abide by the result award." Nicolay and Hay suggested that Lincoln wanted to release the prisoners. They wrote that while Seward was drafting his reply, "It is probable, therefore, that, even while writing this draft, Lincoln had intimated to his Secretary of State the need of finding good diplomatic reasons for surrendering the prisoners."[9] This would be consistent with Lincoln's desire for "one war at a time." In addition to this, Lincoln made a conciliatory comment to Alexander Galt, the Canadian finance minister who was in Washington at the time of the *Trent* Affair. When Galt asked Lincoln what he planned to do, the president characteristically remarked, "Oh, that'll be gotten along with." Lincoln did not say that he favored release. However, this remark is consistent with one war at a time and the wish to see the matter settled in a way did not involve war or even protracted negotiations.

Regarding Seward's intentions, the diary of Edward Bates, however, suggests otherwise. He recorded that the substance of the Seward reply was read to the cabinet for discussion. That discussion focused on the belief that the war of rebellion with the Confederacy would probably be lost if the Union also had to defend itself against the Anglo-French alliance. According to Bates, "There was general reluctance on the part of some of the cabinet – and even the President himself – to acknowledge these obvious truths." Gideon Welles applauded the actions of Captain Wilkes. According to some, Lincoln initially took a hard line over British demands. Some believed that Seward saw his finest hour in recommending the release of the emissaries and avoiding war. Secretary Welles paints another picture, however. According to Welles:

> "The truth is, not only had the president expressed his doubts of the legality of the capture, and had them increased, while Mr. Seward was rejoicing over and approving of the proceeding ... Mr. Seward took a totally different view (to the release of Mason and Slidell); scouted the idea of letting the prisoners go; said that the British did not want them, and we could not think of delivering them up ... Nearly every member of the administration, like Mr. Seward, rejoiced in the capture of these mischievous men."[10]

Wells suggested that Seward was manipulated by the British foreign office rather than the hero who saved the union. According to Welles "Mr. Seward was at the beginning opposed to any idea of concession which involved giving up the emissaries, but yielded at once, and with dexterity, to the peremptory demand of Great Britain."[11] Welles frequently disagreed with the actions of the secretary of state. Like many, Welles considered Seward a politician first and a public servant second. The dexterity Welles mentioned was recognized by many others. Seward had quick political reflexes which allowed him to comprehend issues and their potential impact. This ambitious posture won him few friends. What does Edward Bates say about the issue?

Before the cabinet discussion on the *Trent*, Bates had gone to the Anacostia River with Lincoln to watch the construction of pontoon bridges. While there, he saw a man "walk on water" with a small pontoon on each foot and a paddle to help him remain upright and paddle across the river. In the next paragraph, Bates writes, "1861, December 25 Cabinet Council at 10 a.m. to consider [sic] the relations with England, and on Lord Lyons' demand on the surrender of Mason and Slidell. Long and interesting session lasting until 2 p.m."[12] According to Bates, Lyons' letter was read to the cabinet members. Secretary Seward had already prepared a reply and this was read to the group. At this point, Sumner and Lincoln had already met on the matter, and Sumner had given the president his advice. Seward and Lincoln had also held a discussion prior to the cabinet meeting. Lincoln may have advised Seward as to the position to be taken. Before discussing the reply and the initial opinions of the members of the cabinet, Bates inserted some interesting facts he didn't think were known to the others present. Essentially, he declared that the entire matter had been deliberately staged. At this point, Senator Charles Sumner walked into the cabinet room at Lincoln's request. Lincoln trusted the Senator's judgment, and thought that his presence would help insulate the administration from attack by Congress on the matter. Sumner entered the room and read a letter from member of parliament John Bright which claimed that Mason, Slidell and Captain Wilkes had dined together in Havana and arranged the capture there. Although Bates doubts the allegations, he doesn't doubt the threat the incident posed for the Union. He stated, "But on the part of Mason and Slidell, the policy is obvious, and they could bring on a rupture between us and England – actual war." Bates stated that the matter was further complicated by the fact that France would take sides with England. He believed that the French economy was seriously damaged by the Union blockade of Southern ports.

France couldn't get cotton, and she couldn't sell her commercial goods to any of the Southern states. What is significant about Bates' discussion of the *Trent* is that in the margins of one diary page he repeats a rumor that Seward had authorized the seizure of Mason and Slidell. He stated, "In this same conversation the count said that it was well enough to give Captain Wilkes the credit of originality and boldness in seizing mason and Slidell, but in fact the Secy. Of State sent orders to the consul at Havanna [sic] to notify Wilkes and tell him what to do."[13] The next insertion in the diary relates to the fact that his offices were closed on Thanksgiving Day and he took no exercise. Bates made no further comment on the Seward allegation. The State Department files contain no reference to Seward making any such recommendation to Wilkes. Few historians believe that the secretary of state had anything to do with authorizing the capture of the Confederate envoys. Lyons and Russell were also skeptical. They knew that the previous group of Confederate representatives still in London at that time had achieved little. They didn't think that the addition of Mason and Slidell to that already flat mix would do any harm, nor any good for the Southern cause.

The personality and temperament of Captain Charles Wilkes suggests that he didn't need any help from Henry Seward to take the action he did against the *RMS Trent*. Wilkes was sixty-two years old when the Civil War broke out. He had already achieved success as the man who had accurately charted the waters from Rio de Janeiro to the Arctic. He is credited with discovering the Antarctic. Wilkes, however, was a strict captain and disciplinarian. He was court-marshaled twice for ordering severe punishments of his men and officers. At sixty-two, Wilkes found himself stranded ashore and chairman of the Lighthouse Board. When the *San Jacinto* stopped the *RMS Trent*, Wilkes was supposed to be sailing his boat back to Philadelphia from Africa. He decided to take the long route home and look for Southern blockade runners along the way. While looking for the *Sumter*, he heard about the *Trent*. Warned by his first officer, Donald Fairfax, that seizing the ship of a neutral country was going to cause trouble, Wilkes ignored him and went after the British mail packet anyway.

Senator Sumner maintained his communication with Cobden and Bright during this time. He told Cobden in a letter of December 31, 1861, "On reaching Washington for the opening of Congress, I learned from the President and from Mr. Seward that neither had committed himself on the *Trent* affair, and that it was absolutely an unauthorized act. Seward told me that he was reserving himself in order to see what view England would take."[14] According to Sumner, therefore, Seward at this stage was neither for nor against the release of the commissioners.

On October 18, Mason and Slidell were in Cuba anticipating a successful arrival in England later in the month. They had not run into Charles Wilkes as yet. In Dispatch No.569, Lyons to Russell on October 18, 1861, Lord Lyons wrote about Seward's circular to the governors of seaboard states. Lyons believed that the circular was probably another Seward bluff to help ensure that England did not attempt intervention in the rebellion. The Seward circular of October 14, 1861 went to the Governors of all the eastern seaboard states. Before the departure of Mason and Slidell, Congress in Washington had adjourned. With the fear that Europe may now intervene in the Civil War and break the blockade, Seward warned the states on the eastern seacoast that they should consider improving their own individual fortifications through state funds.

Lyons tells Russell that he doesn't anticipate much disturbance in the North because, "It can hardly be supposed that the government can attribute much importance to the presence of two additional Confederate agents in Europe; or indeed if they did, that they would resort to so futile an expedient to counteract the proceedings of these gentlemen." Lyons underestimated Captain Charles Wilkes.

Faced with what he may have believed would be catastrophic results if the Union went to war with England over the subsequent *Trent* seizure on November 8, William Henry Seward clearly saw that this was not the place for bluster. He was always willing to walk to the edge of the precipice, but not jump over. For Bates, the cabinet discussions clearly outlined the possible results of a war with England. According to Bates, "The first and immediate effect would be, to withdraw all our forces, land and naval from the Southern coast-the suspension of all our revenue from customs. The distruction [sic] of our foreign commerce. The probable capture of our sea ports – and ills innumerable – The scene would be reversed! The Southern coast would be open and the northern blockaded." [15] The actions and words of Seward and the *de facto* secretary of state, Charles Sumner can only be confirmed by the diaries and letters which exist. Adams claimed that Seward saved the day. Welles, Sumner and Bates dispute this. It is believed that Lincoln listened carefully to Sumner's reading of the letters from Cobden and Bright. According to the Senator, his immediate reaction to the seizure of the Confederate commissioners was to release them. Those letters recommend that the matter be arbitrated. Sumner supported this and told Bright in a letter of December 30 that, "I spoke with the President several times on arbitration, and proposed Russia . . ." [16] Sumner tells us that he had many meetings with Lincoln on the matter prior to the Christmas morning meeting at the Executive Mansion. Some of those meetings involved a discussion of the opinions of Cobden and Bright. Writing to Bright on December 30, Sumner stated, "All of the letters, including that of December 14, I have sent to the President . . ." To Cobden on December 31, he wrote, "I cannot thank you enough for your constant and most instructive letters down to 12 December. Not a word has been lost. I have read them all to the President . . ." In the letter to Cobden of the 31st, Sumner claims to speak for the president and his cabinet on the *Trent* matter. Acting as *de facto* secretary of state, he stated, "Will the settlement of the *Trent* case be accepted in England as definitive? I fear not. The war fever is too intense; and I fear there is a foregone determination in the public mind to have war with the United States. Can this be? This must be stopped. We are in earnest for peace. I can speak for the President and his cabinet."[17]

In the end, all agreed that his final response to Lyons was well-written. Adams believed that he saved the day and thus the country. This is disputed by Welles, Bates and Sumner. With Welles and Sumner often at odds with Seward, it is difficult to evaluate their response and reaction to Seward. However, Seward's consistent antipathy and public bluster towards England would suggest that his initial reaction was either to retain the commissioners or at the least, wait and watch England's reaction. Seward's eyes and ears in London was Thurlow Weed. His letter of January 8, 1862 to Seward confirms his understanding that the secretary did not want to give up the commissioners. Weed is irritated and complains, "I ought to be content with being left in the dark as to what you intend, when Mr. Adams continues in 'blissful' ignorance. To be indebted to British ministers for what he knows about negotiations at Washington, is not either profitable or helpful. I infer from the previous private note from you to Mr. Adams that M & S are not to be given up."[17] This letter was written after the decision to release had been made. However, mail communication took time, and Weed could not have known of the decision in Washington. In view of the well-documented penchant for making decisions based upon the politics of the moment, we may reasonably conclude that Seward really didn't know what to do at first. Sumner had stated that the secretary told him that he wanted to wait and see what England was going to do. That was probably Seward's first thoughts to himself. Lincoln's December 3 message to Congress suggested that he was probably for either releasing the commissioners or sending the matter to arbitration. We know that Lincoln wanted one war at a time, and that would be consistent with release or arbitration. Regardless of initial intentions, everyone breathed a sigh of relief. Even the normally nationalistic and combative *Times* commented on page eight of the January 9, 1862 edition, "Twenty-four hours after the message from Washington which we reported yesterday the cabinet of the

Federal States' government broke its silence, and the Old World is no longer at enmity with the New ... We draw a long breath and are thankful." Unfortunately, the *Times* ended the article with a statement that completely ignored the lessons of the war of 1812, "The government of the Federal States has done in mere wantonness what no nation of the Old World had ever dared to do."

The incident involving the *Trent* brings up one of the more mysterious chapters in the diplomatic career of William Henry Seward. In March, 1862, William Schaw Lindsay went to Paris to meet with Napoleon III on his own. Lindsay was a ship owner and former member of parliament with a vested interest in Confederate recognition to help break the blockade and secure cotton. When he returned to London after his meeting, Lindsay sought out Benjamin Disraeli and repeated the substance of his conversation with the emperor. What happened next surprised him. "Disraeli declared that Lord John Russell was bound by a secret agreement with Mr. Seward not to break the blockade and not to recognize the Confederacy." Somehow, this information came to John Slidell who repeated it in Dispatch No.6, April 18, 1862, to Judah Benjamin.[19] Such a secret agreement, if it existed, must have generated a *quid pro quo* at the Foreign Office.

This secret pact raises a number of questions. What did the British get out of this and when and how did they get it? Is it possible that this agreement was part of the deal to release Mason and Slidell? If so, how did discussion of such a sensitive matter take place? How did Seward communicate with Russell? Did Lincoln and Palmerston know?

Government mail to Europe was carried by government steamer. Lyons also sent his dispatches by steamer from New York under the protection of Admiral Milne. Lyons' dispatches make no mention of such an agreement. However, having no necessity to go through Lyons, Seward could have gone through a private envoy and trusted friend like Thurlow Weed.[20] Weed left for Europe on November 8, 1861. This was as the *Trent* crisis was unfolding. Weed remained in Europe until March, 1862. He was Seward's most trusted friend and would have been in a position to discuss a secret deal at that time. Other than the claim by Disraeli as reported by Slidell to Benjamin, is there any other evidence that a deal had been struck? Indirectly, there is language in several dispatches from Lyons to Russell that Seward had softened his attitude towards England at this time. On April 7, 1862, Lyons and Seward concluded the treaty which allowed each country to search each-others ships suspected of carrying slaves. Much of the work was done by Lyons, but he agreed to give the credit to Seward so that passage of the bill would be smoother in the U.S. Congress. Under the circumstances, this is viewed as a reasonable tactic, but may it also suggest that a separate deal had been struck? On April, 18, Benjamin Disraeli repeated remarks made by Napoleon to William Schaw Lindsay about a secret agreement between Seward and Russell. Around this time, one of Lyons' early biographers, Thomas Legh, Second Baron Newton states in early 1862, right after the conclusion of the *Trent* Affair, that "Mr. Seward's demeanor towards England had changed so much, that in early 1862 his friendliness had become actually embarrassing."[21] This represents quite a change from someone who formerly wanted to "eat all Englishmen raw." Something had happened. Although a mission of this type would have been sensitive enough to force Seward to commit his instructions to Weed orally and not in writing, did Weed carry anything in writing with him to Europe? The only written "instructions" Seward gave Weed was a short note to give to Charles Francis Adams to smooth over any apprehension that Weed was sent to supersede the minister. It should be noted that the Weed mission was approved by Lincoln before the *Trent* Affair. Seward's "instructions" are dated November 7. So, at first, Thurlow Weed's only objective was to help Seward better understand the mood in England and counter any anti-Union feeling wherever it may be found. He had his hands full on both counts. Weed arrived at Le Havre on November 24 and first went to Paris, not London. In London, it was believed that battlefield losses and the threat of war over Mason and Slidell would result in Lincoln seeking peace and the recognition of the Confederacy. The *London Star and Dial* reported that, "It is nothing less than the express conviction of Mr. Seward that the United States government cannot succeed in this war, and that the Confederacy will probably be recognized by European powers, and that peace will result in sixty days." This did not happen. Weed left Paris and met with Lord Russell in London. He remained there for four months, and would have had time to receive subsequent instructions from Seward relative to resolving the *Trent* issue. The Seward papers indicate that communication between Henry Seward and his close friend Thurlow Weed ran from May 4, 1831 to the secretary's death in 1872. The largest volume of communication occurred between December 2, 1861 and February, 1862 – right at the height of the *Trent* crisis.[22] Most of the communication from Weed to Seward concerns that excitement for war that was spread by the London papers. One letter contained a warning that Seward's threats to annex Canada if the Confederate States were recognized was generating some of the war fever. If we may assume that Seward's covert instructions to Weed, in a particularly sensitive matter were oral, it is curious that a December 30, 1861 letter to Weed contains an unexpected request. The last two paragraphs of the letter state: "Do tell Mr. Adams that he had known all that I could know here, as fast as I knew it. I have had to feel my way. Don't lose your pocketbook or, if you are going to, *burn my letters first.* (emphasis added)"[23] If Weed offered to make a secret deal with Lord Russell, when would this have taken place? Did Weed have any written notes or comments on the meeting? Thurlow Weed went to the home of Lord Russell on December 13. He met with the head of the British Foreign Office for an hour. In his privately-published account of the meeting, Weed only states, "Although I am not at liberty to give to the readers of the Journal what was said on a question as delicate as that now pending, I may say that the visit in other respects was an interesting one."[24] Also of interest was a meeting between Gideon Welles and Secretary Seward on the subject of the Laird Rams.

Gideon Welles records an intriguing incident in his diary from September, 1862. At a cabinet meeting on the 18th, the matter of the Laird Rams had come up. As navy secretary, Welles was understandably concerned. When he cornered Seward on the matter, an unexpected and strange scenario took place. Not wanting to discuss the Rams at the cabinet meeting, Welles followed Seward back to the state department and questioned him further as to whether or not Seward had any information that the British government was prepared to let the rams depart. Thomas Dudley, the consul in Liverpool, had sent Charles Francis Adams a message indicating that the rams were definitely going to be allowed to leave. When Welles would not allow Seward to avoid the subject, Welles was surprised when Seward, "said he wanted to tell me a secret which I must not communicate to any living person ... . He must enjoin upon me especially not to tell the President, not let him know I had been informed." It seemed that Seward had been keeping a secret from Lincoln. Seward hesitated and took a deep breath. "If England lets these vessels out, we must let loose our privateers. Well, they won't come out ... They will be retained in port, but you must not know this fact, nor must anyone else know it. Mr. Adams is not aware of it."[25] So, immediately after the *Trent* captives were released, relations between England and the Lincoln government begin to improve quickly. The Seward/ Lyons slave treaty was signed, and credit was given to Seward; the Disraeli assertion was made that a secret deal had been struck between Seward and Russell; Seward's attitude toward Britain had softened to the extent that it was considered "embarrassing"; Welles learns of another secret Seward/Russell deal that the Laird Rams will not be allowed to sail – despite Thomas Haines Dudley's statement that they were not going to be detained; Seward's letter to Weed, while in London at the height of the war scare, that he should *burn* his (Seward's) letters; and Weed's evasive comment on the details of his meeting with Lord Russell regarding the *Trent* issue. In the end, it is impossible to confirm whether or not oral instructions were given to Weed relative to proposing a deal with Lord Russell, i.e. the Confederate commissioners will be released and Seward will stop bashing Britain in exchange for retaining the Laird Rams and extending greater diplomatic cooperation with the Lincoln State Department in future matters concerning the war. However, the circumstantial evidence supports the belief that a secret deal was made. Weed's substantial correspondence during the crisis period provide no clues.[26] In fact, he spends much of his time complaining about the fact that Seward's bad-boy reputation has made his (Weed's) job that much more difficult. There are no private Seward letters on this crisis to either Adams, Russell or Palmerston. Nevertheless, the circumstantial evidence strongly suggests that some form of secret agreement had been reached.

This was a difficult time for U.S. and British relations. Shortly after the capture of the Confederate commissioners, (November 21, 1861), an incident began which involved the landing of armed Union soldiers on British soil. Here again, Palmerston had to make a decision about war. British honor was always a significant factor in the conduct of foreign affairs. On November 21, the *CSS Nashville* steamed into the port of Southampton for repairs and refueling. She was spotted by the *USS Tuscarora* who waited outside the three-mile limit to intercept the Confederate ship. Fearing that the *Nashville* might escape during the night, the captain of the *Tuscarora* put an armed guard on shore to keep close watch on the ship. Palmerston was rightly concerned that the presence of armed U.S. soldiers on British soil might provoke a confrontation with local Southampton authorities. The situation was ripe with imminent danger. Lincoln didn't want to fight and neither did Palmerston. The prime minister immediately requested that Russell tell Adams that he needed to get his men out of there. He also told Adams that a British ship of war would be sent to Southampton to ensure that the *Tuscarora* gave the *Nashville* 24 hours to escape before being chased by the Union ship. Palmerston wrote to Russell on January 10, 1862 and complained that, "These Yankee captains stand in need of being dealt with in a summary manner."[27] Palmerston was understandably upset. If he needed an excuse for war, he had it. The prime minister decided to maintain control and back off. That is, unless he was bluffing.

Throughout the crisis of the *Trent*, the threat of war between the Union and England was always present. Fear of war with England helped to shape the form and direction of foreign policy during the administration of Abraham Lincoln. Ultimately, the *Trent* Affair was much more significant for what it revealed about British military weakness than American strength. It may be argued that Great Britain maintained her fragile hold on international power and influence precisely because she stayed out of the American Civil War to the extent that she did. England threatened war with someone who was fully mobilized as a result of war with another. Full mobilization for war takes money, time and the political will that England lacked after the Crimean War. It has been assumed by many that the Lincoln government backed down during the *Trent* crisis because a two-front war would have been disastrous. Perhaps not. There were many, in and out of the Lincoln government, who believed that the Union could beat the South and England at the same time. Seward said this more than once. There were others who believed that a war with Britain would unite the North and South against a common enemy. Great Britain was believed to be the most powerful nation on earth at that time. If the threat of war with England over the *Trent* Affair shaped foreign policy between the two countries, how realistic were Britain's chances of winning a contest with the U.S. in the 1862–1865 period? According to the *Newcastle Chronicle,* British strategy in a possible war with America always seemed to start with blockading the Northern ports as a means of ultimately defeating the United States. The *Chronicle* bragged, "we have estimated to a fraction the facility with which we could destroy the federal fleet, blockade the American ports and devastate the Union."[28] If we are to better understand the prospect of war between Britain and the United States at that time, we must ask ourselves some basic questions. First, what would be the purpose of such a war? Break the blockade and secure cotton, invade and subjugate the U.S., or both? Second, with the Union military already mobilized, what steps would be required of Britain and how long would it take for her to mobilize for war? Third, could England physically get forces to U.S. shores, maintain them here, and still be able to protect her homeland and colonies from France? Finally, was England capable of fighting effectively in U.S. waters with her deep-draft warships?

From a technical point of view, England during the period from 1861–1865 did not have the capability to threaten the U.S. in terms of military power. Her resources were already stretched following the Crimean War, and issues with ship suitability and manpower would prevent her from mounting an effective attack on the East Coast. Palmerston and his government were bluffing, and they knew it.

The existing British "plan" to subdue the United States amounted to a blockade which they believed would cripple America into submission. That scenario assumes that the U.S. did not have the ironclad strength to successfully challenge such a blockade. According to historian Howard Fuller, the Palmerston government lacked the political will to mobilize for an offensive operation. England was an island nation who based her military budget and related ideology on defense.

> "Even in terms of military strategy it was far easier to present a formidable defense to wreck any potential offensive thrust and at least thereby maintain one's political 'independence'. This is what Britain really invested her energies into during the Civil War years, and why. The hallmark of Palmerston's last ministry (1859–1865) was not a coastal assault flotilla of ironclads capable of deadly-efficient

work against distant shores, but a vast and expensive series of coastal fortifications designed to nullify any French naval raid on British dockyard arsenals like Portsmouth or a full-scale invasion of southern England."[29]

Mobilization of armed forces is expensive. The Union army required 1 billion rounds of ammunition, 1 million horses and mules, 1.5 million barrels of pork, 100 million pounds of coffee, 6 million blankets and 10 million pairs of pants.[30] If Britain did not want to risk sending a fleet to U.S. shores thus leaving her colonies unprotected as well as her own homeland from continued suspicion of Napoleon III, was Admiral Milne's North Atlantic fleet, already offshore in the U.S., large enough to break the blockade and, secure cotton exports and repel men like Grant, Thomas and Sherman just waiting to throw him back into the sea? Not only was Milne's fleet too small for the task, he was afraid to get too close to American shores for fear that too many of his sailors would desert. The North Atlantic Squadron was an all-wooden fleet that would have suffered under fire from low-freeboard, turret ironclads. Only eight ships in Milne's fleet had more than 500 men. The flagship, the *Nile*, had 90 guns and 900 men. Although mostly armed with 32-pounders, six ships in the squadron had less than 100 men and as few as two guns. The mission of the fleet was to protect British subjects and commercial interests in North America and the Caribbean dominions.

Could British warships have sailed into New York and/or Boston harbors and subdued either city? Admiralty hydrographer Captain John Washington assessed the odds after reading a study on New York commissioned by Governor William Henry Seward and Major J.G. Barnard of the U.S. Corps of Engineers whose 1861 *Notes of Seacoast Defense* were of special interest.[31] In Barnard's *Notes,* he quotes from a previous British study commissioned to assess British defensive strength. The study concluded, "Having carefully weighed the foregoing considerations, we are led to the opinion that neither our fleet, our standing army, nor our volunteer forces, nor even the three combined can be relied on as sufficient in themselves for the security of the kingdom against foreign invasion." What about U.S. ports? Washington wrote a report entitled *List of the Chief Ports on the Federal coast of the United States showing the Shipping, Dockyards, Population and Defenses etc.* In the case of Boston, "The harbor is safe and spacious once inside, but the entrances are intricate with a depth of only 18 feet in some parts at low water, and twenty-nine feet at high water"[32] With the largest British warships drawing twenty-nine feet of water, Boston was out. What about New York? Seward knew what happened at Sevastopol, and wanted assurances that New York would not suffer the same fate. The report that Seward commissioned ultimately concluded that a mobile army and navy were better protection than fixed fortifications.[33] Admiral Milne knew that water depths and channel breadth at the Narrows were sufficient to allow his larger warships to enter. Getting within close combat range with low-freeboard turret monitors and fixed harbor fortifications shooting back at you was difficult. Even if you landed ashore, the railroads and telegraph would help with rapid and effective ground mobilization and deployment to an extent that New York was also not a good target.

If entering New York and Boston harbors was not realistic, could a British blockade of American ports, as suggested by Richard Lyons and others, be successful? This would probably also fail in view of the comparative size and function of U.S. and British navies at this time. The British Royal Navy was a large fighting force, but most of it was wooden, and most of that was spread out protecting colonies and commercial interests all over the world. If wooden ships attempted a blockade within sight of the American shoreline, the much larger Union ironclad navy would have made quick work of English blockading ships (see appendix C). Between turreted monitors and ironclad broadsides, the powerful Union navy boasted 2,500 smoothbore and rifled guns compared with only 1,300 mounted on British frigates. England would have found it impossible to enter or even get close to strategic U.S. harbors. However, the U.S. ironclad navy was built strictly for harbor and coastal defense. Gideon Welles had no oceangoing ironclads until late 1865.[34] By contrast, Britain had 26 seagoing ironclad warships, and 22 of these could have been detached for offensive service in U.S. waters – if they had sufficient coal to sustain themselves in a protracted blockade effort. Failing this, Britain could have defeated the U.S. Navy in a blue water contest. But why bother to take the bait and fight on the open ocean when this was not necessary? In an Anglo-American naval contest for the integrity of U.S. harbors, that contest would be America's to lose. There would be no reason to take a risk in blue water. Just wait until coal and supplies ran out, and the Royal Navy went home. At this point, the return trip would probably be under sail alone because those Penn Trunk engines used to power the screw propellers would probably have broken down. Even if ships like the *Warrior* could limp into an American harbor for repairs, there were no U.S. dry docks big enough to accommodate her. [35] The single component of naval combat which might have supported Richard Lyons' contention that the Royal Navy could "annihilate at one blow" U.S. commerce and thus the ability to sustain a long war on two fronts would be the commerce raiders like the *Alabama*. By itself, that ship accounted for millions of dollars in damage during two years of warfare. This argument is crippled by the fact that the Union ironclad navy was growing at such a rapid pace, that an armada of British commerce raiders would have been met with many more like the *Kearsarge* and sent to the bottom before making it home. America was safe, and Britain probably maintained her hold on international influence by staying out of the American Civil War and "showing the flag" whenever she could safely get away with it. "Above all, the [Royal Navy] needed to be able to simply 'show the flag', and they did this superbly. When the *Warrior* showed up off your coast or in your port you couldn't help but be impressed."[36]

How much of this did Seward and Palmerston know and take into account in shaping foreign policy? Palmerston was cautious when dealing with the U.S., in part, because he didn't want another Crimea. However, "Even if he knew *Warrior* would have a tough time against *Monitor*, he would play up the former's strengths in Parliament while quietly complaining of her weaknesses to the Admiralty/The Duke of Somerset." Seward knew that important ports like New York and Boston were safe. However, he never contested the spoken fears of men like Edward Bates who urged caution when dealing with British naval power. Richard Lyons, John Laird and many others were justifiably concerned with the rapid growth of the Union navy. Gideon Welles may have been a caustic and partisan critic of Seward and others with whom he had little confidence, but he knew his navy. He recognized a scam when he saw it. Welles ignored Bates and the others who feared British naval strength. Just before First Bull Ruin, his diary states, "A war with England would be a serious calamity to us, but scarcely less serious to her. She cannot afford a maritime conflict with us, even in our time of troubles, nor will she." Nevertheless, Lyons still believed that the Union navy was no match for the ships of the line and frigates of the British Royal Navy. Nevertheless, Seward shared, "the perception that America was now very strong 'at home' and could give the British a good pounding if they came over looking for a fight; the Yankee raiders could give as good as they got on the high seas against commerce, etc."[37] In view of the fact that the well-publicized successes of David Farragut and David Dixon Porter made the Union navy appear invulnerable, Seward suspected he had something to back up his bluff. Palmerston was left with "showing the flag."

CHAPTER 8

COBDEN AND BRIGHT, ET AL.

I venture to say that the affection and veneration which Mr. Bright has inspired are not fully explained either by his eloquence or by the magnificent service which he has rendered to the country. The man is greater than the eloquence. The man is nobler than his service. He never quailed before the power of the great. I believe he has elevated the national ideal of political morality.

Dr. R. W. Dale, August 1882

Secretary of State William Henry Seward had competition in the foreign affairs department from many quarters, including Senator Charles Sumner of Massachusetts and John Bright from Rochdale, England. Sumner was Chairman of the Senate Foreign Relations Committee, and Bright had his picture in Lincoln's office.[1] Lyons discussed with Russell some of the men who had influence in the Lincoln government. He recognized Sumner as someone who would be helpful in controlling Seward. Lyons tells Russell that Sumner "has considerable influence in Foreign Questions ... I think no greater service could be rendered to the cause of peace than to make Mr. Sumner aware of the real perils to which Mr. Seward and the Cabinet are exposing the country."

Sumner also had competition from the lion's den itself. Three liberal reformers from England, John Bright, Richard Cobden, and William Edward Forster, were important members of that British team, which, along with Charles Sumner, helped manage and shape U.S. foreign policy during the Civil War. In addition to this team, both Britain and France attempted to influence events in America through the sometimes ill-conceived efforts of people like William Gladstone, MPs William Schaw Lindsay and George Peacock; newspaper editors like W.J. Rideout (*Morning Post*), John Delane (*The Times*), M.B. Sampson (city editor, *The Times*); bankers like J.S. Gilliat (Director, Bank of England) and another small army of ship owners, stock brokers, barons and baronets, lords and ladies.[2] The opposition was formidable. In addition to competition from Sumner, Cobden and Bright et al, it has also been argued that the U.S. State Department had effective competition from Tsar Alexander II of Russia.[3] Ultimately, France refused to intervene in the Civil War without help from England. In addition, both countries were reluctant to get involved without support from Russia. Bismarck was making noise in Prussia, but few were listening – not yet. It has also been argued by some that regardless of Seward's threats, bluster and "wrapping the world in flames", Lincoln was given a free hand to conduct the war as he saw fit because those desperate for intervention were held back by Russia. Great Britain remained the primary concern, however.

John Bright was a Quaker and Cobden a businessman. Together they served a combined ninety-five years in parliament. Both Cobden and Bright grew up during the age of the Great Reform Act of 1832. This legislation greatly increased the numbers of those eligible to vote, and increased representation from the large cities that emerged from the Industrial Revolution. Cobden and Bright were against slavery, and worked hard to accurately represent the Union to the English populace. The first communication on record between Cobden and Sumner is March 9, 1848 – a letter concerning the threat to peace in Europe due to the build-up of arms by many countries. Cobden complains that standing armies are expensive to maintain. He also fears that standing armies are a potential threat to their respective governments should they chose to depose it. "For surely governments will begin to calculate the cost of these useless armed retainers, whose maintenance causes disaffection to the overtaxed people, and tends, in fact, to produce the very rebellion which they were intended to prevent."

Both Cobden and Bright were in frequent communication with Charles Sumner. The senator from Massachusetts was an outspoken abolitionist, chair of the Senate Committee on Foreign Relations and a powerful legislator. He was handsome and demanded attention. Carl Sandberg tells us that he was "the most elegantly tailored man in the House or Senate, wearing maroon vests, fawn gaiters, blue-violet neckties, high silk hat, cape over shoulders, gold-headed cane, gold watch chain, was born in Boston to money and leisure."[4] Sumner and Lincoln were like two pieces of a jigsaw puzzle that were different, but fit together well. Lincoln was a quiet back-slapper and Sumner had a "natural coldness" about him. He had a rigid, moral side that did not allow compromise. Lincoln appreciated that. His secretary of state sometimes compromised as quickly and successfully as a chameleon changed colors. Sumner was proud of his connection with the president. His letters to Cobden, Bright and the Duke and Duchess of Argyll are full of references to his having spoken to or advised Lincoln about this or that.[5] As an abolitionist, Sumner was colorful and passionate in public. Speaking in Worcester, Massachusetts on October 1, 1861, he told his audience that, "I have exposed the tyrannical usurpations of the Slave Oligarchy; and I have dragged into the light the huge and hideous Barbarism of Slavery"[6] In addition to the president, Sumner is singularly unique in another unexpected way. He was one of the few who were on consistently friendly terms with Mary Lincoln throughout the war years. Mary alienated everyone from her dressmaker to her husband's secretaries.[7] However, according to Mrs. Lincoln, Sumner and her husband were "great chums after they were acquainted ... they were like boys during [Lincoln's] last days." Mary Lincoln's opinion notwithstanding, Sumner was critical of just about everyone he met. He was especially critical of both Abraham Lincoln and Henry Seward. He believed that the president was sincere and had good intentions. However, he saw Lincoln as cognitively slow and lacking in the decisive leadership needed at this time to win the war and bring peace. Sumner believed that emancipating the slaves would immediately bring England to the Northern side, eliminate the warships being built in British shipyards and thus ensure that the Confederacy would see the hopelessness of their cause and give up the fight. Sumner was singularly focused on abolition and peace.

He was bright, blunt in speech and simplistic regarding his remedy for peace. However, at six feet two inches tall, he was bigger than life and could not be ignored. He spoke with a deep voice that commanded attention. An early Lincoln biographer, Albert Beveridge, said of Sumner: "Sumner knew that he was able, knew that he was learned, and he was not unaware that he was handsome. Indeed he seemed to think that anyone who disagreed with him was either a knave or a fool, and probably both." Critical, however, is the fact that Sumner may have played a larger role in specific areas of foreign relations than did Seward and the State Department. According to Pulitzer Prize-winning historian David Herbert Donald, Sumner ran an alternative State Department that Lincoln often consulted. According to Donald, Lincoln was so upset upon reading Seward's confidential memo, "*Some Thoughts for the President's Consideration*" that he immediately sought foreign relations advice elsewhere. The best place for that advice naturally came from the chair of the Foreign Relations Committee, Charles Sumner. Donald states, "Lincoln gave Sumner a virtual veto over foreign policy. Before Congress assembled in July (1861) he authorized the Senator to go through all the foreign correspondence since the inauguration; he asked Sumner's advice on that part of his message to Congress dealing with foreign affairs; and he repeatedly consulted with him on legal questions relating to the blockade."[8]

When considering the influence of Sumner, historians must be careful when making generalizations. It is easy to read and analyze the letters and dispatches that men like Sumner and Seward sent back and forth across the Atlantic. Their motives may be debated, but their words are clear. It is much more difficult to be sure what was said in private conversation at a dinner party, social event or private meeting. Anecdotal comments are difficult to confirm. Yet those comments could carry just as much weight and have the same or more impact on events. It is necessary, therefore, to confirm anecdotal statements with subsequent actions. Seward eventually learned to control his words in print, but after a glass of brandy and a good cigar, he was much less guarded. Sumner was much more direct in speech and print, but he did not have direct access to the London Foreign Office nor the Ministry of Foreign Affairs in Paris. The senator, however, had access to influential members of parliament and some of their wives. Conversely, the Lincoln papers show a relatively small number of official letters that went from the president to Sumner. The Lincoln papers even include social invitations from Lincoln to Sumner, but few related to the foreign relations drama that almost ignited a two-front war with Europe at this time. This is consistent with the assessment of Sumner by his friend Carl Schurz. Ambassador, senator, Civil War general and later cabinet member under Rutherford B. Hayes, Schurz preserved his thoughts about Charles Sumner in his eulogy at Sumner's death. Schurz saw Sumner as a magnet for controversy to the same extent as Henry Seward. Observing Lincoln and Sumner, he remembered two very significant facts. First, "No two men could be more alike as to their moral impulses and ultimate aims; no two men more unlike in their methods of reasoning and their judgment of means." So, Schurz saw similarities and differences between Lincoln and Sumner. Most significant, however was Schurz' comment on Sumner's influence on Lincoln. As well-researched and respected as he was, David Herbert Donald may have overstated his case for Sumner. During the push for the Emancipation Proclamation, Schurz recalls: "The President at first passively resisted the vehement counsel of the senator. But Mr. Sumner [Lincoln] treated as a favorite counselor, almost like a Minister of State outside the cabinet. *Thus Mr. Lincoln while scarcely and ever fully and speedily following Sumner's advice, never ceased to ask for it.*" (emphasis added)

Lincoln encouraged advice and counsel from diverse and adverse sources. He listened to Sumner, but he also took note of many others before making up his mind. The Schurz eulogy of Sumner makes no mention of William Henry Seward, let alone the suggestion that Sumner was the *de facto* secretary of state as proposed by Dr. Donald. Sumner personally knew many of the politicians in Europe with whom Seward was dealing. He was deeply opinionated and outspoken, but he also had sufficient credibility to command attention from Lincoln. In the end, Sumner was an influential voice, but probably not to the extent suggested by some. Perhaps part of the problem lies in the self-serving retrospect with which some cast themselves with the knowledge that they were an important player in a significant, historical drama. Thus, an overstated reference to the influence of Charles Sumner may be found in a letter he wrote to a manufacturer and politician from Massachusetts, Francis

W. Bird. Writing on April 16, 1871, Sumner tells Bird about a trip he made to City Point with the Lincolns aboard the *River Queen*. Sumner was present as a guest of Mary Lincoln. Sumner tells Bird:

> "My dear Bird: My relations with Presdt. Lincoln were of unbroken intimacy always and constantly. I arrived at City Point as one of his party the day after his visit to Richmond, but went with Mrs. Lincoln. For 4 days we were together Thursday, Friday, Saturday and Sunday when he deposited me at my own door. The next Friday he was assassinated. On the Sunday on board the steamer, he read MacBeth aloud, and in private conversation with me said – *they say I have been under Seward's influence; I have counseled with you twice as much as I ever did with him.* And this same remark has been reported to me as said by him to others. I have been more than once told that, had he lived, he would have offered me to the Dept. of State, and his course toward me made me sometimes think that I should be called to decide the question, whether to quit the Senate. My relations with all his cabinet were friendly and confidential – including Blair, who has often said that Mr. Lincoln intended to offer me Seward's place. I send you these facts to be used discretely. Ever yours, Charles Sumner."

If true, this is an extraordinary statement. If Lincoln is accurate, and spoke with Sumner twice as many times as he spoke with Seward, that would be many conversations requiring much time. There would be more written evidence than exists. However, Sumner was present at some of the critical decision-making periods of the war. We know that he was in the Executive Mansion on Christmas morning to argue the case of Mason and Slidell. It is also known that he worked on Lincoln to emancipate the slaves. Sumner's speech on Maritime Rights and Ocean Belligerency[9] left no doubt as to his stand on privateering. Therefore, the Senator and Chair of the Senate Foreign Relations Committee exercised a pacific degree of control over foreign affairs legislation that reflected his own, personal philosophy. Regardless of what Sumner tells us in his memoirs, we have letters from Cobden and Bright which discuss Sumner's presidential contact and implied influence.

For the most part, Seward and Sumner were antagonists during the Civil War. Those who knew the players and published their diaries and memoirs after the war often disagreed with each other on key points. For example, Carl Schurz wrote of Sumner's support of Seward, "But in spite of such serious disagreements he faithfully aided Seward in the conduct of foreign affairs, and far from seeking to undermine the

Secretary's influence abroad … he earnestly labored to disabuse the minds of Englishmen of the unfortunate impression that Seward was bent upon provoking a quarrel with Great Britain."[10] Schurz probably used as one source Sumner's letter of December 31, 1861 to Richard Cobden in which he mentions a dinner party at Seward's right after the *Trent* issues was settled. Seward discussed his note to Richard Lyons releasing the Confederate commissioners, and insisted that his advocacy of release was done "in good faith – laying up nothing for future account or recollection." Sumner relates this incident to Cobden and assures his English friend that, "Seward may be careless or hasty; he is not vindictive." This was a rare moment of praise for Sumner.

The Cobden letter aside, Sumner was often very critical of Seward and his handling of foreign affairs. He thought the secretary was politically motivated. He really didn't trust him because he believed that Seward was "not frank and straightforward; only a cunning conniver of little plots and not a true man."[11] In the end, Sumner was more interested in domestic than state matters.

Charles Sumner constantly urged Abraham Lincoln to issue an Emancipation Proclamation. Lincoln resisted at first. He was concerned about the reaction from border states like Maryland, Tennessee, Missouri and Kentucky. Lincoln finally agreed in the summer of 1862. It would take effect on January 1, 1863. From contact with Cobden and Bright, Sumner believed that the impact on the British would be positive. Even though the battle at Fredericksburg in December, 1862 did not go well for General Burnside and the Union cause, Lincoln went ahead and ensured that the proclamation would take effect on January 1. Seward was against issuing the Proclamation at this time. He favored gradual, compensated emancipation. He was afraid that the proclamation might cause chaos in the South and thus encourage the foreign intervention he worked to avoid. He feared that there would be a "servile insurrection" whereby the slaves would take revenge on their former masters. Some called Seward a coward. "Success" at Antietam in September, however, convinced Lincoln that emancipation was the right course at the right time. Sumner urged an immediate issue. The Proclamation reaction in London was also immediate. Henry Adams wrote to his brother Charles Francis, Jr. on January 30, 1863. He tells Charles, "the Anti-slavery feeling of the country is coming out stronger than ever expected … The cry was Emancipation and reunion and the spirit was dangerously in sympathy with republicanism … Every allusion [sic] to the South was followed by groaning, hisses and howls, and their enthusiasm for Lincoln and for everything connected with the North was immense."[12]

Richard Cobden and John Bright deplored war, the British controlling aristocracy, slavery, and the Union blockade. Their letters to Sumner always recommended care and moderation in all dealings with England and America. Cobden and Sumner trusted each other.[13] Their letters contain intimate details of the thoughts, prejudices and plans of their respective governments. Writing during the *Trent* crisis, Cobden tells Sumner, "I write to you, in confidence; and I write to you what I would not write to any other American – nay, what it would be perhaps improper for any other Englishman than myself to utter to any other American but yourself. But we are, I think, both more of Christians and cosmopolitans than British or Yankee."[14]

Richard Cobden visited the United States in 1835 and 1859. He greatly admired American prosperity and believed that England had much to learn from this young country. His opinion of Lincoln's secretary of state, however, was consistent with the opinions of many others at this time. Writing to Sumner on November 27, 1861, Cobden states, "There is an impression, I know in high quarters here that Mr. Seward wishes to quarrel with this country. This seems absurd enough. I confess I have as little confidence in him as I have in Lord Palmerston. Both will consult Bunkum for the moment …"[15] This was written during the *Trent* crisis. In that context, it is easier to understand Cobden's concerns. Cobden recognized that Seward and Palmerston were both basically politicians who adapted their policies to fit the needs of the howling public. Between Sumner, who advised Abraham Lincoln on foreign policy, and the Cobden/Bright/Forster team, who tried to force their opinions on Palmerston and Russell, these men did much to preserve peace between England and the Lincoln government and thus ultimately help win the war for the North.

The first time that these men had significant influence on the Lincoln administration was during the *Trent* Affair. Lincoln had learned the hard way that his secretary of state was impulsive and was to be handled carefully. Politically, it would have been too dangerous to keep Seward out of the cabinet where the potential for mischief was too great a risk. At the cabinet meeting on December 24, 1861, Sumner arrived and provided an opinion that was based partly on the feedback he had from Cobden and Bright. He read letters from both men to the assembled cabinet members. It has already been established that Abraham Lincoln initially considered submitting the matter to arbitration. This idea may have either come from Cobden, or subsequently reinforced by him. John Bright wrote to Sumner on December 5, 1861, and made a case for arbitration. He told Sumner, "If I were minister or President in your country, I would write the most complete answer the case is capable of, and in a friendly and courteous tone, send it to this country. I would say that after your view of the case is not accepted, you are ready to refer the matter to any Sovereign or two Sovereigns, or Governments of Europe, or to any other eligible tribunal, and to abide by the decision, and you will rejoice to join with the leading European Governments in amendments and modifications of international law in respect to the powers of belligerents and the rights of neutrals …"[16] Bright advocates arbitration. He also suggests that submitting this problem to arbitration would go a long way to settling the difficult issue of the rights of neutral countries. Those rights were a serious issue throughout the war, and threatened to ultimately bring the Union and Great Britain to war. England was "neutral", but was also allowing Confederate privateers, blockade runners and warships to seek shelter and resupply in English ports. Although not official and acting under the authority of the Crown, English ships manned by English crews were either seeking to breach the blockade or were shipping supplies to the Confederacy through Matamoros, Mexico and Nassau, Bahamas. The Palmerston government believed that private citizens could take whatever risks they were prepared to take. They did not represent the government, and were on their own. As a neutral, Britain believed that this was her right in view of the fact that the Lincoln administration was blocking that right through a blockade which was shown to be ineffective.[17] British consuls in Southern ports were always asked to send reports to Lyons regarding the number of private ships breaching the blockade. The Treaty of Paris, 1856, stated that the blockade will be honored if effectively maintained. Claiming that the blockade could not secure a coast as large as that of the Confederacy, England claimed that she was within her rights to circumvent it in any way possible. This helped promote the privateering that was a potential *casus belli* throughout the Civil War.

At the time of the Christmas Day cabinet meeting, England, France, Spain and Russia were the only players on the field. The interest of France and England initially was economic. Their textile mills were idle because the Union blockade had prevented most cotton exports. In an attempt to force the recognition issue, the Davis government recommended withholding cotton shipments. Later, it was recommended that cotton in storage should be burned so that it didn't fall into the hands of Union troops. Cotton was only part of the problem. Spain wanted territory in the Caribbean. Russia was the wild card that the other three looked at to see who she would support. Russia was the most heavily populated of all the European powers, and she was growing at a rapid pace. However, the seizure of the *Trent* raised questions primarily for England and France. Palmerston wanted immediate relief from Lincoln. Stirred up by the *Times*, Englishmen were crying for war. Napoleon often waited to see what England would do before making up his mind.

This was not a good time for the Lincoln administration and the war effort. The Congressional Joint Committee on the Conduct of the War was created to second-guess Lincoln and his generals.[18] From the memory of men and terrified spectators fleeing the field at Bull Run Creek to the death of a U.S. senator at Ball's Bluff, that first year of the war ended in a crisis that could have cost the Union the war. The president knew that Sumner was in regular communication with two members of parliament who were sympathetic to the Union cause. This was Lincoln's pipeline to intelligence from Britain. These two members of parliament supported Sumner in his efforts and advised him as to the action he should take on many matters before the Committee on Foreign Relations. From G.M. Trevelyan, influential biographer of Bright, it is confirmed that, "Bright's letters to Charles Sumner, Chairman of the Senate Committee on Foreign Relations, were read to President Lincoln and Secretary Seward. And they were sometimes read aloud in the U.S. Cabinet."[19] Seward feared that his bluster toward England was a bluff that was about to be called. That would undermine his political position, put his country at risk of war, destroy the entire Lincoln plan to reunite the country, and probably reignite calls for the secretary to resign. He was in a spot. This was no time for bluff and bluster.

At this stage, Richard Cobden was in poor health. His ability to represent the cause of the Union in parliament was limited. Just when Lincoln's cause needed it most, a new member of parliament stepped in to keep up the pressure on the Palmerston government. Cobden, Bright and Edward Forster were Quakers and were drawn to the Civil War because of the Union position on slavery. Their passion wasn't for the balance of power or the balance of trade. They were drawn by the stand taken by Abraham Lincoln on slavery. When William Edward Forster made his first speech to the members of the House of Commons, he quickly demonstrated that he knew the intimate details and consequences of the struggle between North and South. His first speech dealt with an issue that should have been uppermost on the minds of his fellow members. He would wait to address the issue of slavery. Long before that, the problem of to whom should British ship captains, doing business in South Carolina, pay their duties on goods to be imported and sold in the United States. Charleston had seized the port. But Lincoln claimed that the customs regulations of the United States should be honored. Failure to honor these regulations would result in consequences.

South Carolina saw the matter differently. She was owed the customs duties and her regulations would apply. The Confederacy and the Union needed the money. Ironically, the Davis government had intended to finance their military campaign through the customs duties that were being denied by the blockade. Before that blockade was adequately strengthened, however, Forster wanted to know what England should do.

Few in England understood the complexity of this war and its implications for England at this time. Lord Russell saw this war as of one side for empire and the other for independence. The mill workers in Yorkshire quickly sided with the North. The English aristocrat was convinced that the war would bring down what they believed was a dangerous experiment with democracy.

Forster's diary provides specific and interesting detail of his first speech. After breakfast, he wrote out his address. He was anxious about it

'Progressive democracy', Currier & Ives.

because part of it dealt with slavery. At 2pm, he had a few words with Lord Palmerston at his club. By 6pm, he was about to take his seat, but noticing that Cobden's seat was empty, he took his place so he could see the House speaker better. The speaker gave him the nod to stand up at 6:30pm. Two others rose at the same time, but the Commons wanted to hear their newest member. The house wasn't full, but Forster spoke well and was cheered when he sat down. At dinner, later that evening, he was told by one of the members present that he had pronounced the word "lamentable" wrong. Forster smiled and was pleased that someone had listened carefully enough to recognize the mistake. Forster only mentions William Henry Seward on one occasion in his diary. When reading the diaries and personal letters of the men stationed in Europe who were involved in this drama, Seward is frequently mentioned. Lincoln is rarely referenced. Bigelow and Dayton say very little about the president. The secretary of state was still regarded as the grey eminence who really determined foreign policy for the Union. Forster, however, knew the inner workings of the Lincoln administration as did Cobden and Bright through correspondence with Charles Sumner and others. In a letter to his wife on December 4, 1861, Forster briefly comments on Seward in the midst of the *Trent* crisis: "I trust I have won something to combat the foregone conclusion that Seward wishes war."

Sumner, Cobden, Bright and Forster were all concerned with the evils of slavery. Sumner pushed Lincoln to emancipate the slaves. Seward was not opposed to emancipation *per se*. Seward had a long, public history of espousing freedom for those in slavery. In this spirit of freedom and prior to the July, 1862 signing of the Emancipation Proclamation, Secretary Seward signed an historic agreement with Richard Lyons that ultimately enabled the more effective search and seizure of slave ships coming from Africa to the Americas and European colonies in the Caribbean. Secretary Seward is historically given credit for a treaty which allowed British ships to stop and search U.S. merchant ships suspected of carrying slaves. As with other activities of the Lincoln state department, the facts behind the story don't always match the headlines. The *Times* of May 9, 1862, gives credit to Lyons and Seward for concluding the treaty. "There is intelligence which will deeply interest us in the ratification by an unanimous vote of the Senate of a treaty which Lord Lyons has concluded with Secretary Seward for the suppression of the African slave trade."

The background of the treaty is interesting in that it exposes more initiative on the part of the British Foreign Office than the U.S. State Department. It also demonstrates the growing political maturity of William Henry Seward. When a blockade was established around key Southern ports, Lincoln did not have enough ships to make the blockade effective. He knew that Britain and France might not honor the blockade if it was not effectively maintained. In order to strengthen the blockade, U.S. warships that were patrolling the coast of Africa for slave traders, were recalled for duty. As per the Webster-Ashburton treaty with England in 1842, a squadron of U.S. ships with eighty guns was to patrol the coast of Africa in partnership with warships from England. Now, that U.S. force was to be reduced to one ship with twenty-two guns. This gave greater opportunity to the slavers to work the coast of Africa with no interference from the United States. British ships patrolled the coast alone. Under these circumstances, Britain suggested that she be allowed to help out and search suspected ships. Having come close to a serious international crisis in the *Trent* Affair, Seward sought to honor the *quid pro quo* with Russell, and help the Union cause at the same time. He knew that the bold and unprecedented act of allowing British ships to stop and search suspected American slave ships would play well in the English press. He also believed that this may further ease those tense Anglo-American foreign relations which he helped to create.

On February 28, 1862, Russell writes to Lyons about the extraordinary gesture made by Seward regarding the search and seizure of American ships. Russell writes, "I am well aware that Mr. Seward has told you, as Mr. Adams has told me, that the American government has no objection to the overhauling of American ships by British Cruizers, provided there exists good grounds for suspicion." In view of the turbulent history of search and seizure of the United States and Great Britain in the early part of the century, this was an extraordinary offering on the part of the state department. The diary of Richard Lyons explains how a British proposal became an American initiative in the eyes of the public. He states, "On the 21st instant, Mr. Seward told me that he had brought the question of concluding such a treaty as that proposed before the President and the cabinet … One point, however, he deemed essential to success. The proposal must originate with the United States. The great majority, if not all, of the present senators were strongly opposed to slavery and the Slave Trade. But there were no doubt many who retained the old jealousy of Great Britain on the right of search. They would resist all appearance of conceding anything on this subject to pressure from the British government. But the question would present itself in a different aspect if it could be Great Britain that acceded to a requisition from the United States, if it should appear that the proposal had been made spontaneously by the American government from its own desire to suppress the African Slave Trade." Seward then told Lyons that he needed to make some minor changes in the draft that Lyons had produced so that the Seward proposal would not look identical to the Lyons/Russell document. The change inserted by Seward was contained in the last clause of the proposal which stated that the treaty could be vacated by either country after ten years with a notice of one year in advance. Seward believed that the Senate would be more disposed to approve the treaty if there was an escape clause.

Most of the Lyons to Russell correspondence on the Slave Trade treaty was marked "Confidential". Both Lyons and Russell sought to keep their negotiations out of the *Blue Book* so as not to be subjected to the argument and scrutiny that their published correspondence often generated and Lyons feared. Lyons urged Russell to support the Seward proposal right away. He was afraid that adverse public reaction to any action in the Civil War might make it difficult for Seward to move forward with the treaty. Lyons knew that Seward worked both sides of the press. He was sometimes swayed by public sentiment, and other times Seward used the press to mold public sentiment against Britain. On April 25, 1862, Senator Charles Sumner successfully guided the Seward-Lyons treaty through the senate. By 5pm, Sumner walked quickly from the senate chambers to the State Department. He found Seward as he often found him – lounging on the sofa in his office. Both Seward and Lyons were pleased with the result. In his memoir on Lincoln and Seward, Gideon Welles was not as complimentary. He objected to the dangerous precedent of allowing British ships to search and seize illegal slave cargo found on American ships. He was mollified, however, in the knowledge that the treaty would not be implemented because so many American ships, public and private, had been sent to the Southern coast for blockade duty. By 1863, however, the treaty was tested by Spain and Santo Domingo.

Claims by Spain that the U.S. was stirring up trouble for her in Santo Domingo produced a denial by Secretary Seward. Dispatch No.58 on November 23, 1863 to Lincoln's Minister to Spain, Gustav Koerner, makes it clear that "The United States neither contrive, nor aid, nor encourage, nor mix themselves up in civil or international wars of other nations."[20] The problems go much deeper than threats of interference in internal matters in Santo Domingo.

The issue was that Spain was importing slaves to the island to work the sugarcane fields. This was in violation of the Webster-Ashburton treaty of 1842, to which Spain was a signatory. Seward had concluded a treaty with England in 1862, but had no similar agreement with Spain. Spain, however, was still bound by the 1842 agreement which she had signed with England. Seward reminds Koerner in Dispatch No.67 on February 6, 1864, "We have no treaty with Spain on the slave trade;

but as the laws of the United States characterized it as piracy long before our treaty with Great Britain above referred to, we think ourselves entitled to consider that trade an offense against public law."[21] Seward was restrained in his remarks to Koerner. However, he refers to this as an act of piracy. This was punishable by death. Already, slave traders like Nathaniel Gordon were being executed in New York.[22] By this time, however, Seward was more successfully learning on the job. When Santo Domingo appealed to the State Department for help in holding off Spain, Seward refused to meet with her representatives. He was concerned that any official reception would encourage Spain to be more sympathetic to the Confederacy.

By 1863, there were many issues between the United States and Great Britain with which the secretary of state had justifiable concern. These included the building and arming of Confederate privateers, flying the British flag for protection, and the transshipment of contraband supplies to the Confederacy through British dominions in the Caribbean. These ships were listed with the harbormaster as departing from England to Egypt or China, but then head for Barbados where they would unload supplies for the Confederacy in exchange for cotton. Henry Sanford's spies compiled long lists of ships that were sailing from Liverpool to the West Indies. On October 26, 1861, Sanford collected a list of departing ships for Adams. This illegal traffic in contraband goods was common knowledge. All ships departing from British harbors were required to post their ship's name and registry number, captain, cargo, and destination. The eighteen destinations listed on the communication of October 26 include Havana (4) and Vera Cruz (3).[23] Charles Francis Adams complained, and Henry Seward complained. The Crown law officers claimed that the burden of proof was with the moving party, the United States. William Seward correctly countered this with the fact that it was easier and a more secure approach to have British authorities provide the proof and take the necessary action.

On November 20, 1862, Charles Francis Adams tactfully complains to Lords Russell, "My Lord, it is with very great regret that I find myself once more under the necessity of calling your Lordship's attention to the painful situation in which the government of the United States is placed by the successive reports received of the depredations committed on the high seas upon merchant vessels by the gunboat known in this country as *290*, touching the construction and outfit of which in the port of Liverpool for the purpose I had the honor of heretofore presenting evidence of the most positive character."[24]

Adams cautions Russell that this is made worse by the fact that the shipyard in which the warship was built was owned by a member of parliament. The *290*, as well as the many privateers shipping out from British ports, was manned by English crews and piloted by a retired British Royal Navy captain who would hoist the Union Jack whenever they were confronted by a Union gunboat. While running the blockade, local, Confederate pilots were temporarily employed to guide the runner around the reefs and up the narrow channels that brought them to Wilmington, Charleston and Mobile. At one point Adams was so frustrated that he wrote to Richard Russell and complained that if England continued to build warships for the Confederacy: "It would be superfluous in me to point out to your lordship that this is war."

On March 10, 1863, the U.S. Supreme Court got involved with the blockade running issue as well as the scope of presidential authority. Four merchant ship owners of British registry brought an action when a U.S. prize court judgment went against them.[25] All four blockade runners were bound for the Confederacy, and were captured as prizes and brought to court for adjudication. When the court ruled against the owners, they brought an action to recover their ships and cargo. The case was heard by the U.S. Supreme Court. It is significant that the high court elected to hear this case. The action claimed that the blockade was illegal because the president stated that this was not a war but a rebellion. Without a formal declaration of war by Congress, seizure of ships breaching the blockade was illegal. Lincoln and Seward were now caught in a serious war of words, terms and definitions. Losing here would force Lincoln to either defy the court and maintain a blockade that might be declared illegal, or to accept the judgment of the court, lift the blockade and enable the Confederacy to secure the support needed to better prosecute the war and secure recognition. Lincoln and Seward were in a tight spot. This was one battle they could not afford to lose. Ironically, the Supreme Court of the United States relied for guidance on Vattel, the British Admiralty decisions of Lord Stowell and Queen Victoria herself.

The majority opinion was written by Justice Robert Cooper Grier.[26] Although a cousin of Confederate Vice President Alexander Stephens, Grier concluded that the president:

> "... is Commander-in-chief of the Army and Navy of the United States, and of the militia of the several States when called into the actual service of the United States. He has no power to initiate or declare a war either against a foreign nation or a domestic State. But by the Acts of Congress of February 28th, 1795, and 3d of March, 1807, he is authorized to call out the militia and use the military and naval forces of the United States in case of invasion by foreign nations, and to suppress insurrection against the government of a State or of the United States.
>
> "If a war be made by invasion of a foreign nation, the President is not only authorized but bound to resist force by force. He does not initiate the war, but is bound to accept the challenge without waiting for any special legislative authority. And whether the hostile party be a foreign invader, or States organized in rebellion, it is none the less a war, although the declaration of it be "unilateral." Lord Stowell (1 Dodson, 247) observes, "It is not the less a war on that account, for war may exist without a declaration on either side. It is so laid down by the best writers on the law of nations. A declaration of war by one country only, is not a mere challenge to be accepted or refused at pleasure by the other."

Lincoln and Seward won a significant and critical legal decision. However, in 1863, Seward and Adams were making Lord Russell aware that after the conflict was over, they intended to seek redress for the damage done by privateers in the courts. Russell soon took the hint and began legal action against those shipyards in Liverpool which were still provisioning and manning the privateers. Russell was presented with many depositions from English citizens who were serving on Confederate warships. Adams gave him entire crew lists with their positions on board ship and their Liverpool addresses. He even supplied the documentation showing where the wages earned on the privateers were to be sent. In most cases, it was to the seaman's wife who waited for the monthly stipend. Although there would be no more *Alabamas* leaving British yards, the private blockade runners that Alexander Collie was building kept coming. The Davis government sought to circumvent the Foreign Enlistment Act by providing English sailors with Confederate naturalization papers while at sea. The evidence was so strong, and the depositions so voluminous that Seward wrote to Adams threatening that if the Foreign Office did nothing to stop this activity, that he would send

Union warships right into to the docks at Liverpool and arrest those involved.[27] Having taken several steps forward, the secretary now took another one back with his threat to sail right into British dock yards and settle matters with the sailors and dock masters.

Adams cautions Seward to be more careful with his words. In Dispatch No.584, dated January 28, 1864, Adams cautions Seward, "For many reasons, I hold it wise just at this moment, not to crowd too many complaints upon the government here, and especially those which do not rest upon the firmest foundations."[28] Later in February, Adams informs Seward that members of parliament were discussing the fact that he had summarized the Secretary's dispatch about chasing English privateers back into their home ports. Parliament was outraged and wanted to see the original text. They remembered Dispatch No.10. They were fully transparent with the publication of their *Blue Book*, and they wanted to see what Seward originally intended. Adams warns Seward in Dispatch No.595 on February 11, 1864, "The publication of the diplomatic papers annexed to the president's message has elicited much comment in parliament and in the newspapers, upon your instructions to me, in your No.651, of the 11th of July last, and particularly that portion of them which declared the intention of the government, under certain contingencies, to enter English ports and seize obnoxious vessels."

The issue of British-built privateers was long-standing. The activities of Alexander Collie and others was well-known at the foreign office. Allegedly, Palmerston joked, "catch 'em if you can." Although the issue had been addressed by Cobden and Bright, it was first addressed by William Edward Forster. He outlined the issue of England being in violation of the Foreign Enlistment Act by building these ships and manning them with British crews while hiding behind the English flag. Forster began his attack with the following: "[Forster] wished to ask the Secretary of State for the Home Department, whether it is not a criminal offence against the provisions of the Foreign Enlistment Act for any subject of Her Majesty to serve on board any privateer…And also whether any such Privateer equipped in a part of Her Majesty's dominions will not be liable to forfeiture?"

Sir George Cornwell Lewis responded to Forster's questions by stating that, "The General principle of our law is that no British subject shall enter into the service of any Foreign Prince or Power, or engage in any hostilities that may be carried on between any two foreign states."[29]

In an attempt to recover some semblance of neutrality, Lord John Russell responded that he had informed all appropriate departments in the United Kingdom that ships captured by privateers acting on behalf of North or South cannot be taken into a British controlled port for settlement. Russell communicated with the French who indicated that their laws were similar in that a prize could not remain in a French port for more than 24 hours, and no prize court would be authorized to address the capture. Russell had already stopped commerce raiders like the *Alabama*, *Sumter*, and *Florida* from leaving British ports. With help from Edward Forster, smaller, armed privateers were compromised as well.

By late 1862 and early 1863, Jefferson Davis and Judah Benjamin were desperate for help from Europe. The excess cotton supply had run out in Liverpool. Inflation was impacting Confederate currency, and credit was desperately needed. Secretary of State Benjamin conceived the idea of using cotton as credit to secure a loan. Cotton had already been running the blockade and landing in Liverpool. Even though the quantity of cotton making it through the blockade was comparatively small, the quality of Southern cotton was such that there was no really viable substitute. Even the cotton coming from Egypt and India was mixed with Southern cotton to produce the best alternative available at the time. The quality of Southern fiber was so strong that it commanded prices that only increased as the blockade tightened. This afforded Confederate arms agent Caleb Huse the temporary credit necessary to buy thousands of guns and artillery pieces. By 1863, however, the blockade was much tighter. Huse found that he had placed orders for guns for which he had no money to pay. The *Charleston Mercury* and other newspapers began advocating the withholding of cotton from the market in order to force the reluctant Anglo-French alliance to recognize the Confederacy in order to restart the flow of cotton. Jefferson Davis was reluctant to blackmail Europe. Soon, however, wheat and other grain crops were planted in place of cotton in order to feed a slowly starving population. In Richmond, food was now as scarce as good credit. On April 2, 1863, Confederate war clerk J.B. Jones observed, "This morning early, a few hundred women

'*Southern women feeling the effects of the rebellion, and creating bread riots*', *Frank Leslie's Illustrated Newspaper, 2 May 1863.*

and boys met as if by concert at the capitol square, saying they were hungry and must have food. The number continued to swell until there were more than a thousand."[30]

This was the start of the Richmond Bread Riot. With the blockade and scarce food supplies being diverted to the soldiers at the front, the women at home were starving. Shouting "Bread or Blood" they looted bakeries and other shops in downtown Richmond until Jefferson Davis himself came out and begged them to stop. Something had to change. Using his contacts with French bankers in New Orleans, Benjamin began the process of arranging a loan for the cash-poor Confederacy, but was too late. Before making any headway, New Orleans fell to Union troops. Making matters worse was that although the Confederacy was classified as a Belligerent, that status was not recognized by the Union blockade. Jefferson Davis was willing to try anything.

Every time that British Minister Richard Lyons got tired of the dust and heat in Washington and requested leave to rest in London for a few weeks, the pulse in Richmond quickened. Maybe Lyons really wasn't tired. Let's hope he was really going to London to negotiate recognition or at least an armistice. Davis was willing to believe anything that had even the remotest possibility of success. Into this came some relief from an unexpected form. The marriage of John Slidell's daughter to the son of an Erlanger banker did more than her father's futile efforts with the Emperor Napoleon.

CHAPTER 9

PETERHOFF

We may have our own opinions about slavery, we may be for or against the south; but there is no doubt that Jefferson Davis and other leaders of the south have made an army; they are making, it appears, a navy; and they have made what is more than either – they have made a nation.

William E. Gladstone, Newcastle, October 7, 1862

At around the same time that Seward and Russell were working out that secret deal to block the Laird Rams from leaving British docks, an elegantly dressed man walked quietly through a city that had changed much in two years of war. He was going to the Richmond Customs House, but walked by private homes houses with peeling paint and broken clapboards. The homeless sleeping in the streets weren't a threat. The small, outdoor auction businesses with men waving red flags and screaming that an old piece of cotton cloth was going once, twice and three times to the bidder in the back were unexpected, but harmless. Rumors of dangerous street gangs and threats of riot and looting were of much greater concern.[1] Richmond was surrounded and in constant danger. Food was scarce, currency highly inflated and war profiteering was already in full swing.[2]

Nevertheless, the quiet gentleman found the granite building with rounded Italianate arched windows right in front of City Hall. This was the command center of the Confederacy. Offices of the president, quartermaster and state department were housed here. The post office had been here, but was recently moved to the basement of the Spottswood Hotel due to critical space needs at the Customs House. Up on the second floor in the northwest corner, the words State Department had been painted above a door that led into the office of a short, plump man with curly black hair and neatly trimmed whiskers. A large, gold watch chain bounced off that big chest as he rose to shake hands with his visitor. Speaking in French, the visitor was one of the richest men in Europe – Émile Erlanger.[3] The man who rose to greet him was Confederate Secretary of State Judah Philip Benjamin. Erlanger ran the blockade and came to Richmond for several reasons. As head of one of the largest banks in Europe, he saw potential profits in the thousands of cotton bales resting idly in Charleston, Savanah and Wilmington. Jefferson Davis was cash poor, and there was money to be made. Recently divorced, Erlanger was also in the process of chasing after Marguerite, the daughter of John Slidell.[4] Still working to convince the emperor to act with or without the aid of England, Slidell was surprised when he was approached by Erlanger about a loan.

Cotton, and the issue of getting more of it, was a continuing problem in both England and France. Many in Europe had invested in cotton from the farms of South Carolina and Mississippi, but now were financially pinched because of the blockade. The *Times* was as outspoken as the *National Intelligencer* and Secretary Seward. The chancellor of the exchequer, William Gladstone, was always calling for mediation in the conflict,[5] as was former MP and shipping merchant William Schaw Lindsay.[6] When Lindsay saw that the Foreign Office made no move to break the blockade, he went on his own to try and get Napoleon III to do it himself. While in Paris, John Delane, editor of the *Times*, continued to stir up trouble with similar calls for mediation in a conflict that had impacted unemployed Liverpool mill workers and Atheneum Club members alike.

The American Civil War raised many concerns in Europe. Lack of cotton, and its business impact, was a major concern. Moral issues over a fight that was taking thousands of young lives was also a worry with many. Of greater, immediate alarm, however, was the fear that Lincoln's Emancipation Proclamation would result in more bloodshed by angry slaves striking their masters before running away behind union lines. Before Erlanger left Richmond, however, that fear proved to have no merit. Rather than slay plantation wives and daughters, the slaves just ran. Many of the men joined the union army and fought with a skill and bravery that surprised many Northern officers.[7] Nevertheless, calls for either mediation or at least an armistice continued from the mouths and pens of influential men from all over England. Lincoln, in his message to Congress, had already warned that European interference in the domestic issues of America would result in "injury" to those getting involved. Speaking for a president who preferred caution in his written and spoken communication, Henry Seward proclaimed what Lincoln was thinking – that meddling in U.S. affairs would "wrap the world in flames." Lincoln and Seward believed that mediation would ultimately result in recognition of the Confederacy. Both men also believed that the armistice proposed by France would just give Jefferson Davis more time to regroup and fight on. In the middle of all this, Europe still needed cotton and Davis still needed money.

The Confederate treasury, directed by C.G. Memminger, still had two and a half million dollars in gold coin with which to purchase arms in Europe.[8] Barings and Rothschild Banks had both declined to help the Confederacy with credit.[9] Davis, however, had valuable, expensive cotton and a chest full of gold coins. Before the war, Fraser, Trenholm processed 20,000 bales of cotton per day. At that rate, Fraser, Trenholm took in almost 19 million dollars every day. Three million bales of cotton were exported to Britain in 1860. By late 1862, the cotton surplus had run out in Liverpool and France. Jefferson Davis had committed Confederate "suicide" by withholding cotton from the market. He was receiving bad advice and making serious mistakes. His government was a revolving door. In the first two years of life, the Confederate States of America had six secretaries of war, five attorneys general, four secretaries of state and two secretaries of the treasury. The situation was further complicated by the disorganized group of purchasing agents representing the Confederacy both officially and unofficially. Caleb Huse was already at work signing contracts for guns and artillery. Accused of taking bribes from the already clever and successful Alexander Collie, Huse now had to contend with Major J.B. Ferguson who was sent to supplement the efforts of Huse. The two didn't get along. It was Ferguson who accused Huse of taking bribes to steer business to Collie. Nevertheless, Ferguson was given a line of credit through Fraser, Trenholm and Co. in Liverpool. From the CSA Treasury Department, October 28, 1862, Memminger writes to Fraser, Trenholm,"Dear Sirs: You will please extend a credit to Major J.B. Ferguson to the extent of five hundred thousand dollars, and give him any assistance in your power to make his purchases for the Confederate States."[10] Further complicating this overlapping master plan was the supposed voluntary presence of James Spence, self-styled banker for the Confederacy.[11] Spence was a contributing editor of the *Times*, Liverpool businessman, and one who sought to help Confederate purchasing agents with making the contacts necessary to secure their purchases. At this stage, James D. Bulloch was on the scene in Liverpool and London arranging for the construction and purchase of war ships for the Confederacy.[12] Although Huse and Ferguson stayed out of his way, Bulloch could never shake off the spies and detectives that consul Thomas Dudley had arranged to follow him wherever he went. All of this was before the arrival of Colin McRae who was belatedly sent by Judah Benjamin to oversee this overlapping tangle and make sure that Huse didn't get too greedy.[13] With no cotton, and the North apparently unable to subdue the South, calls for mediation got much louder.

The U.S. consul in Paris, John Bigelow, had disturbing information regarding these calls for mediation. While at a party in Paris, Drouyn de Lhuys introduced him to an English merchant who had secret information about some of the subscribers to what became known as the Erlanger cotton loan of 1863. A list of loan subscribers containing many names, including Gladstone, Lindsay and Delane as well as the private secretary of Lord Palmerston himself was sent to Bigelow. On the list, Gladstone was listed as W.E. Gladstone. Concerned that the list might be a forgery, Bigelow wrote to John Bright. He knew that Bright was a friend of Gladstone, and might be able verify or discredit the information. Although Bright wrote back and doubted that Gladstone was involved, he offered that the full name of W.E. Gladstone was the only one of which he was aware. When Bigelow dug further, he found that an organization called the Southern Independence Association had been formed in November, 1863. Its initial purpose was to ensure that the cause of the Confederacy was always before the public through print and other available media.

Despite concerns over the validity of the list, Bigelow took a chance and published the names in the *London News,* and waited to see who would scream in protest. According to Bigelow, "Its publication naturally produced an explosion throughout Her Majesty's dominions."[14] He made a list of those who denied involvement and those who did not respond at all. First to deny any connection was Gladstone. The *Times* immediately called the list a forgery. However, Bigelow began to compare the names of those admitting to taking part in and helping to finance the work of the Southern Independence Association, and the names on the donor list. Many of the names matched. Included in the match were some of those calling loudest for mediation or some form of settlement. They included William Schaw Lindsay, William Gregory, J.S. Gilliat (Director, Bank of England), fifteen members of parliament, and John Laird, son of the original Birkenhead shipbuilder, now the builder of the *Alabama.* Lindsay wrote to the *News* and admitted that he was a bondholder, but for less money than Bigelow quoted. Gilliat never denied his involvement. William H. Gregory, former MP, friend of James Mason and outspoken Confederate supporter, did not deny his place as a bondholder.

As a result of the "explosion" produced by Bigelow's exposé, one may reasonably assume that the high level calls in late 1862 and early 1863 for intervention in the American Civil War were not the result of concern for broken bodies and runaway slaves, but for business. The naïve reality is that the Confederate States of America gained a deceptive, fragile form of "financial recognition" through the discussions then taking place between two French-speaking Jews on the second floor of the Richmond Customs House. Ultimately, a loan for the Confederacy was secured through the issuance of bonds, backed by cotton, and yielding 7% at maturity.[15] Suddenly, the Confederacy has a new lease of life.

In early, 1863, things began to look up for Davis. His clever secretary of state, Judah Benjamin, had negotiated that loan from his friend, Émile Erlanger. Gladstone and Russell kept pushing Palmerston to recognize or at least offer to mediate a war that was finally having a negative impact on the English economy. Ironically, Palmerston began to listen and

'Wanted, a $15.000.000 loan for the C.S.A.', unknown, between 1861 and 1865.

reconsider his caution because of the newly promulgated Emancipation Proclamation. Many in the Palmerston government believed that this edict of Lincoln's would cause the slaves in the South to finally rise up and revolt against their masters. If so, the time for mediation was right now. Before he could savor the victory of the Proclamation, Seward stirred the pot again.

Just as serious as the matter of the *Trent* and the *Nashville* was the incident of the *U.S.S. Peterhoff* in early 1863. Acting as *de facto* president and apparently after no consultation with President Lincoln, the secretary of state made a written promise to Lord Lyons that blockade runners carrying mail to Confederate ports would not be sent to a lawful prize court for examination. Was this yet another dividend of that so-called secret deal between Seward and Russell? The mail would not be opened to determine possible contraband content. Seward assured

Lyons that British mail would be sent to its destination unopened. The navy secretary objected that this was in violation of all historic precedent, international law and accepted practice by both the United States and Great Britain since 1789. Again, the facts of the case are relatively simple, but the long-term implications for peaceful foreign relations and international law were serious.

On January 27, 1863, a British side-wheel steamer left Falmouth, England for Matamoros, Mexico.[16] Matamoros was a problem because it was near the border with Texas, and an easy overland haul of goods from Brownsville to the Confederate armies. It was also a stretch for the Union naval blockade to guard this more remote part of the coastline. Under these circumstances, the British contended that the blockade was not effectively maintained as required by the 1856 Treaty of Paris. England, therefore, felt comfortable in ignoring the spirit of the blockade and engaged in commerce that the Lincoln government considered to be illegal. In addition to this, the distance from Matamoros to Brownsville, Texas was short. En route to Matamoros, the *Peterhoff*, by flying the British flag, made a stop in the Dutch island of St. Thomas. Within the three-mile limit, Captain Wilkes from *Trent* fame was waiting. He took the ship to Key West for adjudication by the prize court there, and seized the mail bags on board.

Prior to this, Seward had sent a letter to Welles telling him to allow British mail bags to reach their destinations unopened. The secretary wrote, "It is thought expedient that instructions be given to the blockading and naval officers, that in the case of the capture of merchant vessels suspected or proved to be vessels of the insurgents or contraband, the mails should not be searched or opened."[17] Four months later when the incident occurred, Welles complained that this was contrary to international law.[18] Seward defended himself. According to Welles, "He was greatly disturbed; said he was committed by his letter to me of the thirty-first of October which had directed and virtually pledged the government that the mails should be given up without search."[19] Seward claimed that he had the approval of the President in this matter.

Both men took their case to Lincoln. The president, absorbed in the war, stated that he had no knowledge of this affair or the issues involved. According to Welles, "The President said he had no distinct recollection that the subject of captured mails had been brought to his notice ..."[20] According to Welles, however, "Mr. Seward wrote me on the 15the that he had submitted the subject to the President who approved his course." This may be further disputed by the fact that Lincoln now directed both men to prepare detailed written answers to questions that the president had asked in order to learn more about the situation and the implications for foreign relations. These questions might not have been necessary if he had been previously briefed as Seward stated to Welles. On the *Peterhoff* situation, Lincoln requested of Wells and Seward:

1. Lists of all similar cases that had already been adjudicated;
2. Lists of all cases either opened or unopened before and during the current crisis;
3. What would be the issue if the mail were forwarded unopened?;
4. What would be the issue if the mail was opened?;
5. Other issues.

Welles' response to the president's questions was detailed and compelling. Other than what we know through Welles, there is no direct, written record of the Seward response. The first hint that the Seward State Department was controlled by the British Foreign Office comes when Seward learned that the prize court in Key West had ruled that the mails may be opened. At a cabinet meeting, Seward "made a passing reply that he had great difficulty in keeping the peace and satisfying foreign demands, particularly the English who were very exacting."[21] The secretary believed that he was keeping the peace and avoiding a war with England by placating and allowing himself to be controlled by these potential enemies. Public threat and private submission was recognized by those "hoary and shrewd" men in London and used to their advantage. Welles cited the law of 1789, enacted by the Second Continental Congress and carried over to the United States Congress. The navy secretary told Lincoln that Congress stipulated: "All papers, charter-parties, bills of lading, passports, and other writings whatsoever found on any ship or ships which shall be taken carefully preserved, and the originals sent to the courts of justice for maritime affairs."[22] Welles reminded the president that an Act of Congress dated April 23, 1800 requires that, "The commanding officer of every ship or vessel in the navy who shall capture or seize upon any vessel as a prize, shall carefully preserve all the papers and writing found on board and transmit the whole of the originals unmutilated to the judge of the district to which such prize is ordered to proceed." Gideon Welles carefully outlined such instances as British ships seizing the mails from the vessels *Romea, Atlanta, Lisette* and *Caroline* operating under the Dutch, Danish or French flags.

Although praising Seward in his 1873 eulogy, Charles Francis Adams admits that when it came to the *Peterhoff* incident, "the subject is one attended by many embarrassments." Welles ultimately viewed the decision to send the *Peterhoff* mails to their final destination unopened as an English victory over the Lincoln government. He complained, "The English government is less willing to renounce a right than our Secretary of State, received with complacency our obsequious surrender in the case of the *Peterhoff*, but entered into no arrangement for renunciation on their part ...".[23]

Welles went further and was clear in his belief that Seward was intimidated and thus controlled by the British Foreign Office. He complained, "the Secretary of State, flattered and seduced, I need not say intimidated by the British legation, had without authority by law or by treaty, abandoned a principal and given the parties immunity by his ill-advised letter renouncing the national right to search the mails."[24]

The incidents with both the *Trent* and the *Peterhoff* are important for several reasons. Seward's bluff was called. Threatening war with England was one thing – loading your guns and manning battle stations was another. Charles Francis Adams was convinced that Seward saved the Union and the United States ultimately by writing a conciliatory note that released the Confederate envoys. According to Bates, Sumner and Welles, he wrote the note, but was personally against the release of the commissioners. Lincoln probably used better judgment in standing by his desire for one war at a time.

The *Peterhoff* situation was similar to the *Trent* Affair in that it demonstrated the extent to which the British Foreign Office was in control of foreign relations between the Lincoln and Palmerston governments. The *Trent* Affair is also significant because of the continuing influence of Charles Sumner in foreign relations. Lincoln valued his judgment, and his contacts with British MPs Cobden and Bright.

Just when things looked dim for the secretary, an unexpected and welcome surprise sailed into New York Harbor. On September 24, 1863, two heavily armed Russian frigates sailed through the Narrows and dropped anchor. Admiral Lisovski rowed ashore to cheering crowds of thousands of New Yorkers. At the same time, Admiral Popov was being hailed in San Francisco. The seven-month visit of the Russian fleet has been controversial as to its purpose for historians ever since they landed. There is no question that Tsar Alexander's consistent declaration of loyalty to the United States stemmed from revenge against England and France for their part in the Crimean War as well as a desire to maintain equilibrium among the powerful nations of the world. The U.S., with its large army and ironclad navy, was someone who could not be ignored in the balance of power struggle at that time. In order to ensure that neither England nor France would bombard Russian cities again, somebody else was needed to give them pause and shake a fist. The Spanish navy was not strong enough to frighten John Bull. Prussia and Austria were emerging as possible game-changers, but neither had a navy to challenge England or France.[25] That left the U.S.

Democratic America and autocratic Russia were strange partners. They were, "Two of the most mismated [sic] bedfellows in all recorded history."[26] If the enemy of my enemy is my friend, then tsarist Russia was the best of friends. Simon Cameron, Bayard Taylor and Cassius Clay have left the historian many written accounts of discussions with both the tsar and the prime minister as to their loyalty to America. Their reasons were self-serving, but emphatic and consistent nevertheless. America helped Russia maintain "equilibrium", in the words of the tsar. It has also been suggested that Russia really sent her fleet to U.S. shores to ensure that they did not get caught in their base at Kronstadt in the Gulf of Finland. During Crimea, as the British fleet was pounding Sevastopol into submission, the Russian fleet was trapped in the Gulf by a British naval squadron and could not help relieve the city. This would never happen again. Historians point to this as the second reason for the visit to New York and San Francisco. When one takes a closer look, the reality is different.

Although the Russian flagship, the *Alexander Nevsky*, made the trip from Kronstadt, some of the rest of the fleet came from duty off the coast of Greece. They could not have been trapped.

Judah Benjamin also recognized the significance of Russia in the foreign relations effort. On November 19, 1862, he appointed Lucius Q.C. Lamar as Special Commissioner of the Confederate States to the Empire of Russia. Furnished with letters of introduction, he set out for Moscow on January 25, 1863. He sailed from Matamoros on the French ship *Malabar* to Havana, Cuba. After a stormy passage, he arrived in London on March 1, 1863. Mason and Slidell were still working against heavy odds to secure some cooperation from England. Soon after arrival, Lamar met and talked strategy with Nathaniel Beverly Tucker. The sympathies of the English for the Confederacy were confirmed. Tucker had been U.S. consul to Liverpool from 1857 to 1861. He was from Virginia. After secession, he was sent as a special agent to London. He was on his way home, and agreed to take some letters and dispatches from Lamar.[27] According to Lamar, "In this country, the leading contestants for power, in both parties, Conservatives and Whigs, supported by the great body of their adherents, are favorable to the success of the south." Further discussion, however, revealed that, "Not only the government party, but even the conservative leaders are exceedingly timid in regard to any movement which give umbrage to the United States. They seem to consider that a war with that country would be the greatest calamity that could befall Great Britain."[28]

Lamar's instructions from Benjamin were similar to those given to prior Confederate commissioners as well as the first dispatches sent by Seward to the U.S. ministers in Europe. Benjamin and Seward wanted to make sure that London, Paris, Moscow and others knew the position of their respective governments in the politics of the Civil War. At this point, however, the Confederacy was desperate, and not in a position to realistically offer Russia the same specifics originally proposed by Toombs to the Yancey commission. Benjamin was left with offering generalities, "The time has now arrived, when in the judgement of the President, he may, without hazard of misconstruction, tender to the Emperor of Russia, the assurances of the sincere desire of this people to entertain with him the most cordial relations of friendship and commercial intercourse, and the President has chosen you to represent this government in conveying such assurances."

Unfortunately for the Davis government, Confederate missions to Europe had not succeeded. Yancey, Mann and Rost had given up. Mason and Slidell were still at it, but also failing in their mission. On July 22, 1863, Lamar failed as well. His lack of success was not from lack of effort, but from the failure of the Davis government to have any confidence in help from Europe. On the 22nd, Lamar acknowledged a dispatch from Benjamin indicating that his commission had not been approved by the Confederate Senate. Although Benjamin and Davis were willing to try anything at this point, the members of the Senate were conscious of the fact that their inability to win support from Europe was public knowledge which made their cause look hopeless. Lamar tells Benjamin that he found the prospect of help from Europe unlikely. He added that, before receiving Benjamin's letter, he had considered giving up his commission and coming home. He ends his final letter to Benjamin, "Shortly after my arrival here, I became convinced that the state of things supposed to promise useful results from diplomatic representations at the court of St. Petersburg had been essentially altered." Those alterations concerned the relations between France and Russia. With new warships being constructed in French yards, Benjamin and Davis believed that an alliance between France and Russia might ultimately benefit the Confederacy. With Sevastopol still in ruins, that was not likely to happen.

There are those who argue that Russian support for the Union backed up by the presence of the Russian fleet in September, 1863 was a controlling factor in restraining England, France and Spain from interfering with the war. Gunboat diplomacy did what words could never do.

It was at this time that one of the Confederate blockade runners was caught attempting to enter the harbor at Charleston. On board were Confederate mail bags from Europe. One of the letters made the headlines in the *New York Times*, and unexpectedly, albeit briefly, outlined the failure of Confederate diplomacy. The aim of such diplomacy was to secure recognition of the sovereignty of the so-called Confederate States of America from at least England and France. Jefferson Davis was slow to recognize the importance of competent foreign relations, and the Confederate independence effort suffered as a result. One of Davis' "commissioners" in Europe was Edwin DeLeon. After the publicity surrounding the mission, capture and release of Mason and

Slidell, Davis decided that he didn't need that kind of advertising. The rest of the world didn't need to know that the Confederate commissioners were being "forced to wait in the back hall like servants." As a result, only secret agents were sent to generate good press, buy guns and ships, and make important friends wherever they could find them. Thus, men like James Bulloch, Caleb Huse, Edwin DeLeon, Colin J. McRae, J.B. Ferguson, Henry Hotze and others were sent with letters of credit on Fraser Trenholm to do what they could. In their own respective areas, each was relatively successful. Bulloch purchased warships and Henry Hotze published a weekly newspaper called *The Index*.[29] The paper was an aggressive attempt to better explain the reasons for Southern secession and the war. Unfortunately, the paper never gained wide circulation, and always faced the inexplicable shadow of slavery with which the British were so opposed. Ferguson and Huse were able to buy a significant quantity of arms, but it took Colin J. McRae some time to straighten out the financial tangle in which the Confederacy had found themselves at this stage. Edwin DeLeon was a private citizen who went to England at his own expense to lobby for the cause of the Confederacy. DeLeon came with credentials much more substantial than Yancey, Rost and Mann. DeLeon was the owner and publisher of several pro-Southern newspapers. Franklin Pierce appointed him consul-general to Egypt. At the outbreak of the Crimean War, the Ottoman Porte expelled all Greeks from his dominions, which included Egypt. Appealing to DeLeon, the Greeks were protected until the end of the war. After secession, DeLeon offered his services to Jefferson Davis in any capacity he selected. Davis decided to send him to Europe. As a private citizen, DeLeon was able to speak with Palmerston and Napoleon. He found Palmerston "a hale, hearty, vigorous-looking old man whose age was only betrayed by his white hair. He received me with great courtesy and kindness, entirely without any pretention."[30] After some small talk and Palmerston complaining of gout, the prime minister set the record straight about Confederate recognition. He said, "The commercial and the cotton manufacturing class, headed by John Bright, are against you; and so are the bulk of the middle class because of your institution of slavery. The Queen, Prince Albert, Lord John Russell are also dead against you."[31]

At this point, DeLeon knew that recognition from Europe was not realistic. The cause of Confederate recognition from England was over – from the highest authority, the queen and her prime minister. In October, 1862, he wrote as much to Jefferson Davis. The Confederate president never received this dispatch because it was found aboard the *Robert E. Lee* when captured by Union patrol boats. That capture was in 1863, and the *New York Times* started publishing excerpts of the DeLeon dispatches at the request of Secretary Seward. The November 14, 1863 excerpt stated, "It is useless to disguise the fact that the men around you do not inspire confidence, and chaos would soon come were your hand withdrawn from the helm. Military ability of the highest order our revolution has produced, out of diplomatic talent it has been most singularly barren. There has been, and is today, as little real intention of a speedy recognition by France as by England."[32] Now the rest of the world knew that the Confederacy was on its own. England would not help. But what about France? DeLeon's interview with Napoleon brought the excuse that France would act, but only in concert with England. However, having said that, Napoleon was at that time already building two of the most powerful warships ever constructed in ship yards in Nantes and Bordeaux.

★

"There are now about 42,000 French troops in Mexico. These are on their march from the gulf coast to Puebla by two routes, one division by Jalapa, the other by Orizaba." This is the opening paragraph of Dispatch No. 36, on November 19, 1862.[33] It was written to Secretary Seward by Thomas Corwin, U.S. Minister to Mexico.[34] This was an active period for Napoleon III, and it brought a new consular official to Paris to assist William L. Dayton, the head of the legation. That new consul, John Bigelow, brought his skills as a writer and newspaper editor to the job. Dayton, Bigelow and Corwin were different. Corwin was a wagon boy who drove a supply wagon for William Henry Harrison in the War of 1812. He was a former governor of Ohio, treasury secretary and strong critic of the war with Mexico in 1848. He took his job as Minister to Mexico seriously and was quoted as saying, "The world has a contempt for the man who amuses it. You must be solemn, solemn as an ass. The great monuments on earth have been erected over the graves of solemn asses." Sitting for Matthew Brady's heavy box camera, Corwin looks solemn. He was a good choice to serve in Mexico because of his stand on the war. Although not in the best of health, Corwin worked hard to make Seward aware of his options under difficult circumstances.

Dayton was similar in temperament and health. He was a Whig vice presidential candidate in 1856 with Charles Freemont. His appointment to the post in Paris was done as a reward for party loyalty and perceived political strength. Dayton was not Seward's choice for the legation in Paris, and some historians downplay Dayton's role in the foreign relations drama that unfolded during the Civil War. He spoke no French and was always in need of a good interpreter. Unfortunately for Dayton, he worked in the shadow of his Paris consul, John Bigelow, but he ultimately proved himself to be a hard-working and dedicated representative to France. His dispatches to Secretary Seward are extensive, detailed and contained the restraint sometimes missing in those from his boss, William Henry Seward. Unlike Charles Francis Adams, however, Dayton's dispatches contain little of the policy advice and direction which is found in the Adams dispatches from London. Dayton provides the facts and leaves policy to Seward. The secretary's responses to Dayton contain none of the praise as found in the dispatches to Adams, Motley, Corwin and Robert Pruyn in Japan. The foreign ministers who knew and worked with Dayton were praiseworthy of his dedication and ability. Although not Seward's choice for minister to Paris, Dayton proved to be substantially more capable than historians have allowed. He was succeeded by Bigelow as attaché *ad interim*. John Bigelow was, "at forty-four, a high-strung, intense, quick-moving Yankee, a long, lean, handsome man of unshakable integrity who made friends easily and had a shrewd grasp of European and American politics."[35]

Bigelow brushed up on his idiomatic French on his sea voyage to France, and wrote books on everything from Jamaica in 1850 to a biography of Benjamin Franklin.[36] Bigelow was a journalist who was sent to Paris to try and influence the French press in favor of the Union. This was not an easy task. France was a tightly-controlled dictatorship under the thumb of Napoleon III. French newspapers were censored.

Writing articles not favorable to the government was risky. Bigelow always struggled to find papers willing to challenge the Tuileries. As a newspaperman from New York, he knew William Seward. The secretary made a wise decision in recommending Bigelow to Lincoln. With Confederate hotheads like William Yancey in Europe trying to garner support for the Confederate cause, someone was needed to promote the case for the Union. Bigelow quickly saw the danger that intervention from Europe would create. He was particularly concerned with the unpredictable emperor of France:

> "At one stage of our Civil War it seemed as though its fate was to be decided less by the belligerents than by the national powers on the other side of the Atlantic. The insurgents, in their desperation, were ready to make any sacrifice to secure their independence. They offered to Spain, as the price of recognition, to guarantee to her the possession of Cuba; to France, they offered to guarantee Maximillian's sovereignty in Mexico, and for the loan of a squadron of the emperor's navy several millions of dollars in cotton; while to England they offered yet greater temptations. It was even rumored that a restoration of British supremacy in the insurgent states would not have been esteemed too high a price to pay for the overthrow of the government at Washington. It was in one of these paroxysms of desperation that the agents of the Confederate States managed to tempt the Emperor of the French to authorize the construction in the dockyards of France of several vessels of war for the Confederate navy more formidable than any then afloat."[37]

At this time, an extensive traffic in dispatches went from Seward to Dayton, and Dayton to Seward regarding three primary issues, all of them French. First, Dayton had evidence, uncovered by Bigelow, that two French shipyards were building several large warships for the Confederacy. These ships were more powerful than anything then available to the Union navy, and Bigelow was convinced that the emperor knew and approved of the work. Second, Napoleon was planning to install a Prussian monarch on the throne in Mexico.[38] Mexico was always borrowing money and failing to repay. Mexican President Jaurez had recently imposed a two-year moratorium on debt repayment. That did it. Her debts and her political chaos were the excuse the emperor required to say that what Mexico needed was a strong European king. That would settle them down. The Lincoln government believed that this plan was too close for comfort.

In addition to this, the French port of Cherbourg was providing safety and resources for the Confederate privateer *Alabama*. This ship was ultimately responsible for the destruction of many millions of dollars of Union commercial ships and their cargo. The prize courts of a technically neutral country like England could not go so far as to allow prize vessels captured by the *Alabama* to adjudicate their plunder in British courts. With few prize courts available in countries having declared neutrality, the *Alabama* looted, burned and sank wherever she could. When threatened, she hid in Cherbourg. Seward and Dayton were both frustrated.

Ship *290*, later known as the *Alabama*, was built under the direction of Confederate secret agent James D. Bulloch. She was captained by "old Beeswax", Raphael Semmes. For two years, the *Alabama* burned millions of dollars of Union commercial shipping on the high seas. Semmes feared confrontation with Union warships, so he focused his attention on vessels carrying much-needed wheat and other commercial goods to Europe.

The *Alabama* was built in the Laird shipyard at Birkenhead, Liverpool, England. She was a sloop powered by steam and sail, and was unique in that she had a double-bladed screw propeller that could be vertically cranked up out of the water into an open housing in the hull. This allowed the ship to take full advantage of good winds and sail without the screw creating drag and slowing her down. She could achieve 13 knots, which exceeded the steam power of any Union commercial ship. The *Alabama* was 235 feet long, but drew only 15 feet of water when her coal bunkers were full. That alone made her a formidable threat. Her crank propeller and shallow draft allowed her to hunt her prey in shallow waters where the heavier warships could not catch her. Her coal bunkers carried enough fuel to last for eighteen days. The *Alabama* was able to extract fresh water from the salty Atlantic and make all needed repairs while at sea. She was a mighty machine. Her captain, Raphael Semmes, was a good match for this ship. He was independent, fearless and bold.[39] After his mustache was waxed to a sharp point every morning, he roamed all over the Atlantic in search of any Union ship that he could find. He believed that damaging Union commerce would weaken the Union war machine by crippling the economy. He also hoped to draw some of the blockade squadron away from their duties and allow more runners to sneak in with badly-needed supplies. A weak economy meant fewer guns and fewer soldiers in the field. Semmes bristled at the caution exercised by the politicians in the *Trent* Affair. Semmes vented his frustration, "Although the world interfered to keep the peace in the *Trent* affair … so goes the world. Well, thank God we are independent of them all, and can whip the Yankees without their assistance."[40]

The *Alabama* was so successful in her work that insurance rates on Northern commercial ships were always being increased.[41] Despite Seward protests, some Union ship owners found ways to register their vessels with England. Flying the British flag gave them the protection of a neutral country. Semmes honored that neutrality when he could determine that the ship was really of English origin. He was not easily fooled.

After the Emancipation Proclamation, Union victory at Vicksburg and the retreat of Lee's army at Gettysburg, the Palmerston government decided to stop the private construction and sale of Confederate war ships. Henry Adams wrote to his brother Charles Jr. on July 17, 1863, "We are in receipt of all your sanguinary letters, as well as of news down to the 4th, telling of Cyclopean battles, like the struggles of Saturn, and Terra Hyperion, for their empire, lasting through sunrise after sunrise."

Victory notwithstanding, many in London were disappointed at the news. Charles Francis wrote to his son Charles Jr. on July 24, 1863, "The salons of this great metropolis are in tears; tears of anger mixed with grief."

The story of the *Alabama* escape is also controversial. Although some historians contend that the *Alabama* was deliberately allowed to sneak out of her British dry dock and create havoc on the high seas, there is no evidence to support this. Through Henry Sanford, Charles Francis Adams employed detectives which were constantly spying on the activity at Birkenhead. Urged by Adams, it appears that the Palmerston government made a sincere attempt to restrain the *Alabama* from sailing, but was too late. Some claim that members of parliament cheered when they learned of the *Alabama* escaping to the open ocean. Even though it would not have been inconsistent for the House of Lords to be openly sympathetic to the *Alabama* escape, there is no evidence to support this. The Confederate secret agent who supervised the construction of the ship explains that he told the Laird foreman that he wanted to take the

290 out for a day- sail. This was to be a casual shake-down cruise which was permitted by contract. To ensure that the ruse worked, a separate ship, the *Agrippina*, was loaded with the arms and powder. Sailing separately from different ports allowed the *290*, now renamed the *Enrica*, a better chance to depart uncontested. Between Adams and the Foreign Enlistment Act, Bulloch had to exercise further caution. When his crew of forty sailors showed up to board the ship, some arrived with a local prostitute on his arm. The ladies refused to leave. Bulloch was initially unsure as to what to do. He finally decided that the presence of the women would add further credence to the story about taking the ship out for a casual cruise. After reaching the open ocean, Bulloch put his passengers aboard the tug boat that eased her out of the channel at Birkenhead and continued to Portugal where she was armed.

Some evidence exists that shows British concern over the *Alabama* and the long-term damage she might do to British and U.S. relations. This helps support the belief that Russell tried, but was too late, in restraining the *Alabama*. Foreign Secretary John Russell expressed his feelings when he wrote to the Duke of Somerset, First Lord of the Admiralty, on September 14, 1863, "It is of the utmost importance that the ironclads building at Birkenhead should not go to America to break the blockade,"[42] Writing a few days later on September 19 to Sir George Grey in New Zealand, he expressed fear for possible war with America.[43] He wanted England to abandon the building and arming of privateers for the Confederacy. "If one ironclad ram may go from Liverpool to break the blockade of the Southern ports, why not ten or twenty? And what is that but war? If ten line of battleships had gone from New York to break the blockade of Brest during the late war, do you think we should have borne it? Do unto others as you wish that others should do unto you."[44] Gradually, the danger of interference in the Civil War shifted from England to France.

CHAPTER 10

FROM COTTAGE TO CASTLES

*It is forbidden to any Frenchman to take orders from either party to arm
ships of war, or to accept Letters of Marque for privateering, or to concur in
any manner in the equipment or armament of a ship of war or corsair,
of either party.*

Code Napoleon, Article 21

Napoleon III decided to ignore the joint decision-making process that
had driven the Anglo-French alliance during the American Civil War.
Although there is nothing directly linking the emperor with the construction of Confederate warships in the ports of Bordeaux and Nantes,
it is difficult to believe that these ships could be built without his tacit
approval. France was controlled enough to force someone as resourceful as John Bigelow to search for newspapers willing to publish articles
that might not please the emperor. Correspondence was collected by
Bigelow in 1888 in preparation for his book on French naval power
during the Civil War. He uncovered many documents which came from
the minister of marine, a man close to the emperor, which clearly show
that French shipbuilders were constructing the largest and most heavily
armed warships then in service anywhere in the world. The documentation discovered by Bigelow clearly show that the ships were being
constructed for the Confederacy.

The 1864 papers of William Henry Seward show that the correspondence between the State Department and the legations in Paris and

London far exceeded that produced in 1861, 1862 and 1863. Union battlefield victories in 1864 (Cold Harbor notwithstanding) should have cooled both sides of the ocean. England had been the greatest threat, and she was clearly not going to interfere. Unfortunately, 1864 suddenly saw the construction of the most powerful warships afloat – in France. In addition to the ships that were being built in France, the files of Lord Richard Lyons show a surprising volume of dispatch communication to and from London. His papers show that in 1864, 14,816 letters and dispatches were sent to and from the overworked British minister. As France was building warships for Jefferson Davis, the English were still allowing blockade runners to refuel and do business in British ports. The fear now, however, was that the new French warships might break the blockade and save the Southern war effort.

The last two months of 1863 produced dispatches from Dayton to Seward complaining of the protection given to the *Alabama* in the French port of Cherbourg. On November 27, 1863, Dayton wrote to Seward that he has complained to Drouyn de Lhuys about privateers being provisioned in private French shipyards. "I called his attention at once to the *Florida* at Brest, and to the repairs and recruitment of her crew." His primary issue, however, was with the private French shipyards constructing warships for the Confederacy, and publicly stating that they were for sale to China. In his dispatch of November 27 to Seward, Dayton included a copy of a letter he wrote to Drouyn de Lhuys on the subject. He stated, "The pretense that they [the ships] are intended for the China seas is yet kept up in this advertisement, though the papers heretofore shown to your Excellency (especially the letter of Mr. Arman) afford the clearest evidence that this pretense is a false one."[1] Seward's initial reaction is to inform Dayton that the United States will pursue redress in the French courts. Realizing the potential futility of that process, he let Dayton know that when the Civil War is over, France and Britain had better watch out. On December 17, 1863, Seward's Dispatch No.446 to Dayton stated,

"During all this time, we have been at peace with France and Britain. We have practiced absolute non-interference between them and their enemies in war ... We have excused the unkindness of which we have complained ... The evil, nevertheless, is becoming very serious, and is rapidly alienating the national sentiments of the United States ... The political drama is inconstant, and the scene may soon change, and in the chances of the hour, maritime powers may become belligerents. Is it wise to leave open between them and the United States questions which, in such an unfortunate conjuncture, would produce confusion in regard to our own practice of neutral rights?"

Seward had learned not to threaten in such a way as to leave his opponents no way out. Unfortunately, however, he sometimes took one step forward and two steps back. Mexico was the next problem.

Politically, Mexico was unstable. She fought for independence from Spain from 1810 to 1821, but having gained independence, Mexico now faced another threat from the Republic of Texas. That threat ended in the famous battle of the Alamo, where Mexican General Santa Anna defeated folk hero Davy Crockett and his small band at the mission. This is where Mexican problems really began. She soon found herself in a border dispute with the United States. Mexico still claimed Texas as part of her territory, but President James K. Polk had other ideas. He firmly believed that America was destined to control her own destiny from the Atlantic to the Pacific – and that that Manifest Destiny included Texas, no matter what Mexico thought.

Polk annexed Texas in 1845. That resulted in a war which ultimately set the boundary at the Rio Grande, meaning that Texas was now firmly part of the United States. Political instability in Mexico resulted, in part, from a weakened economy which came as a result of war with Spain and the United States. Civil war continued in Mexico over land reform measures instituted by liberal President Benito Jaurez. The new President was an educated lawyer and judge who wanted to create a capitalist society on the scale he found in the United States. While living in New Orleans, he saw how strong America had become as a result of her free market economy. Juarez's reforms ran counter to the traditional power held by the church and the military. An expensive civil war erupted, causing the government to borrow heavily from Europe to sustain itself against a military determined to abolish land reforms and return to the old ways. Mexico borrowed heavily from England, France and Spain. There was always a concern that she would not be able to pay back her loans.

U.S. representative to Mexico, Thomas Corwin, was in regular contact with the Seward State Department over the issue. He was also in regular contact with Senator Charles Sumner. In order to restrict the activity and influence of Europe in Mexico and not violate the Monroe Doctrine, Corwin recommended that Lincoln loan Mexico some money so she would not be dependent on Europe. A loan of five million dollars, paid in monthly installments of one half million dollars, was recommended. This loan would be secured by a mortgage on public lands, mineral rights and the property of the Catholic Church. Before further consideration, Lincoln sent the proposal to the Senate for their advice. He knew that Sumner, as chair of the Senate Foreign Relations Committee, would be an important source of advice in the matter. In his annual message, the president stated, "I have heretofore submitted to the Senate a request for its advice upon the question pending by treaty for making a loan to Mexico, which Mr. Corwin thinks will in any case be expedient." Mexican debt was considerable. At rates from 3–4%, she owed England 75 million dollars. To France, she owed five million dollars, and to Spain she owed ten million dollars. In addition to lending Mexico five million dollars, the Corwin proposal agreed to assume the interest on Mexican debt for five years. Clearly, there was great concern in Washington over French troops headed for Mexico.

Napoleon's invasion of Mexico incited a legislative crisis in Washington that resulted in the resignation of Henry Winter Davis as chairman of the House Committee on Foreign Relations. Davis resigned in protest over actions taken by William Henry Seward in direct conflict with a vote of the House of Representatives. The struggle was over who had the final authority in dealing with other nations, the president or Congress. This was the culmination of a political struggle that dated back to the development of the Constitution in 1787. Davis claimed that the will of the people was exercised through the decisions made by the House and Senate. Seward disputed this and stated that this power rested with the executive branch of government, not the legislative.

The Seward State Department during the period 1861–1865 represents a period when the pendulum of authority in foreign relations swung in favor of the president. The emergency demands of war were a factor in this shift. This represented a swing in power from previous administrations. A Republican Congress, seeking to strengthen their Republican president, gets credit for some of this shift in authority from legislature to executive. Seward also receives some of the credit for recommending that the president should have the authority to issue Letters of Marque. This represented an expansion of the war-making capacity from the legislative to the executive branches of government. Before a new Democratic Congress took over as a result of mid-term elections, he sought to ram as much through Congress as he could before time ran out. Lyons saw what was happening, and communicated this to Russell. He warned that before the new Congress could get started that the old Republican Congress decided to take advantage of this and push new legislation while they still could. He told Russell, "The Republicans appear therefore to have resolved to profit by the short term period during which the control of the legislature remained in their hands." Bills were passed which increased military expenditures, allowed the printing of paper money, and made all males between twenty and forty-five liable for conscription into the Union army.[2] Lyons also added a recommendation of the secretary of state. He wrote that "The Act authorizing Letters of Marque has gone far to transfer the war powers of Congress to the President."

The memoirs of Senator Charles Sumner contain many references to the Constitution and the power it confers on Congress. Sumner also tried unsuccessfully to kill a privateering bill that was introduced into the Senate in February, 1863. Nevertheless, the legislative, not the executive, branch of government had the power to grant Letters of Marque. He stated, "Congress shall have the power to declare war … grant Letters of Marque and reprisal, and make the rules of capture on land and on water." The Senate passed a bill authorizing Letters of Marque on February 17, 1863. The bill was introduced at the urging of Secretary Seward. Two weeks after passing the Senate, it passed the House. It appears that Seward was probably bluffing in pressing the matter. In reality, the Confederacy had little commercial shipping which privateers could attack. Gideon Welles laughed at the project and said that this was "the idle scheme of attempting to spear sharks for wool." Sumner was concerned that without commercial shipping, the privateers would go after neutral ships instead. Neutral shipping meant England, and that meant war. Sumner wrote to Lincoln shortly after the Senate passed the privateering bill. He complained that issuing Letters of Marque was a bad idea because:

1. It was not practical;
2. It may possibly involve us with foreign nations;
3. It was counter to the opinion and aspirations of the best men in our history;
4. It was condemned by the Civilization of the age;
5. It will give us a bad name;
6. It will do this without any corresponding good;
7. It will constitute a precedent which we shall regret hereafter and the friends of human progress will regret everywhere;
8. It will pain our best friends in Europe.

In time of war, these were weak arguments. Gideon Welles succeeded in holding off the implementation of the plan. Sumner was happy. Writing to his friend in England, the Duchess of Argyll on April 26, 1863, he stated, "My policy has at last prevailed. There will be no letters of marque at least for the present. Mr. Seward has been obliged to yield."[3] In the end, Seward may only have sought to bluff the Foreign Office. It has been suggested that the threat of Letters of Marque was a major factor in causing Lord Russell to halt the further launching of additional ships of war from the Laird yards. The issue is more complex. It is likely that Sumner's vocal opposition brought the matter to Russell's attention to a greater extent than would otherwise have happened. England did not want a two-front war, which she might have faced with Russia over Poland. Palmerston might have had his bluff called here. As the Anglo-French alliance began to weaken over the French invasion of Mexico, Palmerston couldn't take his eyes off Napoleon either. In his memoirs, he stated that, "It would not be well to tell the French that we could not carry on war in Europe as well as America." He was afraid that Napoleon would take advantage of the situation.

In addition, when the Letters of Marque program was put on hold, privateers sought Letters from Japan. Japan was anxious to rid herself of any foreign influence, especially British and American. England had forty-six commercial vessels working in the Far East. They would be an easy target for privateers. Some have suggested that Seward's bluff worked this time. Others have concluded that England backed off from building Confederate ships of war because she also wanted just one war at a time. European politics, not state department diplomacy, was still in control.

Unfortunately, the secretary's bluster got the better of him again at a later date when he released unpublished documents from deliberations in the House over French incursions in Mexico. He worked hard to strengthen the state department, but did not always use that authority wisely or to his advantage. His questionable judgment and willingness to appeal to the public knew few bounds, even at this late date in the war. The House passed a resolution condemning French activity in Mexico that then went to the senate. Before senate action could be taken, Davis believed that congressional authority was undermined when Seward leaked their incomplete deliberations to the French. Before Mexico, the issue of building warships kept Seward, Dayton and Bigelow busy.

The shipyards of Monsieurs Arman and Voruz were active in Nantes and Bordeaux. Immediately prior to Gettysburg and Vicksburg, the ship builder in Nantes (Voruz) was corresponding with another builder (Arman) in Bordeaux. Documents were secretly sold to Bigelow which clearly implicated the Confederacy:

> "Dear Mr. Voruz: I have received your letter of the 9th, and Bullock's [sic] check for 720,000 francs enclosed. I hasten to send you a receipt, and also, in accordance with your request, the papers which you have signed, in the hand of Bullock for the first payment of two ships of four hundred horsepower which I am building for account of the Confederates, simultaneously with those you are having built with Joliet and Babin and Dubigeon fils. Beg you to arrange with Mr. Bullock to finally reimburse us for the guarantee commissions we pay to Mr. Erlanger. Accept, etc, Arman."[4]

Powerful warships were being built in France which could challenge the Union navy and possibly break the blockade of Southern ports. Blockade-running warships at this time were the only hope the Confederacy had for winning the war. The Davis government did not have an adequate stock of gunpowder and other supplies necessary to support their army. The new ships being built in France for use by the Confederacy were fast. They were being built with engines that could generate 400 horsepower. By contrast, the *C.S.S. Princess Royal*, had outrun the Union blockade in 1863 with engines generating 180 horsepower. The ship-yards of Napoleon III were in the process of building two ships with twice the speed. If completed and delivered, they would easily outrun any Union warship and deliver needed supplies to Davis' army. What was the reaction of the Lincoln Congress and the State Department? Seward first threatened legal action in French courts, then resolved to turn the tables on France and England when the Civil War was over. His fear, however, was that the Davis government was deliberately trying to provoke war between France and the Union through the construction and arming of warships in Nantes and Bordeaux. This was always a sus-picion when England was building privateers. Now that this was shifted to France, the fear rose again.

In Dispatch No. 447 on December 20, 1863, Seward wrote to Dayton, "In the opinion of this government, a toleration by the French govern-ment of the proceedings of the pirates ... would not be neutrality, but would be a permission to the enemies of the United States to make war against them from the coasts of France ... it is a deliberate design of the insurgents ... to involve France in a war with the United States."[5]

The construction of these ships was in conflict with an order from Napoleon III that forbade such construction. His Declaration of June 10, 1863 stated that he wanted to maintain good relations with the United States.

"Article 21 of the Code Napoleon declares: It is forbidden to any Frenchman to take orders from either party to arm ships of war, or to accept Letters of Marque for privateering, or to concur in any manner in the equipment or armament of a ship of war or corsair, of either party."

According to Bigelow, however, the Emperor wanted to have it both ways. "The evidence before me was conclusive that, unless the Emperor himself had been deceived, which was hardly credible, he was treating us with duplicity."[6] Napoleon was active on several fronts, however. First, he was allowing the construction of warships for the Confederacy in violation of the Code Napoleon. Second, his move into Mexico was risky and threatening to the United States as well as the future balance of power in Europe. How did the Union Congress react?

Traditionally, Congress has acted as a watchdog over the executive branch of government. During the Civil War, the Committee on the

Conduct of the War was formed in reaction to initial military disasters at Bull Run and Ball's Bluff.[7] Although the Committee didn't get involved with foreign relations, it had plenty to say about the head of the state department. In addition to oversight on the military side, Congress also maintained two standing committees on foreign affairs. Henry Winter Davis brought a resolution to the House floor condemning French incursion into Mexico. The Davis resolution was mild compared with one proposed earlier on February 3, 1863 by James McDougall, Democratic senator from California.[8] McDougall stated in his proposal that, "Resolved further, that the attempt to subject the Republic of Mexico to French authority is an act not merely unfriendly to this Republic, but to free institutions everywhere; and that it is regarded by this Republic as not only unfriendly, but as hostile." Those were strong words. The subsequent Davis resolution was modest and stated, "The Congress of the United States were unwilling by silence to leave the nations of the world under the impression that they are indifferent spectators of the deplorable events now transpiring in the Republic of Mexico; and that they therefore think fit to declare that it does not accord with the policy of the United States to acknowledge any monarchial government erected on the ruins of any republican government under the auspices of any European power." Either acting as *de facto* president or with the approval of Lincoln, Seward communicated the deliberations of the House to the French in an apparent attempt to mollify the emperor and maintain what he believed would be friendly relations between France and the United States. Dispatch No.525, April 7, 1864, Seward to Dayton stated, "This is a practical and purely executive question, and the decision of it constitutionally belongs not to the House of Representatives, nor even to Congress, but to the President of the United States."[9] Seward communicated the House resolution to Dayton who then made this available to Drouyn de Lhuys. Seward was not objecting to the words or the intent of the resolution, only to the fact that the sentiment was codified in the form of a House resolution. The issue for Davis was the fact that Seward superseded him by making the French aware of the resolution even before a Senate discussion took place. The resolution was voted on by the House and passed to the Senate. It is not unrealistic to believe that Henri Mercier could have heard of the resolution and secured his own copy for transmission to Drouyn de Lhuys. Seward's actions may have been completely unnecessary.

Without Seward's help, the House resolution made its way into the hands of Gustav Koerner in Madrid.[10] Koerner thought the resolution might insult France to the point of war. Writing to Seward, April 2, 1864, he complained, "the attitude assumed by the House of Representatives will produce complications with France, and may lead to a war." Lincoln still wanted one war at a time. Seward was not responsible for the House resolution. But he elevated it to new levels by tipping off France before the matter could be discussed in the Senate and precipitating the resignation of Henry Winter Davis. The official transmission of this resolution by the State Department enabled that document to carry greater weight and further enhance the authority of the secretary. Davis was enraged and made his feelings known. "The Secretary of State, before all Europe, in a matter of the greatest moment, slapped the House of Representatives in the face in his correspondence with the French government, and the House of Representatives says it will not even assert its dignity."

The U.S. Constitution allows for dual authority in foreign policy. Article two, section II of the Constitution states that the president, " … may require the opinion, in writing of the principal officer in each of the executive departments, upon any subject relating to the duties of their respective offices." In 1864, the "final say" issue was argued by Seward and Henry Winter Davis. The secretary advises the president on all matters which concern foreign policy and security issues related to that policy. Guided by the policy of the president in foreign relations, the state department gathers the facts and provides an analysis for the president. When a course of action is agreed upon at the executive level, the secretary of state is responsible for implementing that policy. In addition, the state department is required to apprise the American public, Congress and other appropriate government agencies as to any action taken. The department also negotiates treaties with foreign countries and speaks for the United States at the United Nations. The secretary of state is the first ranking member of the cabinet, and is a member of the National Security Council.

Regardless of attempts by Secretary Seward to strengthen the power of the executive at the expense of the legislative branch of government, the chair of the alternative State Department had other ideas. According to Charles Sumner, the Constitution charges Congress with creating the rules which the executive branch of government must operationalize. Sumner did not dispute the authority of the President as Commander-in-Chief, for example. Sumner stated, "The President, of himself, has no power to do anything. He is the executor of the laws. He has authority to command the army when the army exists, but it can only exist by the law of Congress."[11] When explaining further the war powers of Congress, Sumner stated again, "It is by Act of Congress that the War Powers are all put in motion. When once put in motion, the President must execute them. But he is only the instrument of Congress, under the Constitution."[12] By contrast, Seward saw the executive branch of government as having a degree of authority that exceeded that outlined by Charles Sumner. On one hand, Seward fully recognized and acknowledged the authority of the legislature to have final approval on treaties with foreign countries. In Dispatch No.53 on October 8, 1863, Seward wrote to Gustav Koerner regarding Confederate privateers hiding is Cuban ports under the protection of Spain. There was talk of rewriting various treaties with Spain in order to remedy this situation. Nevertheless, Seward asserted the primacy of the legislative branch in stating, "On the contrary, the United States cannot contract any binding engagement whatever with a foreign power except by a solemn treaty, which in every case must be submitted before ratification to the Senate for its approval."[13] When the matter was not a treaty with a foreign country, Seward was willing to challenge Sumner and the Senate by issuing Letters of Marque, an action reserved for the legislature alone. Both Seward and Sumner were strong-willed, and drew their own line in the sand that lasted for the duration of their public service. Seward, however, remained in a degree of competition with Sumner for the management of foreign affairs.

The biography of Lincoln by his secretaries Nicolay and Hay was sympathetic to Lincoln, but more balanced when analyzing Seward. They saw and heard much of what went on during the war. The secretaries commented on the strongly-worded McDougall resolution and Sumner's part in nullifying its impact.

> "The Senate resolution was referred to the Committee on Foreign Relations, then, as before, under the judicious chairmanship of Mr. Sumner, and were not

again reported to the Senate. But the House Committee on Foreign Affairs of the House of Representatives had a chair of very different temper from Mr. Sumner, Henry Winter Davis. In arriving at the Senate, this resolution was referred to the Committee on Foreign Relations, when in company with the more fiery utterances of Mr. McDougall, it slept unreported until the close of the session."[14]

In this manner, Charles Sumner buried two resolutions that were hostile to France and Mexico. He did this as chair of the committee. He was powerful enough to cause Senator McDougall to complain that his proposals, "… lay buried, not five fathoms deep, but certainly as well buried as if put into the tombs of the Capulets."[15] It may not have been necessary for Seward to leak a copy of the House resolution to France because Sumner took care of it. Sumner and Mexico weren't Seward's only problem, however.

Far from the battlefields of Northern Virginia and the Foreign Office in London, the ancient empire of Japan was creating problems for the state department which foreshadowed a similar issue seventy-five years later. In 1854, Commodore Matthew C. Perry compelled Japan to expand their limited trading policy. Before this, Japan traded with China, Korea and the Netherlands through the port of Nagasaki. This self-imposed isolation was designed to keep Japan free from Western influences that were considered a threat by the emperor and Tokugawa shogunate.[16] The concern focused on religion and economics. At the time of the Civil War, the leaders of the Tokugawa dynasty were concerned that their control and authority might be undermined by Catholic missionaries who preached that there was a deity much more powerful than the emperor. They were also concerned that trade with the West would enrich local warlords and chieftains that would also pose a threat to the authority of the dynasty. Europe had tried for many years to increase trading opportunities with Japan. All were met with sufficient force to deter potential trading partners. Matthew Perry was different, however. He was the younger brother of the hero of the War of 1812, Oliver Hazard Perry. In addition to serving under his older brother, Matthew did battle with the Barbary Pirates and the slave traders working the coast of Liberia. He was a veteran sailor who had seen extensive combat at sea. He declined the offer of a naval commission from Russia, and sailed into Yedo, on July 8, 1853. He carried a letter from

President Millard Fillmore. Perry was better armed and too bold for the shogun to resist the trade agreement that Perry carried from Fillmore. The Treaty of Kanagawa was signed on March 31, 1854. It allowed for trading in additional ports, more favorable import duties, the protection of shipwrecked sailors and the establishment of a U.S. Consulship. Perry's success emboldened England, France and Russia to seek their own trade agreements. Outgunned, the Japanese reluctantly accepted this change in their way of life. Some Japanese embraced the new policy, and some resisted. That resistance was recorded in dispatches from Robert Pruyn to Henry Seward in 1863 and 1864.

Pruyn[17] was from Albany, New York and a good friend of Seward. The secretary recommended Pruyn to Lincoln for the post in Japan. Pruyn's legation and residence had been burned by outlaws who resented the presence of foreigners on their soil. In addition to this, private citizens from England, France and the United States had been beaten and some murdered at the hands of Japanese insurgents. On July 13, 1863, the United States warship, the *Wyoming*, was fired upon by shore batteries from the straits of Shimonoseki. Two American sailors were killed and four wounded in the action. By 1864, things had gotten worse. Pruyn was afraid that war might break out. In Dispatch No.36, May 18, 1864, he informed Seward, "Sir, I have the honor to inform you that affairs wear a most threatening aspect. The government seems to be determined in its efforts to close this port of Kanagawa …"[18] The Port of Kanagawa was the port forced open to trade with the U.S. in 1854. Japan at this time was a medieval society ruled by local clans. The central government in Yedo (Tokyo) was willing to continue trade as outlined in the 1854 and subsequent agreements. Local warlords, however, resented foreign interference and influence. In Dispatch No.38, May 26, 1864, Pruyn summarizes the situation clearly for Seward. He stated, "The two centuries in which Japan remained isolated and unchanged were centuries of unparalleled progress in Europe and America; and now that its ports are opened, the past and the present stand face to face. These two forces will only harmonize as do light and darkness. One or the other must disappear. They cannot quietly coexist when brought into contact."[19] Seward's reaction at this later stage of his tenure at the state department was more restrained. He advised Pruyn to request an indemnity payment from the local magistrate. The magistrate, or Giorgio, told Pruyn that this would be a disgrace for the government. Seward urged his representative on, but did not threaten war or forceful retaliation. He was no longer prepared to send a U.S. warship into the harbor to force a resolution to the problem. Nevertheless, the situation in Japan continued to worsen. Pruyn was always afraid of war between the United States and the other traders in Japan, England and France. Far from the issues Seward faced with the Anglo-French alliance, that same alliance worked cooperatively and successfully in Japan. English and French citizens were assaulted no less than those from the U.S. England maintained a strong naval force in the area which helped moderate the actions of the clans. Unfortunately, Pruyn was not sure he could always count on them for help.

1864 was a year that was consumed with issues over Mexico and Confederate privateers refueling and rearming in French ports. Édouard Thouvanel had been dismissed as Foreign Minister and replaced by someone more aligned with Napoleon's nationalistic outlook, Drouyn de Lhuys. De Lhuys' letters to Dayton initially contained excuses and delaying actions as to why the government didn't stop the privateer activity in Brest and Calais. He did what the minister of Marine told him to do. Thouvanel was too independent for the Emperor. When Britain developed new rules for foreign ships and their business in English ports, business moved the short distance across the channel to Calais, France. Just before the start of the year, Seward was so exasperated by the lack of support shown by the government of France that he complained to Dayton in Dispatch No. 447 on December 20, 1863: " … a toleration by the French government of the proceedings of the pirates … would not be neutrality, but would be a permission to the enemies of the United States to make war against them from the coasts of France."[20] Union commercial shipping captains were so frustrated that they started to register U.S. ships with Britain and France to avoid being hunted and sunk by the *Florida, Rappahannock, Alabama* and others. Britain and France took their money and duly registered the ships, but the French continued to provide protection for the "pirates". When the *Rappahannock* fled England and came to Calais, Drouyn de Lhuys claimed that the ship was in distress and thus had to be sheltered. William Dayton went to discuss the matter with the foreign minister. In Dispatch No. 400,

January 15, 1864, Dayton to Seward revealed the result, "It would seem that upon inquiries made by their own agents they are led to believe that the visit of the *Rappahannock* was causal and of necessity and that they feel constrained, therefore, to treat this vessel like other vessels in distress only."[21] Seward, Dayton and Bigelow's frustration was justified and made clear in their dispatches to de Lhuys. It was equally frustrating for the state department to read the delaying tactics used by de Lhuys to avoid acknowledging French complicity in the construction and harboring of Confederate privateers.

By the summer of 1864, dispatches from Dayton to Seward concerned the privateers being sheltered in French ports from Calais to Cherbourg. Finally on June 13, 1864, Dispatch No.488, Dayton to Seward stated that the *Alabama* was in Cherbourg. Vice-consul in Paris, Edward Liais, immediately contacted Captain Winslow who had been waiting for his chance. Liais states, "I immediately telegraphed Captain Winslow, of the United States ship *Kearsarge*, now at Flushing. Captain Winslow has replied to me that he will be off Cherbourg about Wednesday." In the official report of the *Alabama* Captain Raphael Semmes tells of the fierce battle between the *Kearsarge* and the *Alabama*. William Dayton's son was on shore watching the battle at sea. After the *Alabama* had sunk, Semmes fled to England where he filed his report from Southampton. Seward's first dispatches to Dayton were primarily concerned with ensuring, to the extent that he could, that the battle took place outside the three-mile territorial limit. He was concerned that the two warships would fight it out within French territorial waters, and draw a lengthy protest from Drouyn de Lhuys. At this stage, Seward was focused on maintaining good relations with France, regardless of circumstances. At 9am on the morning of June 19, 1864, the Confederate privateer, *Alabama*, left the protection of Cherbourg harbor and went looking for the *Kearsarge*. She spotted her nine miles distant, and took almost an hour to reach her. Both ships presented their guns on the starboard side and opened fire. According to Semmes, "By this time we were about one mile from each other I opened on him with solid shot, to which he replied in a few minutes, and the engagement became active on both sides." In order to maintain a quarter mile distance between the two ships, they both remained on a starboard tack and circled around each other belching fire and explosive shell. No longer dependent on sail for motion, there was little point in aiming for the enemy's rigging. The intention was to blast a hole in the enemy ship below the waterline and force it to sink. According to Semmes, "The firing now became very hot, and the enemy's shot and shell soon began to tell upon our hull, knocking down, killing and disabling a number of men." Semmes fired up his boilers and made a dash for the French coast. His speed only forced more sea water into his broken hull, and his boilers died under the cool Atlantic water. The fight was over.

The published dispatches from Washington to Paris and back made no mention of any issues with France over the sinking of the *Alabama*. However, the presence of French troops in Mexico remained of concern to the state department. Dispatches for a period of three weeks from Dayton to Seward told of bad relations between French troops and the U.S. consular officials in Mexico. French memos allegedly were sent to the consulate. French officers refused to salute U.S. officials as was the custom. Although honor was at stake, Seward wisely decided to pick his battles. This was not a dispute worth fighting. In uncharacteristic fashion he tells Dayton that, "I approve of the reticence you have practiced on the subject in your communication with M. Drouyn de Lhuys." Reticence was a new term for William Henry Seward. Although very late in the drama, he was learning on the job.

1864 was a difficult year. For Seward, the issues were on land and on sea. They ranged from Mexico to Japan. The extent of correspondence from Seward to Dayton, Bigelow and Robert Pruyn was considerable. A normally busy state department was busier in 1864. Victory in Gettysburg and Vicksburg mattered to Palmerston and Russell, but not to Napoleon III and the Shogun in Yeddo (Tokyo). At this stage, the Anglo-French alliance had begun to crack. Napoleon III had begun to chart his own, separate course. He was allowing the construction of the most powerful steam warships in his shipyards, and he was extending his empire to Mexico. England decided that she wanted no part of this.

After the death of Richard Cobden on April 2, 1865, the responsibility for post-war relations between Britain and the United States fell to Adams, Seward, Bright and Sumner. However, the *Alabama* claims were a serious challenge to the diplomatic skills of Seward and Sumner. The *Alabama* claims also caused a rift in the relationship of Sumner and Bright.

More than state department diplomacy, it was Union military success, the growth of the Union navy, British caution, Lincoln's resolve and distracting issues within Europe that dictated the substance and scope of U.S. foreign relations during the American Civil War. In his dispatches to Charles Francis Adams, Henry Seward often stated that there would be a reckoning after the war. As far back as March 28, 1863, Lord John Russell got the hint. The foreign minister believed that the outcry against the *Alabama* was exaggerated, and he was later to be a factor in denying and delaying the claims settlement effort. Earlier in 1863, however, he thought differently. He wrote to Lyons that, "I must feel that [*Alabama's*] roaming the ocean with English guns and English sailors to burn, sink and destroy the ships of a friendly nation, is a scandal." This was an extraordinary acknowledgment that England was in a *de facto* war with the United States. Nevertheless, Seward was an optimist and always believed in the ultimate success of the Union. This is confirmed in several dispatches from Adams to Seward in the winter of 1865. Dispatch No.874, February 10, 1865, Adams to Seward stated, "The general fear now is that the domestic reconciliation will be simultaneous with a foreign war … It is important, if possible, in some indirect way, to sooth these alarms."

While Robert E. Lee was trying to outrun Grant's army as they raced toward Appomattox Court House, Judah Benjamin tried to save the Confederacy one last time. One of his best friends was Louisiana sugar planter, Duncan Kenner. Both men were connected through association with John Slidell and interested in the more scientific approaches to planting, harvesting and refining sugar. "Kenner was the only one in official Richmond with whom Benjamin could talk frankly about the war, knowing he would protect confidences.[22] By this time, both Benjamin and Kenner were convinced that the Confederacy needed to issue its own emancipation proclamation. The most remarkable aspect of the Kenner mission to Europe was not that final attempt to save the day, but the fact that Kenner was able to reach London and Paris at all. His instructions and credentials were written in cypher. The blockade was so tight that his attempt to run the blockade at Wilmington failed, and he went back to Richmond to figure out what to do next. He thought that the best way to get to Europe now was through New York. Kenner made his way to Washington, and stayed at the home of a family known to be friendly towards the Confederacy. The owner was a woman named Mary Surratt.[23]

Reaching Baltimore, Kenner changed clothes to disguise himself as a Pennsylvania farmer. When he reached New York, Confederate sympathizers bought him a ticket and found a trunk for his clothes en route to Europe. Kenner went first to Paris where both Mason and Slidell were still trying to save their mission. However, both men told Kenner that he was probably wasting his time. They were right. Although the emperor was still playing both sides and encouraged Kenner, Lords Palmerston and Russell were clear that his trip was a wasted effort. England had no intention to recognize the Confederacy. While Kenner was receiving the bad news, Lee was already surrendering to Grant at Appomattox.

One may argue as to where the war began. Was it with the failure of the original constitution to adequately address the issue of slavery back in 1787? Was it the shots fired at Fort Sumter in 1861? It is difficult to determine. However, it ended with the failed mission of Duncan Kenner to Paris and London in the spring of 1865. Although the shooting war was over, the diplomatic war over the *Alabama* claims was just beginning. William Henry Seward always warned John Bull that they could expect a reckoning after the war. The time had come.

★

What has come down in history as the *Alabama* Claims are several issues that go beyond just the claims of American merchantmen whose ships were seized and burned by the *C.S.S. Alabama*. In addition to American claims, the British also had similar claims for the seizure of their ships attempting to breach a blockade that they claimed was ineffective and thus illegal through the Treaty of Paris. There were issues of free trade between Canada and the U.S. as well as the issue of those naturalized American citizens who were originally British sailors who fled her Majesty's lash. England claimed that once a British citizen, always a British citizen. Unfortunately, Seward made what might have been a simple matter much worse by insisting that the claims must address the fact that England's Belligerency declaration was unnecessary, poorly-timed and resulted in prolonging the war. In Dispatch No.1835, August 27, 1866, Seward to Adams wrote:

> "You will herewith receive a summary of claims of the United States against Great Britain for damages which were suffered by them during the period of our late Civil War, and some months thereafter, by means of depredations upon our commercial marine, committed on the high seas by the Sumter, the Alabama, the Florida, the Shenandoah and other ships of war, which were built, manned, armed, equipped and fitted out in British ports, and despatched [sic] therefrom by or through the agency of British subjects, and which were harbored, sheltered, provided and furnished as occasion required, during their devastating career, in ports of the realm, or in ports of British colonies in nearly all parts of the globe."[24]

Adams took exception to Seward's unnecessarily harsh language and said that his dispatch was, "scarcely conciliatory. I don't think so well as I did of our prospect of setting it all up. Another damned rope's-end let loose to trip us up."[25] Richard Russell stated the British position that the British had only built unarmed ships for the Confederacy. They were not warships when they left British docks. England could not be held responsible. The ships were armed either at sea or in other ports over which England had no control. He also pointed out that the *Sumter* was originally a Union ship that was captured leaving New Orleans, and armed outside British jurisdiction or control.

For these reasons, Russell insisted that British claims were the only ones to be settled. American claims had no merit. He refused to submit any claims to arbitration as suggested by Seward. According to Russell, "Her Majesty's government are the sole guardians of their own honor."[26] Ultimately, the roadblock was cleared not directly through negotiations by either Seward or Adams, but by the fall of the Russell government and the installation of a new administration headed by the Earl of Derby as prime minister and his son, Lord Stanley, as foreign secretary. Stanley agreed to arbitrate all British and American claims. Part of his willingness to submit to arbitration certainly came from the consistent pushing by Seward and Adams. Much of the change of heart, however, came from the fact that the balance of world power had changed.

In Dispatch No.1275, November 23, 1866, Adams wrote to Seward that Lord Stanley had asked, " … if I knew whether my government had any plan in view." With this, the process began to move forward. Again, however, ulterior motives on the part of William Henry Seward held up what otherwise may have been a relatively easy process. Seward suggested that all of the *Alabama* claims be exchanged for Britain ceding northwestern Canadian territory to the United States. He had negotiated the annexation of Alaska the year before. He wanted to continue the spirit of Manifest Destiny and further enlarge American borders. Charles Francis Adams was frustrated, and in five months would resign and sail home. In his diary he wrote, "I saw very clearly the drift of this to be a bargain for the British territory in the North West, or the West India islands more or less in lieu of all demands. Mr. Seward's thirst for more land seems insatiable."[27]

Seward's old nemesis, Gideon Welles, was convinced that Seward wanted to run for president and would point to his success in territorial expansion as his platform. There is no evidence to support this. Seward was left with making his mark as secretary of state.

In May, 1868, Charles Francis Adams sailed home to Massachusetts. Many anticipated that the secretary of state would take his place. Seward recommended Hamilton Fish, but the Senate would only confirm Reverdy Johnson. William Henry Seward would retire with the Johnson administration in less than one year. The fall of the Russell government brought Lord Clarendon to the Foreign Office. The *Alabama* issue was still unsettled, however. Reverdy Johnson had worked out a proposal with Lord Stanley that the claims would be heard and settled by a commission. Any disagreement by the commission would send the matter to an arbitrator. The *Alabama* claims, however, were to be settled separately. Seward rightly objected. Under Clarendon, a proposal was agreed upon whereby all claims would be heard by the commission. Two commissioners would be chosen from each country, and a head of state jointly selected as arbitrator. If they could not agree on an arbitrator, one would be chosen by picking names out of a hat. Seward had agreed to this, but Reverdy Johnson took the fall as outrage mounted in America over the proposal. This was when Charles Sumner got into the act and made a strong speech in Congress that in addition to damages from British-manned privateers, England also owed America damages from the increased insurance rates and other matters caused by prolonging the war. He claimed that the war was made worse and longer by Britain's encouraging the Confederacy when she accorded her Belligerent rights. Public opinion forced out Johnson who was replaced by Seward's first choice, Hamilton Fish. At this point, America wanted real peace.

The time was ripe for a settlement. The supplementary claims issue was finally dropped by Fish. The treaty was finally signed in Washington on May 8, 1871. It was a product of the patience and skill of Hamilton Fish, not Henry Seward who was home in Auburn. British commissioner Sir Stafford Northcote said, "If we have not built a castle, we have laid the foundations of a very nice cottage, which might be turned into a castle at some future day."[28] The Treaty of Washington is credited with being the first step in a rapprochement with England that has endured to the present day.

★

Throughout his career as secretary of state, Henry Seward was either loved or loathed. Nobody hated him, but many distrusted him. To this extent, he was like Abraham Lincoln, Jefferson Davis and Judah Benjamin. Men like Charles Francis Adams gave him credit that Gideon Welles claimed belonged to Lincoln. Edward Alfred Pollard, editor of the *Richmond Examiner*, gave no credit to the Confederate president. Abraham Lincoln and William Henry Seward were politicians who were driven by personal ambition and love of country. Like Sun Tsu, Lincoln's strength lay in the fact that he knew himself as well as his enemies. Seward was an enigma to himself who struggled with this knowledge.

President Lincoln generally allowed his department chairmen to run their own shows. Absorbed primarily with the war on land and sea, he became a reactive leader when issues with other departments arose which required his help. The death of one of his sons, a wife who had her own personal issues, and a war which took so many young lives distracted Lincoln from problems like the blockade, belligerency, *Trent*, neutrality and recognition. He was often forced to quickly catch up on these events and make complex decisions that had great impact on the conduct of the war. Jefferson Davis was his own secretary of war and thus fought a two-front battle that created a level of stress that might have killed him. Acting as his own secretary of war, he took the blame politically and militarily for the battlefield losses that distracted him as much as it did Lincoln. Both secretaries of state were thus left to craft their own foreign policy as best they could. For Seward this was simpler than it was for Benjamin. Seward's primary goal was to keep Britain and France out of the conflict. The author believes that this foreign policy was wisely managed by those hoary and shrewd men like Palmerston, Russell and Lyons. Davis and Benjamin both thought they knew their enemy. They believed that cotton was king. They were wrong. Slavery was king. If Great Britain was the single most important piece of this complex puzzle, her antislavery frame of reference enjoined her from the scope of support Davis needed and England would not supply. There may have been cheering in parliament when the *Alabama* escaped into the open ocean, but, "It has been said that the dress suit and digestive apparatus of England were hostile to the United States, but that the cerebro-centers, heart and muscle, were friendly."[29]

After the war, Lincoln was gone, Jeff Davis was in prison and Judah Benjamin was successfully practicing law in England. William Seward had retired. Yet, the *Alabama* claims still threatened to disrupt relations between Britain and the U.S. People then, and some historians now believe that belligerent "recognition" and the British-built commerce raiders like the *Alabama* resulted in a longer war. The cost of that longer war resulted in the Indirect Claims from the *Alabama* et al. Cries of war were heard consistently in Washington and London. When things settled down, a fellow New Yorker, Hamilton Fish, ultimately worked out the complex language of the Treaty of Washington that settled the *Alabama* claims and averted war once again. Both Henry Seward and Charles Francis Adams deserve credit for constantly reminding the British Foreign Office that England must assume responsibility for her actions with the *Alabama* and other privateers.

Seward was good at bringing attention to problems that might otherwise have been ignored. His letters and thousands of dispatches, however, show little evidence of the ability to negotiate like those "hoary and shrewd men" in London. The negotiations were finally left to men like Hamilton Fish who did the slow and pedantic word-smithing that finally crafted a treaty which was approved by all sides.

Many people had an impact on foreign relations during the Lincoln and Davis administrations. The Seward State Department did the day-to-day monitoring of world affairs as they might impact the Union. However, from the *Trent* Affair to the *Alabama* claims, it is clear that the work done behind the scenes by many "key players" really got the job done. Although Seward was learning on the job until at least 1863, his dispatches to London, Paris, St. Petersburg and Tokyo were short, and businesslike. He knew the power of the printed word. It was only in January, 1864 that he finally lost patience with British reluctance to control the private construction of warships that he threatened to sail right into English docks and challenge the privateers. The old Seward was always just under the surface. In addition to foreign relations issues on land and sea, the secretary of state was at odds with Charles Sumner, the man referred to by historian David Herbert Donald as the *de facto* secretary of state. Seward believed that the executive branch of government was the real power broker in foreign relations. Sumner countered by claiming that the Constitution was the final authority. The final act of the duel between Seward and Sumner was finally played over the claims of the *Alabama*.

Judah Benjamin was as active and ambitious as his Northern counterpart. However, his energies were sapped by the three cabinet posts he held during the Davis administration; attorney general, secretary of war and most successfully as secretary of state. Benjamin was as tenacious in diplomacy as was Robert E. Lee on the battlefield. With few resources or even the ability to communicate effectively with his representatives in Europe, Benjamin achieved the only recognition ever realized by the Confederate States of America. This was the "financial recognition" manifested through the Erlanger Cotton Loan. Benjamin was as up-beat as Seward. He always believed that there was hope, even as his representative to Moscow, Lucius Lamar, was sent back home empty-handed by the Confederate Congress. Even as Lee's army was starving and the war nearing an end, Benjamin sent his good friend Duncan Kenner to London to try and work a miracle. When he arrived, both Mason and Slidell told him it was useless.

Period historians and diarists like Gideon Welles, Edward Bates and Charles Francis Adams understandably maintained strong polarizing views of men like Seward. They worked and argued with him. They were often on the receiving end of Seward's actions and reactions. Modern historians have the benefit of more objectivity. Seward spent most of his time and is primarily known for his place in the Lincoln cabinet and the work he did as secretary of state for Abraham Lincoln. If the truth is somewhere in between, William Henry Seward was neither a "vaporing, blustering, ignorant man" as characterized by Lord Palmerston nor was he the *de facto* President he assumed he would be. Seward gets good marks, but not the high marks accorded by Doris Goodwin. Although he learned on the job, some argue that this learning process prolonged the war. Seward was an enigma to himself, but grew in strength and wisdom as he learned on the job. He made some costly mistakes, finally recognized his own limitations, and by his own reckoning, achieved his greatest triumph not during the war under Lincoln, but after it under Andrew Johnson. Before he died, Seward was asked about his greatest achievement as secretary of state. He never mentioned foreign relations. He uttered one word – "Alaska".

EPILOGUE

Abraham Lincoln died of a gunshot wound to the right side of his brain at 7:30am, April 15, 1865. He was fifty-six years old. Preserved in the National Archives are letters of condolence from all over the world. While these letters were still arriving at the Executive Mansion, President Andrew Johnson remained at his room in the Kirkwood House and told Mary Lincoln to take as much time as she needed before vacating the Executive Mansion. Grief stricken, Mrs. Lincoln took many weeks before leaving with sixty-four trunks of clothes and 100 boxes bound for Chicago. It was too difficult to go back to the old life in Springfield.

Jefferson Davis died of natural causes on December 6, 1889. He was eighty-one years old. After Lee's surrender, Abraham Lincoln came to Richmond and had the satisfaction of sitting in Davis' chair in what we now know as the Confederate White House. By this time, Davis and his wife had fled the Union troops searching for them. In early May, when it was still chilly in the morning hours, Davis was captured with his wife's shawl over his shoulders to ward off the cold. The Northern press couldn't resist picturing Davis running away disguised in his wife's dress. He was imprisoned in Fort Monroe for two years, but lived to write his memoirs of the Confederacy. Judah Benjamin survived by disguising himself as a French-speaking servant who managed to get to England via Nassau. Before leaving, he told Postmaster General John Reagan, "I am going to the furthest place from the U.S., if it takes me to the middle of China." The so-called "brains of the Confederacy" was admitted to the bar in England in 1866, and enjoyed a distinguished legal career for the rest of his life. In 1868, he published a text on the statute and common law governing the sale and purchase of property. *Benjamin on Sales* remained a standard for many years. James Bulloch, the man who arranged for the construction of the *Alabama*, remained in Liverpool after the war and became a successful import merchant. Ironically, his half-sister was the mother of President Theodore Roosevelt, and grandmother to Eleanor Roosevelt. It was Theodore Roosevelt who convinced Bulloch to write his memoirs which were published in 1883 as *The Secret Service of the Confederate States of America*. Bulloch's book is used by historians today to analyze the role of the *Alabama* and other commerce raiders during the Civil War.

Unable to get out of bed and unable to attend the funeral, William Henry Seward had lost a friend, mentor and alter ego.

Two years before the assassination of the president and the attempt on his own life, the diplomatic corps began to change in Washington. After several requests to return to Paris, Henri Mercier was finally given permission to leave his post in Washington. Unfortunately, the French invasion of Mexico made for a quiet but hasty departure. When he reached Paris, Édouard Thouvanel was no longer in office, having been forced to resign in 1862. He was succeeded by Drouyn de Lhuys, someone more willing to do the bidding of Napoleon III. Although critical of Seward bluster at the start of the war, he was more charitable in 1863. He even went so far as to say that, "He [Seward] is very wise." Upon reaching his home in Paris, he found a note from Seward asking him to ship "ten or twelve bottles of Burgundy" to Washington. The Seward social machine continued regardless of who came and who went.

After meeting with de Lhuys, Mercier made sure to stop and talk with William Dayton. Hard-working as always, Dayton regarded Mercier and Seward as similar personalities. Both were flamboyant risk-takers, but Mercier had a better appreciation for the diligence Dayton put into the work of Minister in Paris. In October, 1864, Mercier was appointed Minister to Spain. On December 1, shortly after arriving at his new post, he received a sad telegram from Paris. The official history is that Dayton had been quietly working at his desk. A legation secretary sitting next to him assumed that Dayton had fallen asleep. He died of a hemorrhagic stroke that December afternoon. The reality is that Dayton may have died in bed with his lover at his side. His body was secretly carried to the legation to make it look as if he had died at his post. Retiring in 1870 at the age of fifty-three, Henri Mercier was pleased to see his old nemesis, Henry Seward, traveling in Europe. Both men talked about the tense drama that occupied them in younger days. Baron Henri Mercier died on October 16, 1886 at the age of seventy.

Gideon Welles served as navy secretary throughout the Lincoln and Johnson administrations. After Andrew Johnson left the Kirkwood House and moved into the Executive Mansion, he had a difficult time. He lacked the wisdom, vision and patience of Abraham Lincoln. Nevertheless, Gideon Welles liked Johnson and worked hard to serve him as best he could under difficult circumstances. When Lincoln died, the U.S. Navy had grown to 600 vessels. During the war, those ships had captured 1,504 prizes, many of them British blockade runners. Welles was proud of his achievements, but became weary of the constant struggle between Andrew Johnson and Congress. His beard got whiter and longer. He walked slower now and when Johnson left office, so did Gideon Welles. He went home to friends and family in Hartford, Connecticut. Mary Welles had been a friend of Mary Lincoln. She returned to Hartford with a lock of the President's hair which Edwin Stanton gave to Mrs. Lincoln, and she then gave to her friend, Mary Welles. Finding life in the private sector more expensive than anticipated, Welles began writing articles on the war for the *Atlantic Monthly* and other publications. It was in this context that Welles wrote a short book entitled *Seward and Lincoln* to serve as a rebuttal to Charles Francis Adams' view of Lincoln in his 1873 eulogy in Albany. The publication of this book was the first time that most Americans learned enough accurate information about their late President to realize the service Lincoln had performed for the country. The success of the book encouraged Welles to spend time organizing his diary. That effort has since proven to be a valuable source of information on the Lincoln administration and how it functioned at the cabinet level.

When Gideon Welles died on February 11, 1878, many of his colleagues had already passed away. The first was Edward Bates in 1869. Bates was already sixty-eight years old when he joined the Lincoln administration in 1861. He was a devoted family man who tired of the political struggle and retired in 1864. He also kept a diary which historians use as a unique source of information on the Lincoln administration. Bates died in 1869, the same year that William Henry Seward left public life and returned to Auburn.

The years between the Lincoln assassination and Seward's death in 1872 were busy. The secretary was fond of saying that "rest is rust". On Easter Sunday, 1865, the gravely wounded Seward was finally told that Abraham Lincoln was dead. His doctors had withheld that information for fear it would slow his recovery. Restless and always in a hurry, Seward was out riding in his carriage within a week. By July, he was back at work at the State Department working for a new president, Andrew Johnson. Never anticipating that he would take power so quickly, Johnson was unprepared to deal effectively with foreign affairs, and left those issues to his secretary of state. The immediate issues facing the United States were French troops in Mexico and the insurance companies that were screaming for relief from payments made to policy holders with claims against the *Alabama*. Seward is credited by many for coercing France to remove troops from Mexico. The occupation was expensive, and Napoleon finally realized it was a bad idea in the first place. Leaving Mexico in 1867, the U.S. was now faced with the *Alabama* claims. Seward and Adams must receive credit for consistently bringing the claims issue before the Foreign Office. Seward had always warned Russell that after the war was over, Britain might find herself in a bad position with America now selling arms and warships to the Queen's enemies. In 1866, that nightmare came true as the House passed legislation allowing the sale of munitions to belligerents at war.

Seward next turned his attention to his favorite activity, territorial acquisition. The purchase of Russian America might help coax Canada into the Union. Russia was willing to sell, and Alaska was purchased for $7,000,000 in 1867. This was a particularly stressful time for Seward because in addition to the negotiations for Alaska, Andrew Johnson was going through the impeachment process. The president and the secretary of state survived, however. Returning to Auburn, Seward was quickly bored. His health also began to fail. He felt growing paralysis on his right side. It is possible that the attack on April 14 did nerve damage that impacted the right side of his body. Nevertheless, "rest is rust", and on August 9, 1870, Seward began a 14-month trip around the world. From India, China, Japan and the capitols of Western Europe, Henry Seward took the notes which became *William Henry Seward's Travels Around the World,* published in 1873. At the end of his life, he was asked about his greatest accomplishment. Without hesitation, he never mentioned foreign relations, but simply this, "Alaska". Seward's death on October 10, 1872 came as a shock to his friend Charles Francis Adams, who was in Europe at the time.

Charles Francis Adams retired from the diplomatic service in 1868. He returned home to Massachusetts and what he had hoped would be a quiet retirement. Within six months, the Democratic National Committee considered him for president. Harvard College offered him the presidency of their institution. The D.N.C. offer never materialized and Adams turned down Harvard. Retirement didn't last long, however. In 1871, he was appointed as the U.S. representative to the five-person panel on the *Alabama* claims. Adams left for Geneva with some of his family and helped negotiate the Treaty of Washington. He had some tense moments, however, when Grant insisted on extra claims in the belief that England had prolonged the war and caused further financial hardship that needed to be reconciled. Grant dropped his claim, the treaty was settled, and Adams returned home again. He spent his last years organizing his father's papers and revising the biography of his grandfather, John Adams. Unfortunately, his memory began to fail and work ceased until his death in 1886.

Seward complained more than once that there were too many secretaries of state in Washington. His principal rival was Senator Charles Sumner of Massachusetts. Before his death of heart failure in 1874, Sumner remained in the Senate, but had a difficult time with the changing politics. He eventually parted company with his old friend John Bright over the *Alabama* Claims. Sumner spoke against the negotiations in language strong enough to make enemies everywhere. Bright objected. The senator also had difficulty accepting the scandals that plagued the Grant administration. As outspoken as always, Sumner continued to make enemies in Washington and Massachusetts. In 1866, he married Alice Mason Cooper. She was thirty years younger than Sumner, beautiful and wealthy. Cooper thought that marriage to someone as powerful and distinguished as Charles Sumner would help her social standing. They divorced in one year. Charles Francis Adams, never a supporter of the senator, made comments about Sumner's virility. The gossip was rampant and embarrassing. Finally, in 1872, he proposed a resolution that would ban attaching the names of famous battles from their respective regimental colors. He thought this small gesture would help bring more peace to the Union. With Grant as president and the scars of war still fresh in the minds of most Americans, the proposal resulted in a censure by the Massachusetts General Assembly. This hurt the pride and vanity of someone who had once been so powerful. Frequently injected with morphine to dull the pain from angina, Sumner died March 11, 1874.

Lord Richard Lyons served as minister to Washington for six years. He hated the heat and dust that characterized the capitol in summer. Constantly complaining of poor health, he retired from public service in March, 1865, and returned to England. At this point, Lyons and Seward had come to recognize each other's strengths. On March 20, 1865, Seward wrote to Lyons that "I accept your farewell with sincere sorrow." Lyons didn't retire for long, however. By October, 1865, he was posted to Constantinople to clean up a financial mess left by his predecessor Sir Henry Bulwer. Lyons' greatest service in Europe, however, came in 1867 when he was posted to Paris. He served in that capacity for the next twenty years, skillfully steering England through the many crises at the time, including the Franco-Prussian War in 1870. In addition to Abraham Lincoln and William Seward, Richard Lyons also worked with other giants of the age including Otto von Bismarck.

When Richard Lyons left Washington, changes began to take place in London. Sir Frederick Bruce succeeded him in Washington. In London, Lord Palmerston died on October 18, 1865, and was succeeded by Lord John Russell. The foreign secretary was then replaced by Lord Clarendon. Russell was reluctant to submit American claims for *Alabama* damage because he maintained that Britain was only doing what she was entitled to do as a neutral nation. He claimed that the Union blockade amounted to a *de facto* recognition of the Confederacy as a sovereign entity. That "recognition" then allowed England to do business as she wished. He still believed that England sold ships that were not warships when they left British docks. However, he acknowledged that privateers like the *Alabama* were manned by British crews, but not captained by British officers. For this reason, the damage done to Union commercial shipping was done under the direction of the Confederacy, not England. Disagreement aside, the Russell administration fell in less than one year. Before leaving office, however, Russell introduced a modified Reform Bill that would extend suffrage to all but the "feckless and criminal poor". His government collapsed before the bill became law. After leaving office, Russell went into permanent retirement, and John Bright took up the Reform Bill and greatly enhanced it.

After William Henry Seward and Charles Sumner died, John Bright continued to represent Birmingham until his death in 1889. He successfully legislated the Reform Act of 1867 which enfranchised all male householders in England and Wales. His relations with his American friend, Charles Sumner, suffered over the *Alabama* claims, however. In 1869, the successor to Charles Francis Adams, Reverdy Johnson, struck a deal with Foreign Secretary Lord Clarendon. Sumner said the deal was bad because British belligerency recognition had prolonged the war. Under these circumstances, Sumner believed that the costs of the war itself should be adjudicated as well as the damage done by the *Alabama*. London reacted again with cries of war. The Johnson–Clarendon deal was defeated in the Senate. John Bright also reacted in denouncing Sumner and the attitude of America over the claims and British responsibility.

NOTES

Introduction

1   Royale, Trevor. *Crimea, The Great Crimean War, 1854–1856.* New York: Pelgrave, 2000. p.4.

2   James Orr, claimed that the CSA had no foreign policy. Several additional sources also claim that the Confederacy had no foreign policy, including Robert Barnwell Rhett, who advised William Loundes Yancey not to accept his mission to Europe. He claimed that the Davis government would not provide the necessary support for the mission.

3   Lewis Powell a.k.a. Lewis Payne.

4   Emmerich de Vattel and Henry Wheaton were the two leading international law theorists whose guidance was followed closely by the British. Both John Russell and Admiral Milne had copies of Vattel close by to provide guidance.

5   Stahr, Walter. *Seward: Lincoln's Indispensable Man.* New York, Simon and Schuster, 2012. p.308.

6   Stephen Mallory and Christopher Memminger were secretary of the navy and treasury respectively.

7   See, for example, Howard J. Fuller "Iron Lion or Paper Tiger? The Myth of British Naval Intervention in the American Civil. War" in Peter N. Steams (ed.), *The American Civil War in a Global Context.* Richmond Virginia Sesquicentennial of the American Civil War Commission: 2014, 56–79.

8   The *Gloire* was the first oceangoing ironclad warship. She was built in France, and launched in 1859. She was driven by steam and sail with a screw propeller. She was a good example of the extent to which the naval arms race had come by the end of the Crimean War.

9   Emmerich de Vattel, *The Law of Nations,* 1758.

10 Lord Stowell a.k.a. William Scott, 1745–1836, did much to proscribe international law on the seas through his work on the High Court of Admiralty.

11 Prize Courts were set up to settle maritime questions of search and seizure of "enemy" ships and their cargo in time of war and conflict. In the United States, prize courts were set up in most large principal cities.

12 Neutrality was a subject that garnered much attention by Vattel, Wheaton and many before them. During war, many nations wanted to be able to maintain their economic trading status with warring parties. They wanted to do this without becoming engaged in the conflict. The question of what defined those contraband items which neutrals were forbidden to transport or sell to the warring parties was always a question.

13 Donald, David H. *Charles Sumner and the Coming of the War.* New York: Alfred Knopf, 1960.

Chapter 1

1 "A world wrapped in flames" was supposedly uttered by Seward over the prospect of war with Britain over the *Trent* incident in late 1861.

2 Vandiver, Frank. Jefferson Davis: Leader Without a Legend. The Journal of Southern History, vol. 43, no.1, February 1977.

3 Francis Carpenter painted the picture *The First Reading of the Emancipation Proclamation* 1864.

4 Adams, Charles Francis, Adams Papers, Microfilm Edition, Sterling Library, Yale University.

5 Evans, Eli. *Judah P. Benjamin: The Jewish Confederate.* New York: Free Press, 1988. p.150.

6 Butler, Pierce. *Judah P. Benjamin.* Philadelphia: Jacobs, 1907. p.8.

7 In 1861, an article appeared in the New York *Independent.* It was written by a Yale classmate at that time, in 1828. The classmate, Francis Bacon, claimed that Benjamin was suspected of stealing money, jewelry and other valuables from the rooms of Yale students. According to Bacon, when confronted, the students found their stolen valuables in Benjamin's trunk. He was dismissed from Yale.

8 By contrast Lincoln and Seward were earning approximately $5,000 at this time.

9 Evans, Eli. *Judah P. Benjamin, the Jewish Confederate.* New York: Free Press, 1988. p.69.

10 Ibid. p.65.

11 Van Deusen, Glyndon: *William Henry Seward.* New York: Oxford University Press, 1967. p.25.

12 It was assumed by some that Benjamin was gay. His wife used this as her justification for leaving Benjamin and moving to Paris.

13 Thurlow Weed was a powerful and influential New York newspaper publisher and Whig advisor. He is best known for his support of William Henry Seward. Some believe that Weed was Seward's *alter ego.* Weed was sent to Europe during the dangerous period of the *Trent* crisis to learn more for Seward.

14 Welles, Gideon: *Lincoln and Seward.* Freeport: Books for Libraries Press, 1969. (reprint) p.68.

15 Chase, Salmon: *Private Letters and Public Service.* Cincinnati: Wilson Baldwin and Co., 1874. p.11.

16 There were no U.S. representatives with the rank of Ambassador at this time. That was not achieved until the end of the nineteenth century.

17 A comparative list of key diplomatic ministers and their compensation under Buchanan vs Lincoln

	Buchanan	Lincoln
Secretary of State	8,000 USD	8,000 USD
Minister to England	17,500 USD	17,500 USD
Minister to France	17,500 USD	17,500 USD
Minister to Russia	12,000 USD	12,000 USD
Minister to Japan	7,500 USD	7,500 USD
Minister to China	7,500 USD	7,500 USD
Minister to Prussia	12,000 USD	12,000 USD
Minister to Austria	12,000 USD	12,000 USD
Minister to Mexico	12,000 USD	12,000 USD
Minister to Spain	12,000 USD	12,000 USD

18 Seward reference on the work of the State Dept.

19 Blockade runners generally drew 12 feet of water vs the 25-30 feet of water drawn by the ironclad frigates manning the blockade.

20 Frederick Seward served as Assistant Secretary of State under his father during the Civil War. He later served under Andrew Johnson and Rutherford B. Hayes. He was severely wounded by Lewis Powell on the night of April 14, 1865 as he tried to defend his father. Seward wrote his *Reminiscences* about his time during the war. This serves as another tool in understanding the functioning of the State Department and his father at this time.

21 Nicolay, John; and Hay, John: *Abraham Lincoln, A History.* New York: The Century Co. 189. p.266.

22 William Henry Seward Papers Microform Edition, University of Rochester, Rochester, New York. It is interesting to note a pattern of dispatch volume increasing from 1861–65. After the Emancipation Proclamation and the victories at Gettysburg and Vicksburg in 1863, one might expect that the volume would slow down or stay constant. The following volume to London and Paris is typical of this period:

U.S. Minister at London		U.S. Minister at Paris	
1860	73	1860	37
1861	220	1861	144
1862	317	1862	209
1863	380	1863	304
1864	463	1864	304
1865	449	1865	383

The total dispatch volume to all other aforementioned countries barely exceeded 300 per country.

23 Dayton papers, Firestone Library, Princeton University.

24 James Chestnut helped draft the Confederate Constitution. His name may be better remembered today because of the diary his wife kept, Mary Boykin Chestnut. Her published diary provides unique insight into Confederate life at home during the war.

25 Nicolay and Hay write that nobody in the cabinet ever became aware of the memo. They also state that Lincoln and Seward became close confidants after this.

26 Seward to Richard H. Dana, June 30, 1861.

27 Adams, Charles Francis. Eulogy of Seward, New York State Legislature, 1873.

28 Ibid.

29 The reality is quite different. Purchasing agents for the Union purchased thousands of rifled guns from Austria and thousands of pounds of saltpeter and Sulphur from Great Britain. Lincoln and Seward were much more organized than Jefferson Davis and often beat Confederate purchasing agents to the contract.

30 A copy of Helper's book is in the Seward library in Auburn, N.Y.

31 Stovall, Pleasant. *Robert Toombs: Statesman, Speaker, Soldier, Sage.* New York: Cassell, 1892.

32 Approximately 70% of the population are visual learners, and 30% learn better auditorily.

33 Goldwin Smith's book supported the sensational allegations by John Bigelow that people like William E. Gladstone had subscribed to the Cotton Loan in support of the Confederacy. Smith was concerned that the Laird Rams would not be detained by the Palmerston government. Smith also wrote about education reform on a scale also favored by Seward.

34 Welles Diary. p.58.

35 Monaghan, Jay: *A Diplomat in Carpet Slippers.* New York: Bobbs-Merrill, 1945. p.14.

Chapter 2

2 *Free ships make free goods* was codified in the 1856 Treaty of Paris, of which the U.S. was not a signatory.

2 Charles Francis Adams obtained extensive lists of British seamen working on privateers going to the Confederacy. On the lists were also the names of the wives and kin who were to receive the pay of the seaman while working. The lists were submitted to Lord John Russell in an attempt to curtail the activities of the privateers.

3 Barnes James J.: *The American Civil War Through British Eyes.* Kent: Kent State University Press, 2003. p.98.

4 Congress of Vienna ended the Napoleonic Wars in 1815.

5 French naval strength grew under Napoleon III to the point where England and France were engaged in an expensive naval arms race. Ironclad ships were more costly, and strained the budgets of both countries.

6 Blumenthal, Henry. *A Reappraisal of France-American Relations, 1830–1871.* Chapel Hill: University of North Carolina Press, 1959. p.35.

7 Ibid. p.35.

8   Baxter, James Phinney. *The Introduction of the Ironclad Warship*. Annapolis: Naval Institute Press, 1933. p.77.

9   Lyons to Russell, May 20, 1861.

10   Lyons to Russell, October 18, 1861.

11   FRUS, Seward to Motley, December 18, 1861.

12   Rappaport, Mike. *1848, Year of Revolution*. New York: Basic Books, 2008. p.ix.

13   Garibaldi was one of the most popular heroes of the nineteenth century. His fight to unify Italy and make her a sovereign nation attracted the attention of William Seward who asked Henry Sanford to check with Garibaldi to see if he might be interested in becoming a General in the Union army. Later research has shown that it may have been Garibaldi himself who sought to come to America in the name of an abolitionist cause.

14   Smith, Denis: *Garibaldi*. Englewood: Prentiss Hall, 1969. p.69.

15   Like Lincoln who was referred to as "the original baboon" by George McClellan, Napoleon was also satirized by many. John Hay, one of Lincoln's secretaries, called him a "gouty crab". Napoleon was short, thus the title "Napoleon the Little".

16   Subsequent research has shown that it may have actually been Garibaldi who sought a commission in the Union army.

17   Gasparin, Agenor. *America Before Europe*. London: Sampson and Low, 1862.

18   Ibid. p.13.

19   Palmerston, Henry John Temple: *Correspondence of Lord Palmerston and Mr. Gladstone, 1851–1865*. London: V. Gollancz, 1928. p.136.

20   Email communication from Howard Fuller to the author in December, 2014. The question posed to Dr. Fuller was, "At this time (1861–65), did anyone in government (British, Union and/or Confederate) realize that British naval strength was more perception than reality?"

21   Raney, William Francis. The Diplomatic and Military Activities of Canada, 1861–1865, As Affected by the American Civil War. Doctoral Dissertation, University of Wisconsin, 1918. p.4.

22   Ibid. p.5.

23   Vermont town burned by Confederates coming over the border from Canada.

24   Jacob Thompson was a Confederate who sought to organize Southern resistance from bases in Canada. He was called Davis' Head of the Confederate Secret Service. He had developed plans to burn New York City. His plans never materialized.

25   Lyons to Russell, May 6, 1861.

26   Clay, Cassius: *"The Life of Cassius Marcellus Clay: memoirs, writings and speeches, showing his conduct in the overthrow of American Slavery, the Salvation of the Union, and the Restoration of the autonomy of the States."* Cincinnatti: J.F. Brennan, 1886. p.56.

27   Ibid. p.242.

28   Only two original members of Lincoln's cabinet served throughout the war years, William Henry Seward and Gideon Welles. There were three from Treasury, two from War, two Attorneys General, two from Postmaster, and two from Interior.

29   Goodwin, Doris: *A Team of Rivals*. New York: Simon and Schuster, 2005. p.403.

30 Ibid. p.364.

31 Warren Spencer, in his doctoral dissertation, makes the case that Drouyn precipitated the Crimean War through his negative and patronizing attitude towards the Russians.

32 FRUS Appleton to Seward, April 8, 1861.

33 FRUS Seward to Clay, May 6, 1861.

34 FRUS Clay to Seward, November 3, 1863.

35 Bayard Taylor was also a poet, novelist, literary critic and travel author.

36 Russell, John Earl: *Recollections and Suggestions*. London: Spotswoode, 1875. p.331.

37 Governor Joseph E. Brown of Georgia.

38 FRUS Seward to Gorchakov 10/29/62.

39 In April, 1863, Morris Island was pounded into submission by Rear Admiral John A. Dahlgren. Fort Sumter was still in Rebel hands, but with Morris Island in Union hands, blockade runners could not get past the guns to load cargo in Charleston.

40 McPherson, James. *War on the Waters*. Chapel Hill: University of North Carolina Press, 2012. p.122.

41 FRUS Seward to Tessara 7/15/61.

42 Ferris Norman: *Desperate Diplomacy*. Nashville, U. of Tennessee Press, 1977. p.11.

Chapter 3

1 Huse and Bulloch were successful purchasing agents for the Confederacy. Huse bought arms, and Bulloch ships.

2 General George Thomas is not as well- known as Ulysses Grant.

3 Evans, Eli. *Judah P. Benjamin, The Jewish Confederate*. New York, Free Press, 1988. p.156.

4 Spencer, Warren. *The Confederate Navy in Europe*. Tuscaloosa: University of Alabama Press, 1983.

5 The tariff was used as a justification for secession by Jefferson Davis as well as the Yancey commission to Europe in 1861. The tariff was thought to work better for the Confederacy than slavery.

6 Gill, Gillian. *We Two*. New York, Ballentine Books, 2010. p.261.

7 Ibid. p.261.

8 Ibid. p.96.

9 Ibid. p.13.

10 Dayton died of a heart attack under mysterious circumstances. Some histories have him collapsing at his desk at the Ministry. Others, however, have him dying in bed with his mistress. Friends secretly carried his body to the Ministry to make it look like he had died there.

11 Willson, Beckles. *John Slidell and the Confederates in Paris, 1862-1865*. New York: Minton, Balch, 1932. p.292.

12 Clapp, Margaret. *Forgotten First Citizen, John Bigelow*. Boston, Little Brown, 1947.

13 Ibid.

14 *Dangers and Defenses of New York*, U.S. Corps of Engineers, 1859.

15 Ibid. p.297.

16 Welles, Gideon. *Seward and Lincoln*. Freeport, Books for Libraries Press, 1969. p.8.

17 Coski, John. *Capital Navy: The Men, Ships and Operations of the James River Squadron*. New York: Savas Beatie, 1996. p.2.

18 Underwood, Rodman. *Stephen Russell Mallory: A Biography of the Confederate Navy Secretary.* Jefferson: McFarland, 2005. p.54.

19 The papers of Stephen R. Mallory, 1861–1872, Wilson Special Collections Library, University of North Carolina, Chapel Hill.

20 Nicolay, John; Hay, John. *Abraham Lincoln: A History.* New York: Century, 1890.

21 Ibid. p.445.

22 Donald, David Herbert. *Charles Sumner and the Rights of Man.* New York, Alfred Knopf, 1970. p.25.

23 In 1904, an aging Caleb Huse wrote his memoirs about purchasing guns and equipment for virtually every Confederate government department.

24 Ultimately, the London Armory Company was able to produce enough guns to supply orders for both Union and Confederacy. The company claimed to have shipped 70,000 rifles to the Confederacy.

25 Thompson, Samuel Bernard. *Confederate Purchasing Operations Abroad.* Chapel Hill, University of North Carolina Press, 1935. p.6.

26 Alexander Collie and Company along with Willoughbe, Willoughbe and Ponsonby were two of the largest arms and shipping contractors working to make a profit on the Civil War.

27 Ibid. p.25.

28 Russell, William Howard. *My Diary, North and South* (London, Bradbury and Evans, 1863). p.39.

29 Sweeney, Michael. "From the Front, the story of war". National Geographic, 2002.

30 Bostick, Douglas W. *The Confederacy's Secret Weapon.* Charleston, The History Press, 2009. p.81.

Chapter 4

1 The Memoirs of Sir Edward Malet. *See Memoirs and Contemporary Accounts*

2 Austen Henry Layard was an archeologist, author, politician and diplomat. He served as Under Secretary for Foreign Affairs from 1861–1866. He was outspoken and critical of the Crimean War.

3 The *National Intelligencer* often spoke for the Lincoln administration as did the London *Times* speak for Palmerston. Newspapers in France were very tightly controlled. Few dared to speak against the Emperor. William Lewis Dayton once paid 640 francs to have a pro-north article printed in the French press. Several newspapers spoke for the French government including the *Moniteur, Constitutionelle, Pays* and *Patrie*. French newspapers, however, did not have the circulation found in the British papers.

4 Richard Lyons' father was Edmund Lyons, naval officer and diplomat.

5 Lyons to Russell, October 25, 1859.

6 Charles Francis Adams to Charles Francis Adams, Jr. December 20, 1861.

7 Lyons to Russell, January 7, 1861.

8 Carroll, Daniel B.: *Henri Mercier and the American Civil War.* Princeton: Princeton University Press, 1971. p.85.

9 Some historians have suggested that in a civil war as found in America, neutral nations are required to accord Belligerent status. Wheaton states that, "When countries are intimately connected with each other, through situation or commerce,

a revolt of any magnitude in one materially affects the rights and interest of the others, and entails upon them the necessity of pursuing some course of conduct towards the disturbed state. This may be done either by recognizing the insurgents as belligerents, or by acknowledging them to be independent.

10 Gooch, G.P., ed. *The Later Correspondence of Lord John Russell*. London: Longman, Green and Co, 1925, p.79.

11 Elliot, E.N. *Cotton is King and Proslavery Argument*. Augusta, Portland, Abbott and Loomis, 1860.

12 Howard Fuller to the author, December 15, 2014.

13 Case, Lynn. *French Opinion on War and Diplomacy During the Second Empire*. Philadelphia: University of Penn. Press, 1954.

14 Charles Francis Adams to Charles Francis Adams, Jr.

15 Jones, William. *The Confederate Rams at Birkenhead*. Tuscalusa: Confed. Pub. Co, 1961. p.54.

16 Elliot, E.N. *Cotton is King and Proslavery Argument*. Augusta: Portland, Abbott and Loomis, 1860.

17 It is estimated that 6,000 ships cleared Southern ports in 1860. After the blockade, it is further estimated that only 800 got through the blockade. Of 1,300 runner attempts, only 300 got through. Two-thirds of blockade runners were captured. Some were turned around and put into service with the U.S. Navy.

Chapter 5

1 The Willard Hotel in Washington was the site of as much government business as was conducted at the capitol or the White House.

2 Mary Lincoln exceeded her budget for the White House and resorted to hiding her extra expenses in "padded" bills, etc.

3 Aqi Crawford *The Times op cit* p.76. After the initial reception, the prince went to the Academy of Music. A temporary stage had been erected for 3,000 people, but 5,000 showed up and the floor collapsed. Fortunately, nobody was hurt, and the prince continued on his journey.

4 Crook, D.P. *Diplomacy During the American Civil War*. New York: John Wiley, 1975. p.20.

5 Mahan, Dean B. *The Blessed Place of Freedom: Europeans in Civil War America*. Dulles: Brassey's, 2002. p.11.

6 John Crampton was appointed Secretary of the British legation in Washington in 1845. He succeeded Henry Bulwer as Minister in 1852. However, he was forced to resign in 1856 because of accusations that he was trying to recruit Americans into the British army during the Crimean War.

7 Barnes James J. *The American Civil War Through British Eyes*. Kent: Kent State Univ., 2003. p.112.

8 Fraser, Trenholm and Company had offices in Liverpool and Charleston. George Trenholm became Confederate Secretary of the Treasury in 1864. The Liverpool branch was central to securing credit for the CSA in Europe before the Cotton Loan.

9   Kiersey, Nicholas. "The Diplomats and Diplomacy of the American Civil War". BA Thesis, University of Limerick, Ireland, 1997. p.3.

10 Judah Benjamin served first as attorney general, the secretary of war and finally as secretary of state for the Confederacy. With no Supreme Court and little local common law, Benjamin did little as attorney general. As secretary of war, he served under a man who was secretary of war himself under Franklin Pierce. Benjamin often took the blame for battlefield failures that were more attributable to lack of resources than anything else. As secretary of state, Benjamin was bold and creative in concocting plans to save the Confederacy.

11 Leroy, Hubert. *Ambrose Dudley Mann: Ambassador of the Lost Cause.* Brussels, Confederate Historical Association of Belgium. p.47.

12 Doyle, Dob. *The Cause of all Nations.* New York: Basic Books, 2015. p.39.

13 DuBose, John. *The Life and Times of William Loundes Yancey: A History of Political Parties in the United States from 1834 to 1864, Especially as to the Origin of the Confederate States.* Whitefish: Kessinger Publishing, 2007 (reprint). p.600.

14 Ibid. p.596.

15 Richardson, James D (ed.). *A Compilation of the Messages and Papers of the Confederacy.* Nashville: United States Publishing Company, 1905.

16 The Blue Book was first published in the fifteenth century in Britain, and was a book of facts and proceedings of the British parliament.

17 Barnes, James J. *The American Civil War Through British Eyes.* Kent: Kent State Univ., 2003. p.11.

18 John Lothrop Motley, U.S. minister to Austria. He worked with Bigelow and Adams to keep Europe from intervening in the Civil War.

19 Edward Pollard, editor of the *Richmond Examiner* during the war and author of *The Lost Cause.* Pollard was a strong critic of Jefferson Davis.

20 1873 Response by Welles to the Eulogy of Seward by Adams.

21 Evans, Eli. *Judah P. Benjamin: The Jewish Confederate.* New York: Free Press, 1988. p.153.

22 Sumner, Charles. *Selected Letters*, ed. Beverly Wilson Palmer. Boston: Northeastern Press, 1990. p.79.

23 Emmerich de Vattel was a Swiss who published *The Law of Nations* in 1758. Until the American, Henry Wheaton, published in 1836, Vattel was the authority upon which the Crown law officers of the Queen relied for guidance on international legal matters. Prior to Vattel, Hugo Grotius was regarded as the authority on international law.

24 Stahr, Walter. *Seward: Lincoln's Indispensable Man.* New York: Simon and Schuster, 2012.

25 Ibid. p.5.

26 The invasion plan is found in secondary sources, but cannot be verified.

27 Under Kaiser Wilhelm I and President Otto von Bismarck, the German states were finally unified as the German Empire.

28 Britain was very sensitive to the strength of a blockade. During the Crimean War, she successfully blockaded the Gulf of Finland and kept the Russian fleet bottled

up while England and France pounded Sevastopol from land and sea. England had the ships to successfully and effectively blockade the Gulf of Finland. However, the American coast was much longer, and she knew that the U.S. Navy did not have the number of ships necessary to blockade the Southern coast as she had done against Russia. Relying on Vattel, this "ineffective" blockade of the Southern coast was one that could lawfully be ignored. However, to ignore the blockade and challenge it meant certain war with the Union. Palmerston didn't want another Crimea so soon.

29 By contrast, the turreted monitors favored by the Union had low freeboard and their engines below the waterline where they could not be struck.

30 The Mosquito Inlet is now the Ponce de Leon Inlet which has a tall, brick lighthouse which stands on the spot where the original stood. The original was used as a landmark by Maffitt to pilot his boats into safety.

31 Gunboats were shallow-draft warships that were referred to as "90-day gunboats". They were steam-driven.

32 Royce, Shingleton. *High Seas Confederate: The Life and Times of John Newland Maffitt.* Columbia: University of South Carolina Press, 1994. p.40.

33 Sumner, Charles. *Selected Letters*, ed. Beverly Wilson Palmer. Boston: Northeastern Press, 1990. p.131.

34 Ibid. p.148.

Chapter 6

1 Fleet Admiral Sir Alexander Milne is one of the heroes of the foreign relations chapter of the American Civil War. He worked closely with Lord Lyons and was able to carry British consular and Ministry mail back to England without having to run the blockade. He observed strict neutrality and read passages of Vattel to his officers to make sure that they understood the scope of neutrality as it applied to England, the Union and the Confederate States. He commanded the North Atlantic Fleet that was always just off the American coast throughout the war. His home base was in Halifax, Nova Scotia.

2 Adams, Charles Francis. *Seward and the Declaration of Paris: A Forgotten Diplomatic Episode, April-August, 1861.* Boston: Private Printing, 1912. p.23.

3 William Hunter's name always comes up in discussions about foreign relations and the State Department at this time. He was Chief Clerk of the U.S. State Department, and later Second Assistant Secretary of State after Frederick Seward. Hunter died at the age of eighty, still working at the State Department after fifty-seven years. After fifty years at the department, Hunter was referred to in the press as "the mentor and authority of the Department." Seward often relied on him for advice on international law.

4 Welles, Gideon. *Lincoln and Seward.* Freeport: Books for Libraries Press, 1969. p.76.

5 Some historians have argued that international law at this time required recognition under certain circumstances. Wheaton provides some advice, "When the struggle is carried on by sea as well as by land, the interests of neutral commerce

render a recognition of belligerency absolutely necessary." Wheaton talks of recognition as a Belligerent, not as a sovereign nation. However, the benefits accorded under Belligerency and sovereign recognition are very similar.

6   Wheaton, Henry. *Elements of International Law*. London: Stevens, 1916. (Reprint from 1836)

7   Thouvanel to Mercier, May 11, 1861.

8   In the U.S. at that time, Prize Courts were part of the federal judiciary. Prize courts were located in New York, Boston, Philadelphia, Providence, Baltimore, Washington, Key West and New Orleans. If the court decided for the captors, the ship was sold and the proceeds split among the captain and crew of the capturing ship. 45% of the prize value was donated to the Sailor's Pension Fund.

9   Chernow, Ron. *Alexander Hamilton*. New York: Penguin Books, 2004. p.696.

10 Donald, David Herbert. *Charles Sumner and the Rights of Man*. New York: Knopf, 1970. p.21.

11 Everett, Edward. *Address in Commemoration of the Life of Charles Francis Adams*. Cambridge: Wilson and Sons, 1887. p.21.

12 FRUS, Foreign Relations of the United States was originally published as Papers Relating to the Foreign Relations of the United States, starting in 1861.

13 George Dallas was Minister to England prior to Charles Francis Adams. Dallas, Texas is named after him.

14 The Confederate States of America were always referred to by both Union and European diplomats as the "so-called Confederate States". To do otherwise would have implied the recognition that Seward was trying to avoid.

15 It is common at this time to hear of the Laws of Nature, Divine Right Law, and the Law of Nations. Common law in the English tradition refers to laws that were "created" from court decisions. Natural law refers to more generally to common sense – something that is relative and subject to personal interpretation.

16 Napoleon III was quick to make a distinction between the Anglo-Saxons and the Latins. As a Catholic, Latin country, Napoleon believed that France had a special mission to "help" those other supposedly languishing Latin American countries. Napoleon sought to check the growth of America by exercising French authority on as much of Central and South America as he could – Monroe Doctrine notwithstanding.

17 Elliot, E.N. *Cotton is King and Proslavery Argument*. Augusta: Portland, Abbott and Loomis, 1860.

18 Other countries from which England and France were obtaining emergency supplies of cotton at this time include: Russia, Egypt, Spain, Portugal, Italy, Malta, Greece, Turkey, Africa, India, The Philippines, Siam, China, Hong Kong, Japan, Australia, Jamaica, British West Indies, British Guiana, Haiti, Dominican Republic, Central America, Venezuela, Ecuador, Peru, Brazil, Uruguay, Argentina. Although the list of suppliers is long, the quality and quantity of raw cotton imported from these countries was relatively small compared to that which had come from the Southern states of America. Source: George McHenry's *1864 Statement of Facts Relating to the Approaching Cotton Crisis*.

19   Bonham, Milledge. *The British Consuls in the Confederacy*. New York: Longmans Green, 1911. p.51.

20   Meade, Robert. *Judah P. Benjamin: Confederate Statesman*. Baton Rouge: LSU Press, 2001. p.148.

21   Confederate cypher was used in response to the fact that Confederate dispatches to Europe were captured and published in the newspapers. In order to protect dispatch data, Davis and Benjamin wrote all of their instructions in code.

22   Meade, Robert. *Judah P. Benjamin: Confederate Statesman*. Baton Rouge: LSU Press, 2001. p.149.

23   Jones, J.B. *A Rebel War Clerk's Diary at the Confederate States of America* (Philadelphia, Lippincott, 1866). John Beauchamp Jones served as a clerk in the Confederate war department under five Secretaries of War: Leroy Walker, Judah Benjamin, George Randolph, James Seddon and John Breckenridge.

24   The reference is to John Laird, Sr.

25   One of the problems in analyzing the success or failure of the blockade running effort is the fact that privateers and runners purposely did not keep complete and accurate records. The fear was that if captured, their records could seriously compromise and implicate them. The recognized authority on the blockade is Stephen Wise.

26   Admiral Milne was always at risk of losing English sailors to the lure of high profits found in the blockade runners.

27   Peters, Thelma. *Blockade Running in the Bahamas During the Civil War* (A paper before the Historical Society of South Florida, May 5, 1943) p.1.

28   Alexander Collie and Company was a successful shipping company that not only shipped goods to the Confederacy through the blockade, but charged the Confederacy for the construction of the ships as well as the contracts for securing and hauling the goods overland to the port of Liverpool.

29   Thomas Haines Dudley is sometimes referred to as Lincoln's spymaster. The real spymaster was Dudley's boss, Henry Shelton Sanford, U.S. minister to Belgium.

30   Seward to Sanford January 22, 1862, Box 130, reel #2, Sanford Papers, Sanford, Florida.

31   Sanford papers, Box 139, files 6-14. Sanford's account, for example, shows that he paid Ignatius "Paddington" Pollaky 50 francs for each report he submitted. On May 10, 1862, his Secret Service Records show that Sanford paid John Bigelow 1500 francs for *Extraordinary Expenses*. Bigelow, like William Lewis Dayton, found that he needed to pay an "incentive" to French newspaper editors in order to have pro-union articles published.

32   Ignatius Pollaky was a private detective hired by Sanford at £50 per month. Known as "Paddington Pollaky", he started one of the first private detective agencies in London – Pollaky's Private Inquiry Office. Although sending his information on to Adams, Pollaky was hired and paid by Sanford. Sanford's pay register contains the names of all his spies and the amounts they were paid. During the Alabama Claims proceedings, Seward claimed to have paid out over 42,000 USD to spies and detectives in Europe. The funds came through an account Sanford established at the Bank of Belgium.

33 Sanford Letter book, Sanford to Cameron, 11/01/61.

34 Sanford Letter book, Sanford to Cameron, 11/14/61.

Chapter 7

1   FRUS, Clay to Seward, 01/07/62.

2   The Morrill Tariff was passed during the Buchanan administration. It raised taxes on dutiable goods from an average of 20% to 35%.

3   Nevins, Alan. *War for the Union*. New York: Scribner, 1960. p.242.

4   FRUS, Taylor to Seward, 11/12/62.

5   Sears, Louis Martin. *A Confederate Diplomat at the Court of Napoleon III*. The American Historical Review, vol. 26, no.2, January, 1921. pp.255–281.

6   Unfortunately, like his friend and colleague Judah Benjamin, John Slidell destroyed most of his papers at the end of the war. However, Mason preserved his papers as well as some that he received from Slidell.

7   Doyle, Don. *The Cause of all Nations*. New York: Basic Books, 2015. p.81.

8   Nicolay, John George; Hay, John Milton. *Abraham Lincoln: A History*. New York: The Century Co., 1890. p.32.

9   Ibid. p.34.

10 Diary of Gideon Welles.

11 Welles, Gideon. *Lincoln and Seward*. Freeport: Books for Libraries Press, 1969. p.188.

12 Diary of Edward Bates.

13 Ibid.

14 Sumner, Charles. *The Works of Charles Sumner*. Boston: Lee and Shepard, 1873. p.61.

15 At this stage, the *Monitor* and *Merrimac* had not made their debut. Bates could not have been aware of the strategic defensive advantage the north would have in guarding their shallow harbors against the deeper-draft British ironclad warships.

16 Sumner, Charles. *The Works of Charles Sumner*. Boston: Lee and Shepard, 1873. p.59.

17 Ibid. p.60.

18 Weed to Seward, January 8, 1862, Sanford Papers, Sanford, Museum.

19 Dispatch No.6 to Judah Benjamin.

20 Thurlow Weed, Archbishop Hughes and General Winfield Scott all went to Europe as unofficial representatives of Lincoln and Seward in an attempt to better influence public opinion in England and France in favor of the Union.

21 Newton, Thomas. *Lord Lyons: A Record of British Diplomacy*. London: Edward Arnold, 1913. p.79.

22 The scope of Seward/Weed communication was: December, 1861, 14 letters; January, 1862, seventeen letters; February, 1862, 10 letters.

23 Seward to Weed, 12/30/61. Seward papers, Sterling Library, Yale University.

24 Thurlow Weed, *Letters from Europe 1861–1862*. Private Printing. p.40.

25 Diary of Gideon Welles. p.437.

26 Weed writes to Seward every other day during this tense period.

27 Jones, William. *The Confederate Rams at Birkenhead*. Tuscaloosa: Confederate Pub. Co, 1961. p.29.

28 Excerpted from Thurlow Weed's *Letters from Europe 1861–1862*, p.28.
29 Fuller, Howard. "Iron Lion or Paper Tiger", op. cit., 66; *Clad in Iron.*
30 Wilson, Mark. *The Business of Civil War: Military Mobilization and the State, 1861–1865.* Baltimore: Johns Hopkins University Press, 2006.
31 Barnard, John Gross. *Notes on Seacoast Defense: Consisting of Seacoast Fortification, the Fifteen-Inch Gun, and Casemate Embrasures. 1861.* Whitefish reprint, 2009.
32 Fuller, Howard. *Clad in Iron,* The American Civil War and the Challenge of British Naval Power. Anapolis: Naval Institute Press, 2008. Excerpted, p.38.
33 Seward's Defenses of New York
34 In July, 1865, the Dunderberg was launched. However, she was never commissioned in the U.S. Navy, and was ultimately sold to France.
35 Trunk engines were popular in the navy because they were designed with a more horizontal profile which thus allowed it to be housed safely below the water line.
36 Howard Fuller to the author, December 15, 2014.
37 Ibid.

Chapter 8

1 John Bright served in the House of Commons for forty-six years. He was a champion of the middle and lower classes. Bright is best known for his abolishing the Corn Laws which taxed imported wheat and kept domestic food prices high thus benefiting the wealthy landowners. He was a pen-pal of Charles Sumner and a hero to Abraham Lincoln.
2 Some of these names were on Bigelow's list of members of the Southern Independence Association and subscribers to the Erlanger cotton loan.
3 Like Lincoln, Alexander II is known for freeing the Russian "slaves" or serfs and his assassination in 1881.
4 Sandberg, Carl. *Abraham Lincoln, The War Years.* New York: Harcourt, 1926. p.208.
5 The Duke and Duchess of Argyll were both in regular communication with Charles Sumner.
6 Sumner, Charles. *The Works of Charles Sumner.* Boston: Lee and Shepard, 1873. p.1.
7 Her dressmaker was Elizabeth Keckley, or "Lizzie" as Mary Lincoln called her. However, when Mrs. Keckley wrote and published *Behind the Scenes or Thirty Years a Slave and Four Years in the White House,* Mary Lincoln was upset and cut herself off from her dressmaker friend. Keckley knew the Lincolns well, and was very perceptive. She showed the positive and negative sides of both Lincolns.
8 Donald, David Herbert. *Charles Sumner and the Rights of Man.* New York: Alfred Knopf, 1970. p.25.
9 Charles Sumner and others sought to separate the rights of a Belligerent power into Belligerency on land and Belligerency on the ocean. So, by this reasoning, the Confederate States were granted Belligerent status by Britain and France on land, but not on the ocean. This would deprive Confederate ships and privateers of any rights and protection from seizure on the ocean.

10 Donald, David Herbert. *Charles Sumner and the Rights of Man.* New York: Alfred Knopf, 1970. p.96.

11 Ibid. p.20.

12 Ford, Worthington, Chauncy. *A Cycle of Adams Letters 1861–1865.* New York: Houghton Mifflin, 1920.

13 The stress of war ultimately revealed differing opinions on key subjects, and the trust was broken between Richard Cobden and Charles Sumner.

14 Edsall, Nicholas. *Richard Cobden, Independent Radical.* Cambridge: Harvard U. Press, 1986. p.165.

15 Sumner, Charles. *The Works of Charles Sumner.* Boston: Lee and Shepard, 1873. p.343.

16 Ausubel, Herman. *John Bright, Victorian Reformer.* New York: John Wiley and Sons, 1966. p.314.

17 There is much debate as to the "effectiveness" of the blockade. Initially, it was not effective because there was too much coastline to effectively cover. As time went on, however, the Union navy grew in numbers and tactics. It was soon discovered that the entire coastline did not need to be blocked. Just the major ports needed surveillance. This was soon countered by smaller Confederate privateers of shallow draft that could get in and out of many more ports than just the larger ones being blocked by the Union gunboats. By 1863–64, however, most accounts show the blockade to be almost as effective as the British blockade of the Gulf of Finland during the Crimean War. Statistics of "middling cotton" getting through the blockade to the warehouses of Fraser Trenholm show a sharp decrease starting in 1863. The most respected authority on the blockade is Stephen Wise who claims that 77% of the blockade runners successfully breached the blockade. However, these were smaller ships with less cargo.

18 The Joint Committee on the Conduct of the War was formed in 1861 to investigate Union battlefield losses. It remained a constant thorn in Lincoln's side.

19 Travelyan, George. *The Life of John Bright.* New York: Houghton Mifflin, 1913. p.303.

20 FRUS, Seward to Koerner, 09/23/63.

21 Ibid. 02/06/64.

22 Nathaniel Gordon was the only American executed for transporting slaves. He was hung in New York City on February 21, 1862. His supporters appealed to Lincoln, who was known for pardoning soldiers who had fallen asleep while on guard duty. Edwin Stanton complained that he impacted discipline in the ranks with his pardons. However, Lincoln refused to pardon Gordon.

23 Entitled *Vessels loading at or sailed from Liverpool for the West Indies During the Week of Oct. 26, 1861.* The receiving ports are: Havanah [sic], Vera Cruz, Kingston, Barbados, and Tampico. One of the shipping companies, Alexander Collie, is listed. Collie was one of the most active shipping companies for the Confederacy.

24 The *290* was later renamed the *Alabama.*

25 Prize Cases, 67 US 635.

26 Associate Justice Grier had a colorful past. He was accused of accepting a bribe in 1854 to decide a Pennsylvania case. He was cleared, however, by a Judiciary Committee headed by a college classmate.

27 Seward had a habit of threatening to send in a warship to satisfy some grievance or other. At this same time, he did this with Henry Sanford who was working on settling claims that American citizens had against Venezuela for not supporting the terms of the Aves Island Treaty. That treaty was a commercial agreement which compensated Americans for their investment in the guano deposits on the island. They were not being paid, and Venezuela was reluctant to take action – thus the threat to send in a gunboat to help make Venezuela see the light.

28 FRUS Adams to Seward 01/28/64.

29 George Cornwell Lewis was head of the British War Office, and an opponent of intervention in the Civil War.

30 J.B. Jones, Confederate war clerk, published his diary in 1866. It provides personal insight into the Confederate government, and particularly the War Department under Judah Benjamin.

Chapter 9

1 The bread riot, 1863, was not confined to the city of Richmond. Several other cities in the Confederacy experienced similar situations at this stage of the war.

2 From 1861–1863, Confederate paper currency experienced an inflation rate of 300%. When inflation rates reached 700% by January, 1864, the government stopped printing the large volume of paper currency that was driving the problem. This lasted until January, 1865 when inflation again continued to rise.

3 Frederic Emile d'Erlanger took over the banking and brokerage business from his German father. His second marriage was to Margueritte Slidell in 1864.

4 Margeueritte Slidell, daughter of Confederate Representative John Slidell.

5 William Gladstone, chancellor of the exchequer during this period from 1859–1866.

6 William Schaw Lindsay was a merchant and ship owner who was influential in parliament, but out of office during this time.

7 By the end of the war, approximately 10% of the Union army consisted of black freedmen and former slaves.

8 Christopher Memminger served as Treasury Secretary in the government of Jefferson Davis during the Civil War. He was an orphan who emigrated from Germany, and became a successful lawyer in South Carolina. He headed the state's Finance Committee for twenty years. He was against the earlier nullification issues that initially helped divide North and South. He was a moderate on secession.

9 Barings Bank was founded in 1762, but folded in 1995. The Rothschild bank was founded in London in 1798.

10 FRUS, Memminger to Trenholm, 10/28/62.

11 James Spence was a self-styled "banker" for the Confederacy in that he helped arrange and manage the credit arrangements between Fraser Trenholm in

Liverpool and the CSA purchasing agents in Europe. It was always assumed that Spence was working gratis, but later research showed that he was being paid for his work through Fraser, Trenholm.

12 James D. Bulloch was regarded then and now as one of the more creative and successful of the CSA purchasing agents in Europe. He worked primarily in London and Liverpool. He supervised and paid for the construction of ship 290, later the *Alabama*. The files of Henry Shelton Sanford are interesting because they indicate that Bulloch was almost a celebrity among CSA agents in Europe. He was closely watched by detectives like Ignatius Pollaky.

13 Colin McRae was a Confederate finance agent working in Europe at this time. His actions were closely monitored by Thomas Dudley, consul in Liverpool. Dudley was financed through Henry Sanford in Belgium.

14 Bigelow, John. *Lest we Forget, Gladstone, Morley and the Confederate Loan.* New York: Private Publication, 1905. p.18.

15 The Erlanger cotton loan was marketed in London, Liverpool, Paris, Amsterdam and Frankfurt. It ultimately raised approximately eight million dollars.

16 Matamoros, Mexico was on the border with Texas. Matamoros quickly became a strategic port for the import of goods for the Confederacy. By 1863, however, Matamoras (the spelling at that time) was partially shut down when Union forces occupied Brownsville, Texas. The city is now the center of drug wars and the importation of drugs into the United States.

17 Ferris, Norman. *The Trent Affair.* Knoxville: University of Tennessee Press, 1977. p.85.

18 See The Inviolability of Diplomatic Archives,americanarchivist.org/doi/pdf/10.17723/aarc.8.1.k010662414m87w48

19 Diary of Gideon Welles

20 Welles, Gideon. *Lincoln and Seward.* Freeport: Books for Libraries Press, 1969. p.98.

21 Ibid. p.86.

22 Ibid. p.88.

23 Ibid. p.117.

24 Ibid. p.121.

25 Prussia historically concentrated on its army and a merchant fleet.

26 Woldman, Albert. *Lincoln and the Russians.* New York: World Publishing, 1952. p.124.

27 Tucker was later sent to Canada to arrange a scheme of bartering cotton for food for a starving Confederacy.

28 Mayes, Edward. *Lucius Q.C. Lamar: His Life, Times and Speeches, 1825–1893.* Nashville: Methodist Episcopal Church, 1896. p.107.

29 *The Index* was written and published by Henry Hotze in an attempt to better influence European perception of the Confederacy. Although encouraged and financed in this by James Spence, the newspaper never achieved wide circulation.

30 DeLeon, Edwin. *Thirty Years of My Life on Three Continents*, vol. 2. London: Ward and Downey, 1890. p.29.

31 Ibid. p.34.
32 *New York Times*, November 14, 1863.
33 FRUS, Corwin to Seward, 11/19/62.
34 Thomas Corwin, Union representative to Mexico. He opposed the war with Mexico and won favor with Mexicans. He was a good Seward choice for the position.
35 Clapp, Margaret: *Forgotten First Citizen, John Bigelow*. Boston: Little Brown, 1947. p.165.
36 Unlike William Lewis Dayton, John Bigelow's French was excellent. In addition to standard "textbook" French, he also worked hard to master some of the colloquial language.
37 Bigelow, John. *Retrospectives of an Active Life*. New York, Baker-Taylor, 1909. p.1.
38 Maximillian was the younger brother of Austrian Emperor Franz Joseph. At the urging of Napoleon III, Maximillian declared himself Emperor of Mexico in 1864. The regime collapsed and Maximillian was executed in 1867.
39 Raphael Semmes, "old Beeswax", was Confederate commander of the *CSS Alabama* which sank many Union merchant ships worth millions of dollars. In June, 1864, his ship was sunk by the *U.S.S. Kearsarge* off the coast of Cherbourg, France.
40 Roberts, Adolphe. *Semmes of the Alabama*. New York: Bobbs-Merrill, 1938. p.87.
41 Indirect *Alabama* claims refers to the contention by the U.S. government that English building of privateers and warships for the Confederacy prolonged a war that would have ended sooner otherwise. The U.S. sought damages for the extra cost of the war including the extra insurance premiums paid by northern merchantmen to safeguard their commerce from capture by the *Alabama* and others.
42 Russell, John Earl. *Recollections and Suggestions*. London, Spotswoode, 1875. p.335.
43 Sir George Grey, Governor of New Zealand.
44 Russell, John Earl. *Recollections and Suggestions*. London: Spotswoode, 1875. p.335.

Chapter 10

1 FRUS, Dayton to Seward, 11/27/64.
2 *Greenbacks* were used as currency in the Union during the war instead of gold specie which was used for credit in European banks.
3 Sumner, Charles. *The Works of Charles Sumner*. Boston: Lee and Shepard, 1873. p.111.
4 John Bigelow wrote several influential books at this time. For the French audience to better explain the cause of the Union, he wrote *Les Etats Unis D'Amerique*. The quality of the French is excellent and clearly explained the reasons for the actions of the Union. After the war he wrote his *Reflections* and a book on the Confederate Navy. Retiring from service, he lived in retirement in New York City, and is remembered by many as a dignified older gentleman walking briskly up and down the avenues. He died in 1911 at 94.
5 FRUS Seward to Dayton, 12/20/63.
6 Bigelow, John. *Retrospectives of an Active Life*. New York: Baker and Taylor, 1909. p.11.

7   The United States Congress Joint Committee on the Conduct of the War was formed by radical Republicans to place blame for battlefield losses, investigate corruption in war contracts as well as the surprisingly active illicit trade in "cotton for bacon" conducted by merchants North and South. It continued its work until 1865, and was always a thorn in Lincoln's side.

8   James McDougall, Democratic Senator from California.

9   FRUS, Seward to Dayton, 04/07/64.

10 Gustav Koerner was a friend of Abraham and Mary Lincoln. He became a Brigadier General in the Union army and succeeded Carl Schurz as Minister to Spain in 1862.

11 Sumner, Charles: *The Works of Charles Sumner*. Boston: Lee and Shepard. p.274.

12 Ibid. p.139.

13 FRUS, Seward to Koerner, 11/08/63.

14 Nicolay, John George; Hay, John Milton. *Abraham Lincoln: A History*. New York: The Century Co., 1890. p.407.

15 Donald, David Herbert. *Charles Sumner and the Rights of Man*. New York: Alfred Knopf, 1970. p.143.

16 The Tokugawa shogunate was the last of the feudal governing structure in Japan during the Civil War. Shoguns were feudal warlords who acted as governors of Japanese provinces. They were actively attempting to remove all Europeans from Japan. They did not want Western influence to undermine their own personal power.

17 Robert Pruyn was a good Seward recommendation for U.S. minister to Japan. He was successful in keeping the peace between the U.S. and Japan after an American ship was bombed at Shimonoseki Straits in 1863.

18 FRUS, Pruyn to Seward, 05/18/64.

19 Ibid, 05/26/64.

20 FRUS, Seward to Dayton, 12/20/63.

21 FRUS, Dayton to Seward, 01/15/64.

22 Evans, Eli. *Judah P. Benjamin: The Jewish Confederate*. New York: Free Press, 1989. p.119.

23 The Surratt connection put Kenner at risk after the war as it was incorrectly assumed that he was connected to the Lincoln assassination plot.

24 FRUS, Adams to Seward, 08/27/66.

25 Cook, Adrian. *The Alabama Claims*. Ithaca: Cornell U. Press, 1970. p.36.

26 Ibid. p.32.

27 Ibid. p.41.

28 Northcote to Gladstone, April 18, 1871.

29 Callahan, James. The *Diplomatic History of the Southern Confederacy*, Baltimore: The Johns Hopkins Press, 1964. p.101.

ACKNOWLEDGMENTS

My first acknowledgment of thanks must go to my wife Carmen. The job of writing historical nonfiction is arduous and solitary. When the *Bluff, Bluster* manuscript was accepted for publication, Carmen said, "Finally, I am no longer a widow." (At the time, however, I neglected to tell her that my next book was already deep into the research phase.) The topic of foreign policy during the administration of Abraham Lincoln is complex. The primary and secondary resources available to scholars are considerable. First, it is important to thank the following libraries for their assistance: Sterling Memorial Library at Yale University; Rush Rhees Library at the University of Rochester; Firestone Library at Princeton University; The Homer Babidge Library at the University of Connecticut; The Manuscripts Division of the Library of Congress; The Manuscripts Division of the New York Public Library; The John Milton Hay Library, at Brown University; The University of Pennsylvania Library: the interlibrary loan department of the University of New Haven, and the Henry Shelton Sanford Library in Sanford, Florida. Of special note is Sterling Memorial at Yale. Their resources are significant and address many aspects of diplomacy during the American Civil War.

There some special people who were also "key players" in providing encouragement, critical advice and new data on a subject of which much has already been written. First among this group is Dr. Wayne C. Temple, Chief Deputy Director of the Illinois State

Archives. Dr. Temple's advice and encouragement were critical in convincing me that my research was solid and worthy of publication. My three prior journal publications on Abraham Lincoln, John George Nicolay and William Henry Seward were important in that the editors of these publications were also noteworthy in providing helpful criticism as well as significant editing advice. These editors include Dr. Thomas Turner, editor of *The Lincoln Herald*; William Pederson of the *International Lincoln Association Newsletter*; and Laurie Verge of *The Surratt Courier*. Bill was particularly helpful because he took the time to do a line-by-line editing of the initial manuscript. I learned much from his efforts.

An important key in better understanding the role of Great Britain in the American Civil War is John B. Hattendorf, Chairman of Maritime History at the U.S. Naval War College in Newport, Rhode Island; John recommended that I talk with Dr. Howard J. Fuller, Senior Lecturer of War Studies at the University of Wolverhampton, U.K. Howard is the author of *Clad in Iron: The American Civil War and the Challenge of British Naval Power* (Annapolis, Naval Institute Press, 2010) and *Empire Technology and Seapower: Royal Navy Crisis in the Age of Palmerston* (London, Routledge, 2013). His knowledge of the Palmerston era and the British navy during the nineteenth century was essential in recognizing the unique limitations with which the British were dealing at this time. Howard's detailed emails and conversations were invaluable. Alicia Clarke of the Sanford Museum was also helpful. This museum is unusual in that it contains over 2,000 letters and dispatches from William Henry Seward and his ring of spies and secret agents in Europe to Henry Sanford, U.S. minister to Belgium. Some of Sanford's detectives provide a detailed and intimate look into the world of bribery and surveillance of Confederate activities in England and France during the Civil War. Museum assistant at the Sanford Museum, Brigitte Stephenson, was also helpful in making sure that I had work space and access to the Sanford documents. When getting into even a chance discussion with people knowledgeable about the Civil War, interesting things happen. Such a chance discussion took place at the American Civil War Museum in Richmond Virginia. C.E.O, S. Waite Rawls III, took the time to explain how the retractable screw propeller worked on Confederate ironclads. His accurate explanation was different from what I had imagined. We continued with a discussion of Confederate public relations. Some of that is included herein. A chance conversation also took place with Dr. John Coski, Confederate Civil War historian and author of *Capital Navy: The Men, Ships and Operations of the James River Squadron*. Having read John's book, I was curious as to his thoughts on British and Confederate naval strength during the Civil War. I looked up his number on the internet, called him and had an informative discussion of commerce raiders like the *Alabama* as well as the unfortunate Confederate habit of scuttling more of their own ironclads than Farragut could sink. Laura D'Amico of the Seward House Museum in Auburn, New York was helpful in providing me with information on Seward's "diplomatic gallery". The gallery consists of signed and unsigned pictures and photos of important people who Seward knew during his life. Of particular interest were the pictures of Lincoln and Seward numbered 66 (Lincoln) and Seward (66 ½). Whether this represented Seward as a close friend of Lincoln or Seward as the *de facto* president as he sought to be is open to debate. Nevertheless, Laura's detailed description of the people in the "gallery" was helpful, interesting and revealing. In addition to the creative side of historical non-fiction research and writing, there is a technical side of manuscript preparation that can be vexing at best. My thanks go to tech support specialist Sandy Selders whose unique skills unraveled some of the daunting mysteries of Word.

Finally, I would like to thank the late Pulitzer Prize winner and Harvard professor, David Herbert Donald. Knowing the significance of his research on Charles Sumner, I was anxious to speak with him and have him read my manuscript. Not knowing Dr. Donald personally, I also looked him up on the internet, and found his phone number. I then took a chance and slowly dialed it – anticipating that either his "butler" would answer the phone, or caller ID would warn him not to bother. The phone rang and was immediately picked up by a soft-spoken man who identified himself as David Herbert Donald. I will always remember his kindness and patience with a stranger who had challenging questions about Lincoln, Charles Sumner and the American Civil War. Finally, posthumous thanks must go to Carl

Sandburg. His books on Lincoln (*Prairie Years* and *War Years*) were an early model of peerless English prose and good Lincoln scholarship. Sandburg had an immediate and lasting impact on me. His words are multicolored and restrained at the same time. This is a skillful treatment of language. I owe a great debt to someone I could not look up on the internet and give a quick call.

Thank you all.

GLOSSARY

Note: The Congress of Vienna in 1815 formally established diplomatic rank in Europe. However, the United States did not use some of these positions until later. The rank of ambassador was established in Europe in 1815, but not until after the Civil War in America.

Ambassador: An ambassador is the highest ranking diplomatic representative of one country to another. He/she represents the head of state of their respective country. The ambassador works at an embassy, not a legation. An embassy is sovereign territory of one country within another. Ambassadors enjoy sovereign immunity.

Belligerent: A state of Belligerency existed when two or more sovereign nations were at war. Belligerency rights allowed those nations at war to access privileges in foreign ports without molestation. When the Confederacy was recognized as a Belligerent by England and France, William Henry Seward was justifiably upset because, although not outright recognition, Belligerency implied the status of a sovereign nation. The Lincoln government insisted that the Confederacy was not a sovereign entity entitled to Belligerent rights and protection.

Blue Book: A record of parliamentary debates and activity recorded since the 15th century.

Chargé d'Affairs: The Chargé is an accredited representative who takes over when the minister or head of the legation is away from their duties. He is ranked below the minister. Both Henri Mercier and Richard Lyons took time from their duties in Washington to go home to Paris or London. Mercier went back to Paris for the winter of 1864, and the Chargé in Washington took over for him. Lyons, when feeling ill, went back to London and was supported by the Chargé d'affairs of his legation. When Cassius Clay was temporarily recalled from St. Petersburg, his work was taken over by Bayard Taylor who wanted to replace him. Clay was recalled to Russia again within two months.

Circular: The Circular was a generic notification sent to representatives and consuls about matters common to all. The first Circular sent by William Seward related to the causes for the "rebellion". Ministers and consuls were told not to talk of this as a war. Seward also sent out a circular to the mayors of all major eastern seaboard cities and towns to warn of possible attacks from Confederate agents in Canada.

Consul: A representative of one country to another whose responsibilities include the safety of foreign citizens living in another country, and the monitoring of business and commercial activities between the two countries. Unlike a minister, a consul was subject to the law and punishment of the state in which he operated. Consuls were often able to select their own vice-consul. Consuls were citizens of the country represented. Vice-consuls were often local citizens of the host country. (Control of consular activity gave minister Richard Lyons many sleepless nights while serving during the war in Washington.)

Dispatch: Dispatches were hand-written letters from the secretary of state to his ministers in Europe, and those from the ministers to Seward. In the actual document, they were referred to as "dispatches" and sometimes "despatches". In the published diplomatic papers, they were referred to as "Correspondence".

Emissary: An emissary was a diplomatic representative who was sent on a specific mission. That mission might include the negotiation of a commercial agreement or a peace treaty.

Envoy: The envoy is ranked below the ambassador, and above the minister. He represents his country, not a specific head of state. However, U.S. representatives often mixed the terms envoy, minister and representative together. Charles Francis Adams often did this.

Exequatur: This is basically an official license issued by a head of state to a foreign consul to conduct consular business in the respective country or state. Some states in the U.S. specifically proscribed consular duties and the limits to those duties. Other states allowed great latitude. In 1861, William Seward revoked the exequatur of Robert Bunch, British consul in Charleston because of suspected espionage activities on behalf of the Confederacy.

Legation: Before the establishment of the rank of ambassador, the legation was the office of the minister, representative or envoy. The ambassador occupied an embassy, and a minister occupied a legation.

Letter of Marque: Letters of Marque and Reprisal were approved by the Lincoln Congress but never used. These Letters allowed a privateer to seize an "enemy" ship at sea and bring it into an authorized prize court for adjudication. The court would make sure that the ship was seized outside the protected territorial waters of a host or protecting nation. The court would also decide who would get how much of the prize money from the sale of the ship and cargo.

Minister: The representatives of England, France and the United States sent ministers to the capitols of the respective countries. Ministers, envoys and/or minister plenipotentiary monitored the politics of the respective country and maintained contact with their consuls and sent information as requested back to their secretary of state, Foreign Office or Ministry of Foreign Affairs. The minister represented the country, the ambassador represented the president, emperor or head of state.

Privateer: Privately owned ships that were legally authorized, through Letters of Marque, to capture and seize the cargo of an enemy ship. Privateers were generally used by governments who had an inadequate navy. Ship owners sold shares to investors who profited from the sale of the cargo and ship. The difference between a privateer and a pirate is that the privateer is legally authorized through Letters of Marque to seize other ships on the sea. A pirate has no such authority, and is executed if caught. Privateer crews were usually set free on land to find their own way home. During the Civil War, however, Union commercial ships were burned after their cargo was seized. Privateers had operated from the sixteenth century to the nineteenth.

Prize: Commercial ships that were doing business with countries at war were subject to capture if they were dealing in war contraband. International law at the time of the Civil War called for the captured "prize ship" to be taken to a neutral port to have their case heard before an impartial prize court. The court might decide to have the ship and cargo sold and the funds received divided among the captain and crew of the capturing ship. A definition of what constituted contraband items became an issue because William Seward believed that coal should be considered contraband goods. Coal was used to power the steam ships at the time. Some of those ships were privateers that were sinking Union commercial shipping.

Representative: A term sometimes used in place of minister or envoy. Charles Francis Adams, however, referred to himself as both minister, representative and minister plenipotentiary.

Supplementary Correspondence: Supplementary Correspondence generally referred to consular messages from the respective consul to and from the secretary of state. Correspondence also included Circulars which were notices that were sent by the State Department to all legations throughout the world. Circulars often outlined new administration policy, but were included under Correspondence in the Foreign Relations papers published by the Seward State Department.

Union/United States/Confederacy: The Union consisted of twenty free and five border states. The Confederacy consisted of eleven Southern states. Nevertheless, dispatches to and from Europe always referred to America as the United States. The Southern states were referred to as the "so-called Confederacy".

BIBLIOGRAPHY

Adams, Charles Francis: *An Address on the Life, Character and Services of William Henry Seward. Delivered at the Request of Both Houses of the Legislature of New York, at Albany New York, April 18, 1873.*
——. *Charles Francis Adams.* Boston: Houghton Mifflin, 1900.
——. *The Trent Affair: An Historical Retrospect.* Boston: Houghton Mifflin, 1912.
——. *Seward and the Declaration of Paris.* Boston: Massachusetts Historical Society, 1912.
——. *The Crisis of Foreign Intervention in the War of Secession.*
Adams, Ephraim: *Great Britain and the American Civil War.* New York: Russell and Russell, 1924.
Ammen, Daniel: *The Navy in the Civil War: The Atlantic Coast.* New York: Charles Scribners, 1883.
Anderson, John. (ed.): *The Journal of Kate Stone, 1861–1866.* Baton Rouge: University of Louisiana Press, 1955.
Ausubel, Herman: *John Bright, Victorian Reformer.* New York: John Wiley and Sons, 1966.
Baker, Lafayette: *The United States Secret Service in the Late war.* Chicago: L.P. Miller, 1889.
Bancroft, Frederick: *The Life of William Seward.* New York: Harper Brothers, 1900.
Barnes, James; Barnes, Patience: *Private and Confidential, Letters from British Ministers to the Foreign Secretaries in London, 1844–1867.* Toronto: Susquehena University Press, 1993.
Barnes, James J: *The American Civil War Through British Eyes.* Kent: Kent State University Press, 2003.
Barry, Patrick: *Dockyard Economy and Naval Power.* London: Sampson Low, 1863.

Baumgart, W: *The Peace of Paris 1856: Studies in War, Diplomacy and Peacemaking.* Oxford: ABC–CLIO Ltd., 1981.

Baxter, James Phinney:. *The Introduction of the Ironclad Warship.* Annapolis: Naval Institute Press, 1933.

Beale, H.K.: *The Diary of Edward Bates, 1859–1866.* Washington, Government Printing Office, 1933.

Beckles, Wilson. *American Ambassadors to France 1777–1927.* New York: Frederick Stokes, 1928.

Benjamin, Judah P. (Edmund Bennet, ed.): *Treatise on the Law of Sale of Personal Property, With References to the American Decisions, to the French Code and Civil Code.* Boston: Houghton Mifflin, 1888.

Berwanger, Eugene H: *The British Foreign Service and the American Civil War.* Lexington: University of Kentucky Press, 1994.

Bigelow, John: *France and the Confederate Navy.* New York: Bergman Publishers, 1888.

——. *Retrospectives of an Active Life vols. 1,2,3.* New York: Baker–Taylor Publishers, 1909.

——. *Les Etats-Unis D'Amerique en 1863.* Paris: Impremerie de Ch.Lahure, 1863.

——. *Gladstone, Morley and the Confederate Loan of 1863.* New York: DeVinnie Press, 1905.

Blackett, R.J.M.: *Divided Hearts.* Baton Rouge: Louisiana State University Press, 2001.

Blumenthal, Henry: *France and the United States, Their Diplomatic Relations 1789–1914.* New York: Norton, 1970.

——. *A Reappraisal of Franco-American Relations 1830–1871.* Chapel Hill: The University of North Carolina Press, 1959.

Bonham, Milledge, L.: *The British Consuls in the Confederacy.* New York: Longmans, Green, 1911.

Bostick, Douglas W.: *The Confederacy's Secret Weapon.* Charleston: The History Press, 2009.

Brock, Sallie: *Richmond During the War.* New York: Carelton, 1867.

Brogan, Hugh (ed.): *The Times Reports the American Civil War.* London: Times Books, 1975.

Brooks, Noah: *Washington in Lincoln's Time.* New York: Century, 1895.

Budeit, Janice L (ed.): *Index to the Papers of William Henry Seward.* Woodbridge: Research Press, 1983.

Bulloch, James D.: *The Secret Service of the Confederate States in Europe.* New York: Sagamore Press, 1883.

Burnett, Lonnie A.: *Henry Hotze, Confederate Propagandist.* Tuscaloosa: University of Alabama Press, 2008.

Butler, Pierce: *Judah P. Benjamin.* Philadelphia: Jacobs, 1906.

Cable, James: *The Political Influence of Naval Force in History.* London: MacMillan, 1998.

Callahan, James: *The Diplomatic History of the Confederacy.* Baltimore: Johns Hopkins University Press, 1901.

Campbell, Duncan: *English Public Opinion and the American Civil War.* Suffolk: Boydell Press, 2003.

Capers, Henry D.: *The Life and Times of C.G. Memminger.* Richmond: Waddey and Co., 1893.

Carroll, Daniel B.: *Henri Mercier and the American Civil War.* Princeton: Princeton University Press, 1971.

Case, Lynn M.: *French Opinion on War and Diplomacy During the Second Empire.* Philadelphia: University of Pennsylvania Press, 1954.

———. *French Opinion on the United States and Mexico.* New York: Century, 1936.

Cecil, Algenon.: *British Foreign Secretaries 1807–1916.* London: G. Bell, 1927.

Chamberlain, Muriel E.: *Lord Palmerston.* Washington, DC: The Catholic University of America Press, 1987.

Chase, Salmon: *Private Letters and Public Service.* Cincinnati: Wilson Baldwin and Co., 1874.

———. *Inside Lincoln's Cabinet, the Civil War Diaries of Salmon P Chase,* ed. David H. Donald. Oxford: Oxford University Press, 1955.

Clapp, Margaret: *Forgotten First Citizen, John Bigelow.* Boston: Little Brown, 1947.

Clay, Cassius: *The Life of Cassius Marcellus Clay.* Cincinnati: J.F. Brenan, 1886.

Cleveland, Henry: *Alexander H. Stephens in Public and Private with Letters and Speeches Before, During and Since the War.* Philadelphia: National Publishing, 1866.

Connell, Brian (ed.): Regina versus Palmerston: *The Correspondence between Queen Victoria and Her Foreign and Prime Minister.* New York: Doubleday, 1961.

Cook, Adrian: *The Alabama Claims.* Ithaca: Cornell University Press, 1975.

Crawford, Martin: *The Anglo-American Crisis of the Mid-Nineteenth Century.* Athens: University of Georgia Press, 1987.

———. *William Howard Russell's Civil War.* Athens: University of Georgia Press, 1992.

Crist, Lynda (ed.): *The Papers of Jefferson Davis.* Baton Rouge: Louisiana State University Press, 1992.

Crook, D.P.: *Diplomacy During the American Civil War*. New York: John Wiley and Sons, 1975.

———. *The North, The South and The Powers*. New York: John Wiley and Sons, 1974.

Davis, Henry Winter. *Speeches and Addresses*. New York: Harper Brothers, 1867.

Davis, Jefferson. *The Rise and Fall of the Confederate Government*, Vol. 1. Boston: Da Capo Press, 1990.

Dayton, William Lewis. *Papers, Personal and Diplomatic* Princeton: Firestone Library, Princeton University.

Dodd, William. *Jefferson Davis*. Philadelphia: G.W. Jacobs, 1907.

Dodge, Berthe. *Cotton, The Plant that Would be King*. Austin: University of Texas Press, 1984.

Donald, David Herbert. *Charles Sumner and the Coming of the Civil War*. New York: Alfred Knopf, 1960.

———. *Charles Sumner and the Rights of Man*. New York: Alfred Knopf, 1970.

———. *Lincoln*. New York: Simon and Schuster, 1995.

———. *Inside Lincoln's Cabinet: The Civil War Diary of Salmon P Chase*. London: Longmans, Green, 1954.

Donaldson, Jordan and Pratt, Edwin: *Europe and the American Civil War*. Boston: Houghton Mifflin, 1931.

Duberman, Martin: *Charles Francis Adams 1807–1886*. Stanford: Stanford University Press, 1968.

Edsall, Nicholas: *Richard Cobden, Independent Radical*. Cambridge: Harvard University Press, 1986.

Elliot, E.N.: *Cotton is King and Proslavery Argument*. Augusta: Portland, Abbott and Loomis, 1860.

Evans, Eli N.: *Judah P. Benjamin: The Jewish Confederate*. New York: The Free Press, 1988.

Everett, William. *Address in Commemoration of the Life and Service of Charles Francis Adams*. Cambridge, Wilson and Sons Publishers, 1887.

Ferris, Norman. *Desperate Diplomacy*. Nashville: University of Tennessee Press, 1976.

———. *The Trent Affair*. Knoxville: University of Tennessee Press, 1977.

Fischer, LeRoy. *Lincoln's Gadfly, Adam Gurowski*. Norman: University of Oklahoma Press, 1964.

Figes, Orlando. *The Crimean War: A History*. New York: Metropolitan Press, 2010.

Foner, Philip. *British Labor and the American Civil War*. New York: Holmes and Meier, 1981.

Ford, Worthington. *A Cycle of Adams Letters, 1861–1865*. New York: Houghton Mifflin, 1920.

Foreman, Amanda. *A World on Fire*. New York: Random House, 2010.

Fuller, Howard J: *Clad in Iron, The American Civil War and the Age of British Naval Power.* Annapolis: Naval Institute Press, 2008.

———. *Empire, Technology and Seapower, Royal Navy Crisis in the Age of Palmerston.* New York: Routledge Press, 2013.

Gasperin, Agenor: *America Before Europe.* London: Sampson and Low, 1862.

———. *The Uprising of a Great People* (Mary L. Booth, ed.) New York: Scribner, 1861.

Gavronsky, Serge: *The French Liberal Opposition and the American Civil War.* New York: Humanities Press, 1968.

Gibson, Thomas: *The Declaration of Paris, 1856.* London: Sampson Low, 1900.

Gobineau, Arthur de (Collins, Adrian, ed.): *The Inequality of Human Races.* London: Heinemann Publications, 1854.

Gooch, G.P. (ed.): *The Later Correspondence of Lord John Russell.* London: Longmans, Green and Company, 1925.

Goodwin, Doris Kearns: *A Team of Rivals.* New York: Simon and Schuster, 2005.

Greeley, Horace (ed.): *Charles Congdon, Tribune Essays, Leading Essays from the New York Tribune from 1857 to 1863.* New York: Redfield Publishers, 1869.

Hammond, James H.: *Selections from Letters and Speeches.* New York: Trow and Company, 1866.

Harris, Thomas: *The Trent Affair.* Indianapolis: Bobbs-Merrill, 1896.

Hay, John Milton: *Papers, Hay Library*, Brown University, Providence, R.I.

Hobson, J.A.: *Richard Cobden, the International Man.* New York: Barnes and Noble, 1919.

Holzer, Harold: *Lincoln President Elect.* New York: Simon and Schuster, 2008.

Hudson, Eduard Maco: *The Second War of Independence in America.* London: Longmans Green and Company, 1863.

Huse, Caleb: *The Supplies for the Confederate Army.* Boston: T.R. Marvin, 1904.

Isley, Jeter Allen: *Horace Greeley and the Republican Party.* New York: Octagon Books, 1965.

Isreal, F.L. (ed.): The State of the Union Messages of the Presidents 1790–1966. New York: Chelsea House, 1967.

Jenkins, Brian: *Britain and the War for the Union.* Montreal: McGill University Press, 1974.

Jones, John B.: *A Rebel War Clerk's Diary at the Confederate States Capitol.* Philadelphia: Lippincott, 1866.

Jones, William: *The Confederate Rams at Birkenhead.* Tuscaloosa: Confederate Publishing Company, 1961.

Jones, Howard: *Union in Peril: The Crisis Over British Intervention in the Civil War.* Chapel Hill: University of North Carolina Press, 1992.

——. *Blue and Grey Diplomacy*. Chapel Hill: University of North Carolina Press, 2010.

Kaplan, Fred: *Lincoln, The Biography of a Writer*. New York: Harper Collins, 2008.

Kaufman, Michael: *American Brutus*. New York: Random House, 2004.

Keckley, Elizabeth: *Behind the Scenes*. New York: Penguin (reprint), 2005.

Kiersey, Nicholas: "The Diplomats and Diplomacy of the American Civil War" (BA Thesis, University of Limerick, Limerick, Ireland, 1997).

Kingsley, Vine Wright: *French Intervention in America*. New York: Richardson, 1863.

Knott, Stephen: *Secret and Sanctioned: Covert Operations and the American Presidency*. New York: Oxford University Press, 1996.

Labovitz, Laura: "For the Benefit of Others: Harriet Martineau: feminist, abolitionist and travel writer" (2011, Masters Dissertation, UNLV).

Lang, Jack H.: *Lincoln's Fireside Reading*. New York: World Press, 1965.

Long, David F.: *Gold Braid and Foreign Relations*. Annapolis: Naval Institute Press, 1988.

Lewis, Gilbert Frankland: *Letters of the Right Honorable Sir George Cornwell Lewis*. London: Longmans Green, 1870.

Lincoln, Abraham: *The Abraham Lincoln Papers at the Library of Congress,* Manuscript Division (Microfilm).

Lonn, Ella: *Foreigners in the Confederacy*. Chapel Hill: University of North Carolina Press, 1940.

Lothrop, Thornton: *William Henry Seward*. Boston: Houghton Mifflin, 1899.

MacGilchrist, John: *Richard Cobden, The Apostle of Free Trade, His political Career and Public Services*. Charleston, Nabu Press, 2012.

McHenry, George: *Statement of Facts Relating to the Approaching Cotton Crisis*. Richmond: Government Printing Office, 1864.

McMahon, Robert J.; Zeiler, Thomas V.: *Guide to U.S. Foreign Policy: A Diplomatic History*. Thousand Oaks: CQ Press, 2012.

McPherson, James: *Battle Cry of Freedom*. New York: Ballentine Press, 1988.

——. *War on the Waters, The Union and Confederate Navies*. Chapel Hill: University of North Carolina Press, 2012.

Mahin, Dean: *One War at a Time*. Washington DC: Brasseys Press, 1999.

——. *The Blessed Place of Freedom: Europeans in Civil War America*. Dulles: Brasseys Press, 2002.

Marx, Karl: *The American Civil War*. Die Presse, No.293, 1861.

May, Robert E. (ed.): *The Union, the Confederacy and the Atlantic Rim*. Lafayette: Perdue University Press, 1995.

Mayes, Edward: *Lucius Q.C. Lamar: His Life and Speeches*. Nashville: Methodist Church Publications, 1896.

Meade, Robert. *Judah P. Benjamin: Confederate Statesman.* New York: Oxford University Press, 1943.

Milton, David: *Lincoln's Spymaster: Thomas Haines Dudley and the Liverpool Network* Mechanichsburg: Stackpole Books, 2003.

Monaghan, Jay: *A Diplomat in Carpet Slippers.* New York: Bobbs-Merrill, 1945.

Nevins, Alan: *War for the Union.* New York: Scribner and Sons, 1960.

Newton, Thomas: *Lord Lyons: A Record of British Diplomacy.* London: Edward Arnold, 1913.

Nicolay, Helen: *Lincoln's Secretary.* Westport: Greenwood Press, 1949.

Nicolay, John George: *Papers, Library of Congress*, Manuscripts Division, Washington, DC.

Nicolay, John George; Hay, John Milton: *Abraham Lincoln: A History.* New York: The Century Company, 1890.

Niven, John: *Gideon Welles, Lincoln's Secretary of the Navy.* New York: Oxford University Press, 1973.

Owsley, Frank: *King Cotton Diplomacy* . Chicago: University of Chicago Press, 1931.

Officer, Lawrence; Smith, Lawrence: "The Canadian-American Reciprocity Treaty of 1855–1866" *Journal of Economic History* (Vol. 28, No.4, December, 1968).

Palmerston, Henry John Temple: *Gladstone and Palmerston, Correspondence of Lord Palmerston and Mr. Gladstone, 1851–1865.* London: V. Gollancz, Ltd. 1928.

Parker, Joel: *International Law: The Case of the Trent.* Cambridge: Welch and Bigelow, 1862.

Perret, Geoffrey: *Lincoln's War.* New York: Random House, 2004.

Perry, David: "Abraham Lincoln and John George Nicolay, The Impact of Auditory and Visual Learning Styles on the Civil War". Harrogate*: Lincoln Memorial University Press,* 2010

——. "American Braggadocio: The Lincoln Administration Foreign Policy" in Clinton (ed.): *The Maryland-National Capital Park Commission,* 2010.

——. "Dispatch Number 10 and What it Reveals About William Seward and Abraham Lincoln" Shreveport*, International Lincoln Association,* 2012.

Pierce, Edward: *Memoir and Letters of Charles Sumner.* Charleston, Nabu Press, 2012.

Pinkerton, Alan: *The Spy of the Rebellion.* Hartford: Winter and Hatch, 1883.

Pollard, Edward: *The Southern Spy: Letters on the Policy and Inauguration of the Lincoln War.* Richmond: Qwest and Johnson, 1961.

Poore, Benjamin P.: *Reminiscences.* Chicago: Hubbard Press, 1886.

Porter, David Dixon: *The Naval History of the Civil War.* New York: Sherman Publishing, 1886.

Prest, John: *Lord John Russell*. Columbia: University of South Carolina Press, 1972.

Read, Donald: *Cobden and Bright*. New York: St. Martin's Press, 1968.

Reed, E.J.: *Our Ironclad Ships: Their Qualities, Performance and Cost*. London: John Murray, 1869.

Reed, William Bradford: *A Review of William Seward's Diplomacy*. Philadelphia: Private Printing, 1862.

Reid, Stuart: *Lord John Russell*. London: Sampson Low, Marston and Company, 1895.

Reid, Thomas: *The Life of the Right Honorable William Edward Forster, vols. 1-2*. Charleston, Nabu Press, 2011.

Ridley, Jasper: *Lord Palmerston*. New York: E.P. Dutton, 1971.

Roberts, Adolphe: *Semmes of the Alabama*. New York: Bobbs-Merrill, 1938.

Royale, Trevor: *Crimea, The Great Crimean War, 1854–1856*. New York: Pelgrave, 2000.

Rush, Richard: *Official Records of the Union and Confederate Navies in the War of the Rebellion* Washington: Government Printing Office, 1894.

Russell, William Howard. *My Diary, North and South*. London: Bradbury and Evans, 1863.

———. *Civil War in America*. Boston: Gardner Fuller, 1861.

Russell, John Earl: *Recollections and Suggestions*. London: Spottswoode, 1875.

Schroeder, P.: *Austria, Great Britain and the Crimean War: The Destruction of the European Concert*. Ithaca: Cornell University Press, 1972.

Schuckers, J.W.: *The Life and Public Service of Salmon P. Chase*. New York: Appleton, 1874.

Scott, Stephan: "Spur Up Your Pegasus": Family Letters of Salmon, Kate and Nettie Chase, 1844–1873 (The Journal of Southern History) Kent: Kent State University Press, 2009.

Schwab, John Cristopher: *The Confederate States of America 1861–1865: A Financial and Industrial History of the South During the Civil War*. New York: Scribner's, 1901.

Sears, Louis Martin: *John Slidell*. Durham: Duke University Press, 1925.

Seward, Frederick: *Seward at Washington: As Senator and Secretary of State*. New York: Derby and Miller, 1891.

———. *Reminiscences of a War-time Statesman and Diplomat*. New York: Putnam and Sons, 1916.

Seward, William Henry: *Papers Relating to the Foreign Relations of the United States*. Washington: U.S. Government Printing Office, 1861–1870.

———. *Personal Papers*, University of Rochester, Auburn, New York (Microfilm Edition).

Shingleton, Royce: *High Seas Confederate: The Life and Times of John Newland Maffitt*. Columbia: University of South Carolina Press, 1994.

Siedman, Belle; Friedman, Lillian: *Europe Looks at the Civil War*. New York: Orion Press, 1960.

Sigaud, Louis: *Belle Boyd, Confederate Spy*. Richmond: Dietz Press, 1944.

Smith, Denis: *Garibaldi*. Englewood: Prentiss-Hall, 1969.

Smith, Goldwin: *A Letter to a Whig Southern Independence Association*. Boston: Ticknor and Fields, 1864.

Spencer, Warren: *The Confederate Navy in Europe*. Tuscaloosa: University of Alabama Press, 1983.

Stanton, Edwin McMasters: *The Diary of a Public Man*. New Brunswick: Rutgers University Press, 1946 (reprint).

Stern, Philip V.: *Secret Missions of the Civil War*. New York: Bonanza Press, 1959.

Stoddard, Henry Luther: *Horace Greeley, Printer, Editor, Crusader*. New York: Putnam, 1946.

Stoddard, William O.: *Inside the Lincoln Whitehouse*, (ed. Michael Burlingame) Lincoln: University of Nebraska Press, 2000.

Strode, Hudson: *Jefferson Davis*. New York: Harcourt Brace, 1955.

Stovall, Pleasant A.: *Robert Toombs: Statesman, Speaker, Soldier, Sage*. New York: Cassell Publishing Company, 1892.

Sumner, Charles: *Selected Letters* (ed. Beverly Wilson Palmer). Boston: Northeastern Press, 1990.

———. *The Works of Charles Sumner*. Boston: Lee and Shepard, 1873.

———. *Our Foreign Relations, Speech of Hon. Charles Sumner, before the Citizens of New York, at the Cooper Institute*, September 10, 1863.

———. Speech at Cooper Union.

Tap, Bruce: *Over Lincoln's Shoulder*. Lawrence: University of Kansas Press, 1988.

Thomas, Emory: *The Confederate State of Richmond: A Biography of the Capitol*. Austin: University of Texas Press, 1971.

Thompson, Robert; Wainwright, Richard: *Confidential Correspondence of Gustavus Vassa Fox, Assistant Secretary of the Navy, 1861–1865*. New York: De Vinne Press, 1920.

Thompson, Samuel: *Confederate Purchasing Operations Abroad*. Chapel Hill: University of North Carolina Press, 1935.

Thouvanel, Édouard: *Le Secret de L'Empereur, 1860–1863*. Paris: Calman Levy, 1889.

Todd, Richard Cecil: *Confederate Finance*. Athens: University of Georgia Press, 1954.

Travelyan, George: *The Life of John Bright*. New York: Houghton Mifflin, 1913.

Tyrnauer-Tyner, A.R: *Lincoln and the Emperor*. New York: Harcourt Brace, 1962.

Underwood, Rodman: *Stephen Russell Mallory: A Biography of the Confederate Navy Secretary* Jefferson: McFarland, 2005.

Van Deusen, Glyndon: *William Henry Seward*. New York: Oxford University Press, 1967.

———. *Horace Greeley Nineteenth Century Crusader*. Philadelphia: University of Pennsylvania Press 1953.

Vattel, Emer de: *The Law of Nations or, Principles of the Law of Nations Applied to the Conduct and Affairs of Nations and Sovereigns*. (Kapossy, Whatmopre ed. 1797, reprint) Indianapolis: Liberty Fund, 2008.

Villiers, Brougham; Chesson, W.H. *Anglo-American Relations 1861–1865*. London: T. Fisher Unwin, 1919.

Walpole, Spencer. *The Life of Lord John Russell*. London: Spottswoode, 1891.

Warren, Louis. *Lincoln's Youth*. Indianapolis: Indiana Historical Society, 1959.

Weed, Thurlow: *The Life of Thurlow Weed* Vols. I and II. Boston: Houghton Mifflin, 1884.

———. *Thurlow Weed's Letters from Europe, 1861–1862* (private publication).

Welles, Gideon: *Lincoln and Seward*. Freeport: Books for Libraries Press, 1969 (reprint).

———. *The Diary of Gideon Welles*. Boston: Houghton Mifflin, 1911.

Whiting, William: *The War Powers of the President and the Legislative Powers of Congress in Relation to Rebellion, Treason and Slavery*. Boston: Shorney, 1862.

Willson, Beckles: *John Slidell and the Confederates in Paris ,1862–1865*. New York: Minton, Balch, 1932.

Wilson, Mark: *The Business of Civil War: Military Mobilization and the State, 1861–1865* Baltimore: Johns Hopkins University Press, 2007.

Woldman, Albert: *Lincoln and the Russians*. New York: World Publishing, 1952.

Woodman, Harold: *King Cotton and His Retainers*. Lexington: University of Kentucky Press, 1968.

Wriston, Henry M.: *Executive Agents in American Foreign Relations*. Baltimore: The Johns Hopkins Press, 1929.

Young, Robert W.: *James Murray Mason, Defender of the Old South*. Knoxville: University of Tennessee Press, 1998.

Private Paper Collections (U.S.)

The Papers of Charles Francis Adams, Microfilm Edition, Sterling Memorial Library, Yale University.

The Abraham Lincoln Papers, Library of Congress.

The Papers of John Bigelow, Manuscripts Division, New York Public Library, New York City, New York.

The Papers of James Dunwoody Bulloch, Mariners Museum, Christopher Newport University. Newport News, VA.

The Salmon P. Chase Papers, Correspondence 1865–1873, vol. 5. John Niven ed. Kent State University Press, 1998.

The Messages and Papers of Jefferson Davis and the Confederacy, Including Diplomatic Correspondence 1861–1865. Manuscripts Division, New York Public Library, New York, N.Y.

The Papers of William Lewis Dayton, Manuscripts Division, Firestone Library, Princeton, New Jersey, Box 1, folders 1, 2, 4, 5. Box 2, folders 1-5, 7-9.

The Papers of John Milton Hay, Hay Library, Brown University, Providence, Rhode Island.

Transcribed Letters of Caleb Huse (James Austin Anderson) University of Alabama, Tuscaloosa, Alabama.

The Papers of Stephen R. Mallory, 1861–1872, Wilson Special Collections Library, University of North Carolina, Chapel Hill, North Carolina.

The Papers of John George Nicolay, Manuscripts Division, Library of Congress, Madison Building, Washington, D.C.

The Papers of Henry Shelton Sanford, Sanford Memorial Library, Sanford, Florida.

The Papers of William Henry Seward, Microfilm Edition, Sterling Memorial Library, Yale University.

The William Henry Seward Papers, Microfilm Edition, Rush Rhees Library, Rochester University, Rochester, New York.

The Papers of Nathaniel Beverly Tucker, College of William and Mary.

Dissertations

Baker, Edith Ellen: The Relations of Great Britain and America, 1861–1865 (Doctoral Dissertation, University of Birmingham, 1920).

Bonham, Milledge: The British Consuls in the Confederacy (Doctoral Dissertation, Columbia University, 1911).

Cairns, Scott: Lord Lyons and Anglo-American Diplomacy During the American Civil War, 1859–1865 (Doctoral Dissertation, London School of Economics, 2004).

Kearns, Mary Pinckney: Secession Diplomacy, A Study of Thomas Butler King, Commissioner of Georgia to Europe, 1861 (Master's Thesis, Georgia Southern University, 2006)

Mitton, Steven. The Free World Confronted, The Problem of Slavery and Progress in American Foreign Relations 1833–1844 (Doctoral Dissertation, Louisiana State University, 2005).

Oosterlinck, Kim; Weidenmier, Marc: Victory or Repudiation? The Probability of the Southern Confederacy Winning the Civil War (Doctoral Dissertation, Rutgers University, 1969)

Raney, William Francis: The Military and Diplomatic Activities of Canada, 1861–1865, as affected by the American Civil War (Doctoral Dissertation, University of Wisconsin, 1919).

Reinecke, J.A. The Diplomatic Career of Pierre Soule (Master's Thesis, Tulane University, 1914)

Spenser, Warren F. Edouard Drouyn de Luhys and the Foreign Policy of the Second Empire (Doctoral Dissertation, University of Pennsylvania, 1955)

Zucconi, Adam. The Ideology of Equality: James Murray Mason and Antebellum Politics (Master's Thesis, Clemson University, 2011)

Symposia

Golove, David: Leaving Customary International Law Where it is: *Goldsmith and Posner's The Limits of International Law.* New York University School of Law, 2014.

Periodicals

American Heritage
Blackwood's Magazine
Harpers Weekly
Journal of the Civil War
Journal of the Abraham Lincoln Association
McClure's Magazine
North American Review
Prologue Magazine
Scientific American
The Atlantic Monthly
The Century Magazine

Journals

International Studies Quarterly
Illinois State Journal
Journal of the Civil War
Journal of the Abraham Lincoln Association

Journal of Southern History
Journal of the Louisiana Historical Association
Revue Belge de Philologie et d'histoire
The North American Review
The Northern Mariner
The Atlantic Monthly
The Historical Review
The Tablet
The Opinionator
The Journal of Illinois History
William and Mary Quarterly

Articles

Bauer, Craig: The Last Effort, The Secret Mission of the Confederate Diplomat, Duncan F. Kenner (*The Journal of the Louisiana Historical Association*, Vol. 22, No.1, Winter, 1981).

Baxter, James P.: The British Government and Neutral Rights, 1861–1865 (*The Naval Review*, Vol. 17, No.2, May, 1929).

Blackburn, George: Paris Newspapers and the American Civil War (*Illinois Historical Journal*, Vol. 84, Autumn, 1991).

Block, W.T.: "Prince Polecat": A Sketch of General Camille Armand de Polignac at the Battle of Mansfield, Louisiana. http://www.wtblock.com/wtblockjr/polecat.htm.

Blumenthal, Henry: Confederate Diplomacy: Popular Notions and International Realities (*The Journal of Southern History*, vol. 32 No.2, May, 1966).

Boklan, Kent: How I Broke the Confederate Code (Taylor and Francis Group, LLC, 2006).

Bourne, Kenneth: British Preparations for war with the North, 1861–1862 (*The English Historical Review*, Vol. 76, No.301, 1961).

Brook, Daniel: The Forgotten Confederate Jew (*The Tablet*, 2012).

Bunch, Robert: Dispatch from the British Consul at Charleston to Lord John Russell, 1860 (*The American Historical Review*, Vol. 18 No.4, July, 1913).

Buzan, Barry; Lawson, George: The global transformation: the nineteenth century and the making of modern international relations. (*International Studies Quarterly*, 59 (1), 2013).

Case, Lynn M: Édouard Thouvenel et le Diplomatie du Second Empire (*Revue Belge de Philologie et d'Histoire*, Vol. 57, 1979).

Clark, Michael; Collie, Alexander: The Ups and Downs of Trading with the Confederacy (*The Northern Mariner*, Vol. 19, No.2, April, 2009).

Clark, Michael (ed.): William Schaw Lindsay: Righting the Wrongs of a Radical Shipowner (*The Northern Mariner*, No.3, July, 2010).

Cobden, Richard: Letters of Richard Cobden to Charles Sumner, 1862–1865 (*The American Historical Review*, Vol. 2, January 1, 1897).

Cox, Christopher: Belle Boyd: Confederate Patriot or Pseudo-Celebrity? (*Saber and Scroll*, Vol. 1, Issue 2, April, 2015).

Dattel, Eugene: Cotton and the Civil War (*Mississippi Historical Society*, July, 2008).

Dodd, William E. Jefferson Davis, Constitutionalist: His Letters, Papers and Speeches (*The American Historical Review*, Vol. 29, No.2, January, 1924).

Ferris, Norman B.: Lincoln and Seward in Civil War Diplomacy: Their Relationship at the Outset Reexamined. (*Journal of the Abraham Lincoln Association*, Vol. 12, Issue 1, 1991).

Foster. Kevin J.: The Diplomats Who Sank a Fleet: The Confederacy's Undelivered Fleet and the Union Consular Service (*Prologue Magazine*, Vol.33 No.3, Fall 2001).

Fuller, Howard J.: "The *Warrior's* Influence Abroad: The American Civil War", *The International Journal of Naval History*, Vol. 10., No. 1 (October 2013)

_____, "Iron Lion or Paper Tiger? The Myth of British Naval Intervention in the American Civil War", in Peter N. Stearns (ed.), *The American Civil War in a Global Context* (Richmond: Virginia Sesquicentennial of the American Civil War Commission: 2014)

_____, " 'The absence of decisive results': British Assessments of Union Combined Operations", in Craig Symonds (ed.), *Union Combined Operations in the Civil War* (New York: Fordham University Press, 2010)

_____, " 'This country now occupies the vantage ground': Union Monitors vs. the British Navy", in Harold Holzer and Tim Mulligan (eds.), *The Battle of Hampton Roads: New Perspectives on the USS* Monitor *and CSS* Virginia (New York: Fordham University Press, 2006)

_____, " 'The whole character of maritime life': British Reactions to the U.S.S. *Monitor* and the American Ironclad Experience", *The Mariner's Mirror*, Vol. 88, No. 3 (August 2002)

French Navy 1852–1870 – Second Empire. http://www.globalsecurity.org/military/world/europe/fr-marine-nationale-2empire.html

Golder, F.A.: The Russian Fleet and the Civil War. (*American Historical Review*, 20, 1915).

Hubert, Leroy: Ambrose Dudley Mann: Diplomat of the Lost Cause (*Confederate Society of Belgium*).

Jenkins, Brian: The Wise Macaw and the Lion: William Seward and Britain 1861–1863 (University of Rochester Bulletin, Vol. 31, Autumn, 1978, No.1).

Jones, Howard: Union and Confederate Diplomacy During the Civil War (*Essential Civil War Curriculum*, August, 2010).

Jones, Terry: The Jewish Rebel (*Opinionator*, April, 2012).

Jones, William: Britain's Surrogate War Against the Union, 1861–1865 (*Executive Intelligence Review*, August 12, 2011).

Kelly, Patrick: The American Crisis of the 1860s (Journal of the Civil War, Vol. 2, Issue 3, 2012).

Le Duc de Morny - Histoire du Second Empire (1852–1870). http://secondempire.voila.net/pagesempire/ducdemorny.html.

Lodge, Henry Cabot: William H. Seward (*The Atlantic Monthly*, May, 1884).

Moore, J. Preston: Pierre Soule: Southern Expansionist and Promoter (*The Journal of Southern History*, Vol. 21, No.2, May, 1955).

Nacouzi, Salwa: Les Creoles Louisianais Defendent la Cause du Sud a Paris (Transatlantica, 1, 2002). http://transatlantica.revues.org/451.

Nepveux, Ethel: The Economist, Workhorse for the Confederacy (*Confederate Historical Society of Belgium*, https://www.google.com/webhp?sourceid=chrome-instant&rlz=1C1LENN_enUS507US617&ion=1&espv=2&ie=UTF-8#q=Nepveux%2C+Ethel%3A+The+Economist%2C+Workhorse+for+the+Confederacy+(Confederate+Historical+Society+of+Belgium%2C).

———. Eugene Tessier, A French Blockade-runner (*Confederate Historical Society of Belgium* http://www.chab-belgium.com/pdf/english/Tessier.pdf).

———. George A. Trenholm, Last Secretary of the Treasury (Anderson, South Carolina: Electric City Printing Company, 1999).

Noirsain, Serge: The Blockade Runners of the Confederate Government (*Confederate Historical Society of Belgium* https://www.google.com/webhp?sourceid=chrome-instant&rlz=1C1LENN_enUS507US617&ion=1&espv=2&ie=UTF-8#q=Noirsain%2C+Serge%3A+The+Blockade+Runners+of+the+Confederate+Government+(Confederate+Historical+Society+of+Belgium).

———. The Index: Henry Hotze, Southern Propagandist (*Confederate Historical Society of Belgium*).

Palen, William-Marc: The Civil War's Forgotten Transatlantic Tariff Debate and the Confederacy's Free Trade Diplomacy (*Journal of the Civil War Era*, Vol.3, Issue 1, March, 2013).

Peters, Thelma: Blockade-Running in the Bahamas During the Civil War (A paper read before the Historical Association of Southern Florida, May 5, 1943).

Rathbone, Mark: Lord Palmerston (*History Review*, 2002).

Rice, A.T.: A Famous Diplomatic Dispatch (*North American Review* 353, April, 1886).

Schraffenberger, Don: Karl Marx and the American Civil War (*International Socialist Review*, Vol. 80, January 11, 2012).

Sebrell, Thomas E: The American Civil War Ended in England (posted March 23, 2011 http://www.americansc.org.uk/Online/Sesquicentennial.html).

Spiegel, Steven: British Foreign Policy During the American Civil War: January 1860 to September 1862 (*The Concord Review*).

Still, William. The Confederate Ironclad Navy (*Naval History Magazine*, vol. 28, No.1, February, 2014).

The French Navy of the Crimean War. http://www.cyberironclad.com/crimea/french_fleet_crimea.php.

Titus, Katherine: The Richmond Bread Riot of 1863: Class, Race and Gender in the Urban Confederacy (*The Gettysburg College Journal of the Civil War Era*, Vol. 2, Issue 1, 2011).

Vandiver, Frank. Jefferson Davis- Leader Without Legend (*Southern Historical Association*, Vol. 43, No.1, p.3-18).

Whiteridge, Arnold: The Peaceable Ambassadors (*American Heritage*, 1957).

Published Collections

Basler, Roy P. (ed.), *The works of Abraham Lincoln, 9 vols*. New Brunswick, N.J.: Rutgers University Press, 1953–1955.

Beale, Howard K. (ed.): *Diary of Gideon Welles: Secretary of the Navy under Lincoln and Johnson, 3 vols*. New York: W.W. Norton and Co. 1960

Corwin, Thomas (Josiah Morrow, ed.): *Life and Speeches*. Cincinnati: W.H. Anderson and Co., 1896.

Ford, Chauncy Worthington (ed.): *A cycle of Adams Letters, 1861–1865, 2 vols*. Boston: Houghton Mifflin, 1920.

Gooch, G.P. (ed.): *The Later Correspondence of Lord John Russell, 1840–1878, 2 vols*. London: Longmans, Green and Co., 1925.

Herbert, H.A. (ed.): *Official Records of the Union and Confederate Navies in the War of the Rebellion*. Washington, Govt. Printing Office, 1894.

Lapsley, Arthur. *The Writings of Abraham Lincoln*. New York: Putnam, 1906

Orr, James L.: *Speech of the Hon. James L. Orr, of South Carolina, on the Slavery Question. Delivered in the House of Representatives*, May 8, 1850.

Palmer, Beverly Wilson (ed.): *The Selected Letters of Charles Sumner, 2 vols*. Boston: Northeastern University Press, 1990.

Rhys, Ernest (ed): *Selected Speeches of the Rt. Honorable John Bright, MP, on Public Questions*. London: J.M. Dent, 1907.

Russell, John Earl: *Recollections and Suggestions, 1813–1873*. Boston: Roberts Brothers, 1875 (reprint of London, Longmans, Green, 1873).

Russell, William Howard (Eugene Berwanger, ed.) *My Diary North and South*. Baton Rouge: Louisiana State Press, 2001 (reprint of Alfred Knopf, 1988).

Senior, Nassau W.: *Conversations with M. Thiers, M. Guizot and other Distinguished Persons During the Second Empire, 1860–1863* (London, Hurst and Blackett, 1880).

Papers Delivered

Bridges, Peter: Three Great Civil Servants: William Hunter, Augustus Adee, and William J. Carr (DACOR Bacon House, Washington, D.C. October 11, 2005).

Kennedy, David: International Law and the Nineteenth Century: History of an Illusion (Quinnipiac College School of Law, 1995).

Vail Kellen, William: Henry Wheaton: An Appreciation (Address at Brown University, *1902*).

Pamphlets

Hallek, H. W.: Laws of War and Martial Law (Boston, Williams, 1863).

Lowrey, Grosvenor Porter: English Neutrality: Is the Alabama a British Pirate? (New York, Anson Randolph, 1863)

Parker, Joel: International Law – Case of the *Trent*: Capture and Surrender of Mason and Slidell (Cambridge, Welch Bigelow, 1862).

Collected Works, Government and Public Documents

Benson, A.C. and Viscount Esher: *Letters of Queen Victoria*, Vol.3, 1854–1861, London: J. Murray, 1907.

Blue Book or Register of Officers and Agents, Civil, Military and Naval in the Service of the United States, Corrected to November, 1862 (New York, Colton, 1863)

Bourne, Kenneth; Watt, Cameron (ed.): *British Documents on Foreign Affairs: Reports and Papers From the Foreign Office Confidential Print, Part One, Series F, Europe 1848–1914*. Bethesda Maryland: University Publications of America, 1988.

Correspondence Concerning Claims Against Great Britain. Washington, Government Printing Office, 1870.

Executive Documents of the House of Representatives, 1861–1862, Washington, Government Printing Office, 1862.

Irwin, Douglas: The Optimal Tax on Antebellum U.S. Cotton Exports (Cambridge, National Bureau of Economic Research, 2001)

Journal of the Congress of the Confederate States of America, 1861–1865 (Washington, Government Printing Office, February 1, 1904.)

Lamont, Daniel: The War of the Rebellion, A Compilation of the Official Records of the Union and Confederate Armies (Series II, Vol. II, Government Printing Office, 1897).

Lawrence, William: *The Indirect Claims of the United States Under the Treaty of Washington of May 8, 1871.* Providence: Rider Brothers, 1872.

Leader, Robert: *The Life and Letters of J.A. Roebuck.* London: Edward Arnold, 1897.

Morley, John: *Life of William Ewart Gladstone*, 3 vols. London: Macmillan, 1903.

Philips, Ulrich R. (ed.) The Correspondence of Robert Toombs, Alexander H. Stephens and Howell Cobb (Washington, Annual Report of the American Historical Association for the year 1911. Vol. 2, 1913)

Register of Officers and Agents: Civil, Military and Naval in the Service of the United States (Washington, Gideon, 1851)

Register of Officers and Agents: Civil, Military and Naval in the Service of the United States (Washington, William Harris, 1859)

Register of Officers and Agents: Civil, Military and Naval in the Service of the United States (Washington, Government Printing Office, 1862)

Richardson, James D.: *A Compilation of the Messages and Papers of the Presidents.* Vol. 6, Part 1, Abraham Lincoln, Online Books http://onlinebooks.library.upenn.edu/webbin/metabook?id=mppresidents.

——. A compilation of the Messages and Papers of the Confederacy including the Diplomatic Correspondence 1861–1865. (Nashville, United States Publishing Company, 1905).

Seward, William H. (George Baker, ed.) *The Works of William H. Seward, _5 vols.* (Boston, Houghton Mifflin, 1884).

Memoirs and Contemporary Accounts

Argyll, George Douglas, Duke of Argyll (The Dowager Duchess of Argyll, ed.): *Autobiography and Memoirs.* 2 vols. London: J. Murray, 1906.

Bigelow, John: *Some Recollections of the Late Edouard Laboulaye.* New York: Putnam's Sons, 1888.

Bright, John: *Selected Speeches of the Rt. Hon. John Bright, MP. On Public Questions.* London: MacMillan, 1970.

Brooks, Noah (Herbert Mitgang, ed.): *Washington in Lincoln's Time.* Chicago: Quadrangle Books, 1971.

Dana, Charles A.: *Recollections of the Civil War*. New York: Collier, 1963.

Davis, Jefferson (Dunbar Rowland, ed.): *Jefferson Davis, Constitutionalist, His Letter, Papers, and Speeches*. Jackson: Department of Archives and History, 1923.

Davis, Jefferson (Hudson Strode, ed.): *Private Letters 1823–1889*. New York: Harcourt Brace and World, 1966.

deLeon, Edwin: *Thirty Years of My Life on Three Continents*. London: Ward and Downey, 1890.

Dennett, Tyler (ed.): *Lincoln and the Civil War in the Diaries and Letters of John Hay*. New York: Dodd Mead, 1939.

Dodson, S.H.; Denison, G.S. (eds.): *The Diary and Correspondence of Salmon P. Chase*. Washington, D.C., Government Printing Office, Annual Report of the American Historical Society, Vol. 2, 1902

Johnston, William E. (R.M. Johnston, ed.): *Memoirs of Malakoff: Being Extracts of the Correspondence of the Late William Edward Johnston*. London: Hutchinson and Co., 1891.

Malet, Sir Edward: *Shifting Scenes or Memories of Many Men in Many Lands*. London: J. Murray, 1902.

Motley, John Lothrop. (G.W. Curtis, ed.): *The Correspondence of John Lothrop Motley*. New York: Harper Brothers, 1889.

Seward, Frederick: *Reminiscences of a War-time Statesman and Diplomat, 1830–1915*. New York: Putnam, 1915.

Seward, Frederick: *Seward's Folly, A Son's View*. Rochester: University of Rochester Library Bulletin, Spring, 1967.

Schurz, Carl: *Eulogy of Charles Sumner*. Boston, Lee and Shepard, 1874.

Victoria, Queen (Brian Connell, ed.): *Regina vs Palmerston: The Correspondence Between Queen Victoria and Her Foreign and Prime Minister, 1837–1865*. Garden City: Doubleday, 1961.

Parliamentary Papers

Correspondence Relating to the Civil War in the United States of America. London: Harrison and Sons, 1863.

Further Correspondence Relating to the Civil War in the United States of America. London: Harrison and Sons, 1862.

Hansard Digitized Parliamentary Debates, 1860–1865.

Hansard, Vol. clxx. Session 1863 (2) and vol. clxxii. Session 1863 (4).

Hansard Session 1863 (August 6) "The Debate on the Foreign Enlistment Act".

Newspapers

Daily Picayune
Die Presse
Harper's Weekly
Hartford Daily Courant
Illinois Journal
New York Times
New York Daily Herald
London News
London Star and Dial
London Spectator
The Times (London)
Morning Herald (London)
Newcastle Daily Chronicle
Pike County Free Press
Reynold's Weekly Newspaper (London)
Richmond Daily Dispatch
Richmond Examiner
Sheffield and Rotherdam Independent
The Index
The Toronto Leader
Washington National Intelligencer

Reference and Official Records

A Compilation of the Official Records of the Union and Confederate Armies, 70 vols. Washington D.C., Department of War, 1891.

Barnard, J.G.: *The Dangers and Defenses of New York*. New York Chamber of Commerce, 1859.

Convention with the Republic of Venezuela for the Adjustment of Claims of Citizens of the United States on the Government of that Republic Growing out of their Forcible Expulsion by Venezuelan Authorities from the Guano Island of Aves in the Caribbean Sea; January 14, 1859. 36th Congress, 1st Session. Confidential Executive No.193.

Foreign Relations of the United States. Washington D.C., U.S. Government Printing Office, 1861–1866.

Mallory, Stephen R.: *Report of the Secretary of the Navy*. Committee on Naval Affairs, 1864.

Munden, Kenneth White; Beers, Henry Putney. *Guide to the Federal Archives Relating to the Civil War*. Washington D.C., National Archives Records Service, General Services Administration, 1962.

Official Records of the Union and Confederate Navies in the War of the Rebellion. 30 vols. Washington D.C., Navy Department, 3rd ed., 1927.

Papers Relating to the Foreign Relations of the United States, Washington D.C., U.S. Government Printing Office, 1861–1870.

Seward, William H.: *Circular No. 19 to the Diplomatic Officers of the United States in Foreign Countries*. U.S. Government Printing Office, 1861–1865.

Welles, Gideon. *Report on the Secretary of the Navy*. Washington D.C., U.S. Government Printing Office, 1861–1865.

US Code

67 US 635 Prize cases: The Brig Amy Warwick; The Schooner Crenshaw; The Barque Hiawatha; The Schooner Brilliante

APPENDICES

Appendix A
"Dramatis personae" of U.S. Foreign Policy 1861–1865
Heads of State

Abraham Lincoln	President of the United States
Jefferson Davis	President of the Confederate States of America
Napoleon III	Emperor of France
Queen Victoria	Queen of the United Kingdom

Government Ministers/Cabinet Members

William Henry Seward	U.S. secretary of state
Frederick Seward	Assistant U.S. secretary of state
Gideon Welles	Secretary of the U.S. Navy
Alexander Stephens	Confederate vice president
Judah Benjamin	Confederate attorney general, secretary of war and later of the Confederate State Department
Stephen R. Mallory	Secretary of the navy, Confederate States of America
Lord John Russell	British foreign secretary
Henry John Temple	3rd Viscount Palmerston, British prime minister
William Ewart Gladstone	Chancellor of the exchequer during the American Civil War (later prime minister)
Benjamin Disraeli	Conservative member of parliament, later prime minister
William Schaw Lindsay	Member of parliament, shipping merchant selling blockade runners to the Confederacy
Édouard Thouvanel	French minister for foreign affairs (1861–1862)
Édouard Drouyn de Lhuys	French minister for foreign affairs (1862–1866)

Jean Gilbert Victor Failin	Duc de Persigny, influential friend of Napoleon III and minister of the interior

Legation Heads/Consuls General

Lord Richard Lyons	British minister to Washington (1858–1864). Left post in 1864 due to ill health. Succeeded by Sir Frederick Bruce
William Stuart	Acting minister to Washington during leaves of absence of Lyons
Charles Francis Adams, Sr.	Envoy extraordinary and minister plenipotentiary to British Dominions/England
Henri Mercier	French minister to Washington
Baron Eduard de Stockel	Russian minister to Washington
William Lewis Dayton	Envoy extraordinary and minister plenipotentiary to France, 1861–1864
Thomas Corwin	Envoy extraordinary and minister plenipotentiary to Mexico
Henry Shelton Sanford	U.S. minister resident to Belgium and unofficial head of U.S. Secret Service
Carl Shurz	Envoy extraordinary and minister plenipotentiary to Prussia
Robert Pruyn	U.S. minister resident to Japan
Ambrose Dudley Mann, William Loundes Yancey, Pierre Rost	Confederate Representatives to England, France, Belgium and the Vatican
John Bigelow	U.S. consul to Paris, succeeded Dayton upon his death in 1864 as minister
Cassius Marcellus Clay	Envoy extraordinary and minister plenipotentiary to Russia
John Slidell	Confederate representative in Paris
James Mason	Confederate representative in London
Robert Bunch	British consul general in Charleston, South Carolina
H. Pinkney Walker	Succeeded Bunch as consul in Charleston. Served until 1886
Edward Archibald	British consul general in New York

Politicians

Charles Sumner	Senator from Massachusetts, chair of the Senate Foreign Relations Committee
Henry Winter Davis	Representative from Maryland, chair of the House Foreign Relations Committee
John Bright	Liberal member of parliament, 1843–1889

| Richard Cobden | Liberal member of parliament, 1841–1865 |
| William Edward Forster | Liberal member of parliament, 1861–1886 |

Other Legation Officials/Consular Agents

Henry Adams	Secretary to his father, Charles Francis Adams, Sr.
Thomas Haines Dudley	U.S. consul at Liverpool
Benjamin Moran	U.S. legation secretary, London
Louis Heyliger	British consul in Nassau
Ignatius Pollaky	Union spy, reported to Sanford
Edouard Alean	Union spy, reported to Sanford
Edward Brennan	Union spy, reported to Pollaky
Louis A. Dochez	Union "immigration consultant", reported to Sanford

Confederate Purchasing/Financial Agents

James Bulloch	Confederate purchasing agent for Confederate navy
James Spence	Banker for the Confederacy based in Liverpool, wrote pro-Southern articles for the *London Times*. Services terminated by Judah Benjamin
Colin J. McRae	Chief Confederate financial agent, took over from Spence in 1863
William Crenshaw	Purchasing agent for blockade runners in England
Caleb Huse	Confederate purchasing agent
J.B. Ferguson	Agent for cotton bonds in England

Other

John Laird	Member of parliament and ship builder for the Confederacy
Wharncliffe, 1st Earl, 3rd Baron	Founder of the *Southern Independence Association*
Emile Erlanger	Head of French bank that made Cotton Loan to the Confederacy
George Trenholm	Head of Fraser, Trenholm and Co. in New York office, bankers for the Confederacy in Europe
Charles Prioleau	Head of Fraser, Trenholm and Co. in Liverpool, banker for theConfederacy
Edward Alfred Pollard	Editor of the *Richmond Examiner*
Edwin De Leon	Confederate "commissioner" to London and Paris
Henry Hotze	Confederate publicist in Europe and editor/publisher of *The Index*
Alexander Collie	Cotton broker, purchasing and shipping agent for the Confederacy

| Jacob Thompson | Confederate secret agent in Canada. Sensitive records burned after the war |
| Sir Edward Malet | Secretary to Lord Richard Lyons in Washington during the Civil War |

Appendix B

Staff at the British legation in Washington during the tenure of Richard Lyons

1859

William Douglas Irvine	Secretary of the legation
William Synge	First paid attaché
Fredrick Warre	Second paid attaché
George F.B. Jenner	Attaché
Edmund J. Monson	Private secretary

1860

| Henry Francis Manley | Attaché |
| Gerard F. Gould | Attaché |

1861

| William Brodie | First paid attaché |

1862

William Stuart	Acting secretary of the legation
H. Percy Anderson	Temporarily attached
Ernest Clay	Temporarily attached
George Sheffield	Temporarily attached

1863

H.P. Anderson	Acting second secretary
Edward Baldwin Malet	Acting second secretary
J.G. Kennedy	Attaché
Charles Heneage	Attaché

1864

J.H. Burnley	Secretary of the legation
W.G.C. Eliot	Acting secretary of the legation
H.P. Fenton	2nd Secretary
Arthur H. Seymour	3rd Secretary
William B. Smith	3rd Secretary
Edmund Cope	Attaché

Appendix C

British Consuls and Consulates During the War

Note: The most critical consulates were New York City and Charleston. New York was large and busy enough to require a vice-consul. Charleston was key in keeping the legation in Washington accurately informed about activities in the Confederacy. The consul here was officially recalled in 1861. However, William Seward did not act on the recall, and Consul Bunch continued to unofficially perform his duties.

New York	William Archibald
	Pierpont Edwards, vice-consul
Boston	Francis Lousada
Chicago	John Wilkins (St. Louis after 1861)
Philadelphia	Charles Kortwright
Buffalo	Denis Donohoe
Portland (Me.)	John Henry Murray
San Francisco	William Booker
Baltimore	Frederick Bernal
Charleston	Robert Bunch, 1860–1861
	H. Pinkney Walker, acting consul, 1861–1863
Richmond	George Moore, 1860–1863
	Frederick Crindland, vice-consul, 1860–1863, acting consul, May–June, 1863
Savanah	Edward Molyneux (Allan Fullerton on death of Molyneux, 1862–1863)
	William Tasker Smith, 1865
Mobile	James Magee, acting consul, 1861–1863
	Charles Labuzan, acting consul, 1860–1861
New Orleans	William Mure (George Coppell after departure of Mure, 1861–1865)
Galveston	Arthur Lynn

Appendix D

Union vs Royal Navy: 1861

	Union Navy	Royal Navy
Ships	264	42
Ironclad	49	26
Men	22,000	14,551
Guns	2,557	1,319
Tonnage	218,016	70,456

Note: The chart does not tell a complete story. The British ironclad navy was more offensive. Of the 26 ironclads, 22 were oceangoing, and four were for coastal defense. The British oceangoing ironclad was a steam and sail craft with high freeboard. They were iron-plated, and could attain speeds greater than the Monitor-style ironclad. The Union navy contained 10 seagoing ironclads of the Passaic class and many more Monitor-/turret-style ironclads for harbor and river defense. Generally, The Union Navy was, by comparison, more defense-oriented. However, she also launched two large, seagoing monitors, the Dictator and the Puritan. Both ships had 15-inch guns and 1,000 pounds of coal capacity which allowed them to reach British bases north and south with little difficulty. This was a distance of over 2,000 miles. She also employed six broadside and 15 side and paddlewheel ironclads for river use as well as 60 "tinclads" or protected riverboats. The Confederate navy had no oceangoing ironclads. However, she employed 33 steam and floating batteries as well as 19 wooden/sailing cruisers – used as privateers. Although offensive by design, the most powerful British seagoing broadside ironclad, the Warrior, drew 26ft 9in. The most valuable prize in a naval contest between England and the Union was New York City. The harbor channel in New York was only 17ft in depth in 1861, 24ft in 1880 and 30ft in 1891. Thus, even as late as 1880, the mightiest British warship could not get within "combat range" of Manhattan to have done serious damage. The threat of a British attack on the Atlantic seaboard was thus unrealistic. In addition, the Palmerston government knew the difficulties in winning a contest when the attacking navy was confronted with the heavier guns found in land-based fortifications. Palmerston, unlike the British populace, was not unduly impressed with the new Monitor-style ironclads that made their debut at Hampton Roads in 1863.

Appendix E
British Bondholders to the Erlanger Cotton Loan, 1863

*Note: The following list comes from John Bigelow, Paris consul in 1863. Bigelow was justifiably concerned about the validity of the names on the list because among the names were that of chancellor of the exchequer, William E. Gladstone. Gladstone claimed that the list was a forgery. The list also contained the names of several prominent lords, ladies, members of parliament, bank directors as well as influential newspaper editors and contributors. Several of these worked for the London Times – a paper generally critical of the Union government. Bigelow questioned whether those people (on the list) calling for recognition for the Confederacy were really interested in the survival of the CSA or more concerned about making sure that their bonds would mature and yield par value. Recognition would enable and help justify breaking the blockade and releasing the cotton that guaranteed the loan and supported the bonds. Bigelow asked John Bright to publish the list in the newspapers. He believed "proof" of whether or not the names were legitimately on the list would be achieved by waiting to see who publicly denied their involvement. Believing that this was not the most credible method of determining whether or not the list was a forgery, Bigelow compared the names on the list with names on another list of subscribers to the newly-formed Southern Independence Society. Of the 28 names on the bond list, 22 of these also appeared on the list of the Society. At least one name on the list, John Laird, may have been the son, not the MP father. However, the names of many with a vested interest in the economic survival of the Confederacy are clearly in evidence. Those with an * next to the name published a denial of their involvement in the cotton loan.*

Sir Henry de Houghton
Isaac Campbell and Co. (army contractors)
Thomas Sterling Begbie (ship owner)
The Marquis of Bath
James Spence (*Times* correspondent)
Mr. Beresford Hope (initially denied, but later shown to be a contributor)
George Edward Seymour (stock broker)
Alex Collie and Partners (ship owners)
Messrs. Fernie and Co.
Fleetwood, Patten, Wilson and Schuster (directors of Union Bank, London)
W.S. Lindsay (merchant and former MP)
Sir Coutts Lindsay (baronet)
John Laird ★ (MP and ship builder of *Alabama*. His son by the same name was a contributor)
M.B. Sampson ★ (city editor, the *Times*)
John Delane ★ (editor, the *Times*)
Lady Georgiana Fane
J.S. Gilliat ★ (director, Bank of England)
D. Forbes Campbell
George Peacock MP
W.J. Rideout ★(proprietor of the *Morning Post*)
Edward Ackenroyd
Lord Campbell
Lord Donoughomore
Hon. Evelyn Ashley (private secretary to Lord Palmerston)
Right Hon. William Ewart Gladstone ★

Appendix F
Confederate Purchasing Agents in England During the American Civil War

James Bulloch
Captain W.D. Crenshaw
Major J.B. Ferguson
Caleb Huse
Colin J. McRae
John N. Moffitt
M.F. Murray
Lt. James H. North
George T. Sinclair
James Spence
John Wilkinson

Appendix G

Confederate "special" agents in the West Indies

Charles J. Helm   Havana: lawyer, consul under Buchanan, special agent under Jefferson Davis

Louis Heyliger   Nassau: appointed December, 1861

Norman Walker   Bermuda

Appendix H

Report of the Crown law officers to the Trent crisis and the right of seizure

THE LAW OFFICERS OF THE CROWN IN THE CASE OF THE "TRENT" NOVEMBER 12 ,1861.
Printed for the use of the Cabinet, November 29, 1861.
Confidential.

THE LAW OFFICERS OF THE CROWN TO EARL RUSSELL
Received November 12.
DOCTORS' COMMONS, November 12, 1861.

My Lord,

We were honoured with your Lordship's commands, signified in Mr. Hammond's letter of the 9th instant, stating that he was directed by your Lordship to request our immediate attention to the following case :-
The Confederate States of North America have recently appointed two gentlemen, Messrs. Mason and Slidell, to proceed to Europe, accredited to the English and French Governments respectively. These gentlemen embarked on board the steamer Nashville,' which' vessel appears from accounts in the daily papers successfully to have run the blockade of Charleston, and to have conveyed the two gentlemen to Cardenas in Cuba. It appears also from accounts published in the daily papers that the Federal Government immediately on hearing of the escape of the Nashville dispatched three vessels of war to intercept her.

Within these few days a duly commissioned Federal steamer of war, mounting eight guns of heavy calibre, made her appearance at Falmouth, and she has since arrived at Southampton, where she has coaled, and is now ready for sea at a moment's notice.

Private information has been received that the object of this vessel is to capture the two Envoys before they arrive in Europe. It is not improbable that Messrs. Mason and Slidell will have embarked at Havana on board the west India mail-steamer now on her passage to Southampton.

That steamer is one of those under contract with Her Majesty's Government for the conveyance of Her Majesty's mails, which mails are exclusively under the charge of a commissioned officer of Her Majesty'snavy, acting on behalf of the Postmaster-General. In other respects the steamer is a mere merchant steamer, and is not authorized to display a pennant as a ship of war.

Assuming, therefore, that the United States' man-of-war steamer now lying at Southampton, or any other similar steamer of the United States, should attempt to intercept the West Indian mail-steamer, with a view of getting possession of the persons of Messrs. Mason and Slidell, or of their credentials or instructions,"Your Lordship wished to be informed to what extent, under the Law of Nations, a man-of-war steamer of the United States would be entitled to interfere with the mail-steamer if fallen in with beyond the territorial limits of the United Kingdom, that is, beyond three miles from the British coast.

Whether, for instance, she might cause the West Indian mail steamer to bring-to, might board her, examine her papers, open the mailbags, and examine the contents thereof, examine the luggage of passengers, seize and carry away Messrs. Mason and Slidell in person, or seize their credentials, and instructions and dispatches, or even put a prize crew on board the West Indian steamer, and carry her off to a port of the United States. In other words, what would be the rights of the American cruiser with regard to the passengers and crew, and lawful papers and correspondence on board our packet, on the assumption that the said packet was liable $0 capture and confiscation on the ground of carrying enemies' dispatches: would the cruiser be entitled to carry the packet, and all and everything in her, back to America, or would she be obliged to land in this country, or in some near port, all the people and all the unseizable goods?"

Mr. Hammond was further to inquire "whether, supposing one of Her Majesty's ships of war should be sent to follow the movements of the United States' steamer of war, or should have been ordered to meet the West Indian steamer, and escort her into port, such ship of war of Her Majesty would be justified, and to what extent, in preventing the United States', steamer of war from interfering with the West Indian mail steamer?"

In obedience to your Lordship's commands, we have the honour to Report: That your Lordship's first question may, in our opinion, be answered to the effect that the United States' man-of-war falling in with the British mail-steamer beyond the territorial limits of the United Kingdom might cause her to bring-to, might board her, examine her papers, open the general mail-bags, and examine the: contents thereof, without, however opening any bag or packet addressed to any officer or Department of Her Majesty's Government.

The United States' ship of war may put a prize-crew on board the West India steamer, and carry her off to a port of the United States for adjudication by a Prize Court there; but she would have no right to remove Messrs. Mason and Slidell, and carry them off as prisoners, leaving the ship to pursue her voyage.

On the assumption that the West India packet is liable to capture and confiscation, on the ground of carrying enemies' despatches, the cruiser would, in strictness, be entitled to carry her, and all and everything in her, to America.

We have, etc,
(Signed) J.D. HARDING,
W.M. ATHERTON,
ROUNDELL PALMER.

INDEX